JOHN MILTON'S
ARISTOCRATIC ENTERTAINMENTS

JOHN MILTON'S ARISTOCRATIC ENTERTAINMENTS

CEDRIC C. BROWN

CAMBRIDGE UNIVERSITY PRESS

CAMBRIDGE
LONDON   NEW YORK   NEW ROCHELLE
MELBOURNE   SYDNEY

Published by the Press Syndicate of the University of Cambridge
The Pitt Building, Trumpington Street, Cambridge CB2 1RP
32 East 57th Street, New York, NY 10022, USA
10 Stamford Road, Oakleigh, Melbourne 3166, Australia

© Cambridge University Press 1985

First published 1985

Printed in Great Britain at
the University Press, Cambridge

Library of Congress catalogue card number: 84-27468

British Library cataloguing in publication data
Brown, Cedric C.
John Milton's aristocratic entertainments.
1. Milton, John, *1608–1674*
I. Title
822'.4   PR3588
ISBN 0 521 30440 7

WV

To J. M. N.

CONTENTS

List of illustrations	*page* viii
Acknowledgements	ix
Abbreviations	xii
Introduction	1
1 Contexts and occasions	12
2 The Arcadians	41
3 *Kōmos* – the adversary for the occasion	57
4 The young heroes – realism and idealism	78
5 Spiritual instructions	104
6 1634 and 1637 – texts, epilogues, audiences	132
7 The sense of vocation in the 1630s	153
Appendix: The authenticity of the Bridgewater manuscript and the idea of the censor	171
A note on the Golden Grove portrait	179
Notes	181
Index	205

ILLUSTRATIONS

between pages 52 and 53

Plate 1. Henry Lawes (School of Music, Oxford)
Plate 2. Alice, Countess of Derby. Zucchero threequarter-length (Lord Leigh)
Plate 3. Alice, Countess of Derby. Engraving with arms
Plate 4. Monument of Countess of Derby, Harefield church. Engraving
Plate 5. Elizabeth, Countess of Huntingdon. Portrait attributed to van Somer
Plate 6. George, Lord Chandos. Engraving
Plate 7. John, Earl of Bridgewater (Tatton Park portrait)
Plate 8. Frances, Countess of Bridgewater (Ellesmere 1939 Settlement)
Plate 9. John, Lord Brackley, as infant (Ellesmere 1939 Settlement)
Plate 10. Thomas Egerton, as infant (Ellesmere 1939 Settlement)
Plate 11. Lady Alice Egerton, as infant (Ellesmere 1939 Settlement)
Plate 12. John, Lord Brackley, as young man (Ellesmere 1939 Settlement)
Plate 13. Thomas Egerton, as young man (Ellesmere 1939 Settlement)
Plate 14. The Golden Grove portrait (Earl of Cawdor)

ACKNOWLEDGEMENTS

A VERSION OF some of the materials on *Arcades* was previously published in *Renaissance Drama*, ns VIII (1977), 245–274. These materials have however been redistributed and revised. A version of the discussion of the Haemony crux was published in *JEGP*, LXVIII (1979), 522–544. Again, there have been revisions. I have to thank these journals for permission to re-use those parts which have remained substantially the same.

There are two other past publications of relevance to the book. A transcript of the Chirk Castle entertainment was published in *Milton Quarterly*, XI (1977), 76–86. It should be noted that the dating of the entertainment in this book is more precise than it was in the previous article. Some of the material about the presidential progress of 1634 was first made public at the International Milton Symposium in Cambridge in 1983.

The argument of the book also relates to several forthcoming articles. One of these, on the date of *Arcades* and the first entries in the Trinity manuscript, is still in draft. Another, ' "Arcades" in the Trinity manuscript', mentioned below, is to appear in *The Review of English Studies*. The material on prophetic gesture in *Lycidas* is similar to that used in a forthcoming article on Henry Vaughan's *Daphnis* and Milton's *Lycidas* in a special number of the *George Herbert Journal*, edited by Jonathan Post, to be devoted to the poetry of Vaughan. A fuller discussion of *kōmos* than there was room for in this book is to be found in a forthcoming article entitled 'Milton and the *kōmos*: invention, scholarship, and the limits of iconography', to appear in a special number of the *John Donne Journal*, edited by Richard S. Peterson, to be devoted to iconographical studies.

I have a large number of acknowledgements to make for help with, and in some instances permission to reproduce from, various

Acknowledgements

manuscript documents. These are chiefly to: the Huntington Library; the British Library; the National Library of Wales; the John Rylands Library, Manchester; the Public Record Office; Shropshire Record Office; Middlesex Record Office; Leicestershire Record Office; the Rector of Harefield; Lord Newton; and the Fitzroy-Newdigate family of Arbury Hall, Warwickshire.

For financial help and many kindnesses I must thank the Huntington Library and its staff, for a fellowship I held there and for further help given by mail and during a second visit to the library. I must also thank James Riddell for doing some checking for me there. I wish to thank the Andrew W. Mellon Foundation and the staff of the William Andrews Clark Library for allowing me to escape during some afternoons to do some further reading of documents in the Huntington, whilst I was actually being supported by a fellowship to study Swift at the Clark.

I owe a particular debt to colleagues past and present at the University of Reading. Some of them, in particular Andrew Gurr and Ronald Knowles, and other members of the Renaissance Research Seminar, have had parts of these materials tried upon them. Whatever it was that first kindled my interest in these texts, a part of that curiosity was probably created, quite unconsciously, many years ago, by the late Donald Gordon, who had himself struggled with Milton's masque and who was sometimes heard to remark darkly that no one had yet got *Comus* right. Then also, whenever I have felt the drift of my evidence to be towards the language of Protestantism, I have felt the particular support and expertise in these matters of Anthea Hume.

I must thank Joe Trapp, of the Warburg Institute, for encouragement in the form of arranging a lecture there some years ago. Amongst American scholars I wish to thank French Fogle, with whom I compared notes, only too briefly, on the familial background and who gave me one splendid new lead. More recently, I owe a significant debt of gratitude to John Creaser, of Mansfield College, Oxford, for his patient encouragement of my work, some of which runs parallel to some of his own.

I would like to acknowledge the help of the following persons and institutions in tracing portraits or supplying or arranging for photographs: the National Portrait Gallery, the National Portrait Gallery of Scotland, the Courtauld Institute, W. B. Hunter, Jr,

Acknowledgements

and the office of Sudeley Castle. For permission to reproduce portraits my thanks are due to the Heather Professor of Music at Oxford, Lord Leigh of Stoneleigh, Christie's, the National Trust, the Duke of Sutherland and Mr Cyril Egerton. Particular thanks must be given to the Earl of Cawdor, the owner, and Sir Oliver Millar, Surveyor of the Queen's Pictures, for their generous help with the ex-Golden Grove portrait supposedly of Lady Alice Egerton.

Lastly, but by no means least, I have to thank friends for much forbearance over many years, and especially my wife and family.

ABBREVIATIONS

Sprott	John Milton, *A Maske: the earlier versions*, ed. S. E. Sprott (University of Toronto Press, 1973).
TMS[1]	The earliest stage of development of the masque text as recorded in the autograph Trinity College manuscript, using Sprott's definition: 'the whole manuscript as it read after being revised during the first complete writing'. For further details and subdivisions, see Sprott, pp. 5–7.
TMS[2]	A later state of the Trinity manuscript text of the masque, but still in 1634, as it seems to have stood before the Bridgewater manuscript text was derived from it, apparently via an intermediate copy. For further details and subdivisions, again, see Sprott, pp. 7–8.
the '1637' changes	Those revisions in Milton's own hand in the Trinity manuscript which postdate performance and seem to be preparations for publication; called by Sprott (pp. 8–12) TMS[3a-f].
1637	*A Maske presented at Ludlow Castle, 1634: on Michaelmasse night* (London, 1637). The first anonymous publication of the masque text.
1645	*Poems of Mr John Milton, both English and Latin* (London, 1645). Milton's first published collection of verse.

INTRODUCTION

MIXED IN MODE and expressing their unique occasions, combining arts of poetic celebration with drama, spectacle, music and dance, masques and aristocratic entertainments are rarely simple to describe from the page. When the poet concerned is John Milton, the poetry offers to stand out more self-sufficiently than usual, and Milton clearly thought about the self-sufficiency of his texts, especially when he revised them for publication. Yet in other ways the task of assessing his entertainments is more difficult than usual, since this poet who used many conventions rarely used them uncritically, and his response to occasion was likely to be more than a matter of form.

In fact, Milton's three major occasional texts in English of the 1630s – *Arcades*, *Comus* and *Lycidas* – have, in their various ways, presented persistent difficulties to understanding. With the entertainments the problems are not so much, as they once were, with understanding the modes of masquing itself. It is true that there are peculiarities of situation behind *Arcades* and *Comus*, which gave them unique forms. There are, in other words, adjustments of customary organisation to note. Nevertheless, the modes of masquing in general, which still apply to his texts, have attracted ample critical attention in recent years. The particular difficulties of Milton's pieces would seem to be more to do with the independent and even revisionary characteristics of his writing for aristocratic occasions. They are to do with his attitude, and his sense of his own role as a poet.

The main part of this book attempts a comprehensive examination of both Milton's aristocratic entertainments, that is, the verses which formed part of a family entertainment at Harefield, in Middlesex, in the early 1630s and which Milton

Introduction

himself subsequently called *Arcades* (the Arcadians), and the masque performed at Ludlow Castle on Michaelmas night, 1634, which literary tradition has called *Comus*. *Lycidas*, the Cambridge elegy for Edward King, occupies a special place at the end of the book, which finally provides an overview of Milton's sense of vocation in the 1630s, as it is expressed in his three major occasional compositions of that period.

In assessing the entertainment texts in their various states, before and after performance, and in publication, I find that one characteristic emerges as of central importance: their ardently, idealistically reformist spirit. Delicately though he managed effects of celebration in his texts – and I would not want to belittle his courteous arts in that regard – Milton did not simply celebrate his noble patrons. Young though he was, the independence of his celebratory writing exceeds even that of 'laureate' Ben Jonson. If we call his entertainments aristocratic, then it must be in the sense not that they merely rehearse or consolidate social ideals of nobility but rather that they insistently prescribe the reformation of the leading class considered as a whole, just as parts of *Lycidas*, rather less delicately, prescribe the reformation of most of the clergy. Through festivity, nobility itself is seriously evaluated, its education under particular scrutiny. Milton's entertainments are peculiarly, and in the end problematically, reformist in intent. Problematically, because the evidence of the Bridgewater manuscript of *Comus* suggests that the zealousness and stringency of Milton's text were modified by the organisers in the interests of more conventional social decorum in a celebratory situation. It would seem, also, that Milton himself experienced problems of accommodation between exhortation and celebration in the composition of the Ludlow masque, and in its revisions.

One may illustrate this reformist exploitation of convention from the peculiarly Protestant signature at the very end of the masque. The cast of Milton's language can be shown by comparing it with the song of Michaelmas day in the popular *Hymns and Songs of the Church* of the ardently reformist George Wither, another poet with a sense of a mission. Wither's last stanza, which is about angelic offices remembered on that day, begins:

Introduction

> For, many of that glorious Troope,
> To bring us Messages from Thee,
> From Heav'n vouchsafed have to stoope,
> And clad in human shape to be – [1]

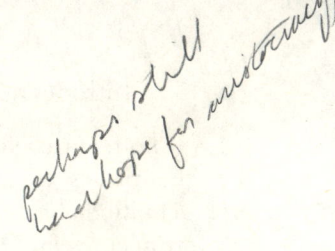
perhaps still had hope for aristocracy(?)

For all the superiority of style, the stooping of heaven in Milton's last line is of the same kind as Wither's: 'or if vertue feeble were / heaven it selfe would stoope to her'. Throughout the action of the masque, the stooping of heavenly grace has been by the agency of an angelic being. This couplet is Milton's sealing mark, and he re-used the lines in 1639 in his entry in the autograph book of Count Camillo Cerdogni in Geneva, on the return leg of the Italian tour. He had not forgotten the doctrinal characteristics of his longest composition to date:

> If Vertue feeble were
> Heaven itself would stoope to her.
> *Coelum non animum muto dum trans mare curro.*
>   Joannes Miltonius Anglus

The familiar tag from Horace – 'I change my sky but not my mind, when I travel across the sea' – would seem to indicate that John Milton, Englishman, was asserting that, by the grace of God, his faith had been uncontaminated by his sojourn in popish lands. His other extant autograph – Ἐν ἀσθενείᾳ τελειοῦμαι – also signifies grace and leaves a distinctly Protestant mark.[2]

Yet there was also play with conventional modes of masquing in that last couplet of Milton's masque. As a spirit ascends to the heavens, the lines recall the mechanical inventions of court masques, which more and more in the Caroline period gloried in their ability to lower and raise from the heavens, contriving to suggest thereby that heaven itself had indeed come to earth in that court. With some wry irony Heaven's stooping recalls the language of such court ritual. Thus, for example, when Inigo Jones brought the queen and the lady masquers down on clouds, surrounded by stars, in the most spectacular such effect yet, Aurelian Townshend had dutifully written in 1631:

> Where Divine Beautie will vouchsafe to stoope
> And move the Earth, 'tis fit the Heavenly Spheres
> Should be her Musick, and the Starrie Troope
> Shine round about them like the Crown she weares.[3]

Introduction

At both Harefield and Ludlow, Milton's special wit was to infuse the rituals of masquing with the live language of religious definition. Especially at Ludlow, it is masquing, but in a more stringent vein. One could say in fact that the whole 1645 volume corresponded to a model of gentlemanly occasional writing, but that it also carried a disturbing reformist spirit in its major compositions.

Some of the specific features of the religiousness of Milton's programme in the Ludlow masque have not been adequately appreciated. Hence, for example, my initial approach to the masque is to highlight the challenge of the adversary, Comus, the spirit of customary degeneracy in festivity in palace halls. An iconographical approach to Comus is insufficient in itself to realise the place of the *kōmos* as badge of degeneracy in Milton's continuing thought about the fate of nations, distinguishing those which had a true magistracy from those that did not. A more philological approach, based on a sense of history, and mixing literary and biblical sources, can realise the urgency of this reformist thought. To centre on the generally instructive idea of the *kōmos*, which is also to see the particular relevance of chastity, gives us one way, too, in which we can escape too specific a topical reference to the infamous Castlehaven scandal, or even the rape case of Margery Evans in the Welsh court.[4] What Milton offers, in *Comus*, and what is of continuing importance in his political thought, is a general analysis of the importance of aristocratic example, as tested in the conduct of the feast.

I feel also that the consistent strength of spiritual instruction must be felt throughout the action of *Comus*. It is mediated through the Attendant Spirit but derives from the idea that religious education is the basis of exemplary conduct, even in the leading class. With the two boys in particular, the Spirit plays substitute for pastor, and acknowledges that he is doing so in his deference to his authority, 'a certain shepheard lad'. Many readings of the masque have failed to acknowledge how the ministry of the word underpins the education and readiness described in the action of the boys, yet Milton is clearly indicating that godliness should be seen as support to all other educational achievements or qualities of mind. As for the Lady, one can hardly miss the pious orientation

Introduction

of her social thought: where in masque but in Milton's masque would one find expounded so openly, if at all, how luxury for the few means deprivation for the many? The Lady's arguments about the use of nature show in themselves a radical reorientation of the emphases of celebration in masque. Even in the slighter *Arcades*, nightly pieties are at the centre of the true Arcadianism.

Also exemplifying the idealistic, reformist imperatives of the masque, the use of Sabrina opens the vision into the national, showing an ideal of a prosperous land on the banks of the river, pitied of God and resting on pious temperance. Confusions about specific applications of the doctrine of grace in connection with Sabrina have often served, in the past, to obscure the realisation of this public aspect of the Welsh presidential masque. Again, Milton's celebratory method here approaches some norms of masque and idealistic pastoral drama, offering a pointed adaptation of common pastoral figures, but now distinctively allied to a historical vision based on pious idealism. *Arcades* plays out a similar idealism, though concerning a class rather than a whole people.

The Sabrina section of the masque also gives full and explicit expression to Milton's pastorly ideal of the role of poetry to instruct the nation, the ideal expressed so clearly also in *Lycidas*. In the magical displays of this part of the masque, the power of poetry is being suggested for all to contemplate, a poetry which forges ideal images to move the mind. The idealism about the functions of poetry is akin to Sidney's apology and Spenser's practice. It is an issue keenly debated by Milton himself in his Commonplace Book and in other writings. Again, I do not think that Milton's statements about the power of the 'true poet' have been sufficiently realised as being embodied in the scheme of the masque; neither have the dynamics of what I have called the suasive design of the masque, by which stringent realism is finally supplanted by idealism in pastoral formulations.

Yet, vital though these instructional, reforming functions were in Milton's texts, their effects can only truly be seen against the demands of writing for the original occasions. Throughout this book I have assumed that there are particular arts of occasional writing, which the modern reader would do well to appreciate

Introduction

before judging some aspects of Milton's entertainments. The challenge of realising occasion in relation to Milton's texts is however no simple matter.

For the Harefield entertainment of which Milton's verses formed a part we seem to need to understand a familial gesture on a private occasion. One's sense of the situation and attitudes of a large family at a particular time is bound to be conjectural, especially considering the relatively modest amount of documentation. Nevertheless, we know enough of the situation at Harefield at the time that *Arcades* was performed to make sense of some of the features of Milton's text, especially with regard to the ideas of bringing courtly festivities to the house and of the happiness of a residence at Harefield for some of the younger members of the family. Accordingly I have provided what is I think the fullest account yet of the familial situation and of its possible relevance to Milton's 'Part of an Entertainment'.

For the Ludlow masque there are various aspects of occasion to consider. With regard to the known roles of Henry Lawes as Attendant Spirit and of the three youngest children of the Earl of Bridgewater, criticism has always known what it needed to know. Nevertheless, accounts seem often to have forgotten the modes of pretence and have often ignored the delicacies of tone in the writing for these roles, especially in relation to the Elder Brother. Anyone who has seen the masque performed sympathetically with children of approximately the right ages will understand how plausible and delightful, as well as intricate and exemplary, Milton's writing for the young Egertons was, whilst his exploitation of the protean part for Henry Lawes remains one of the most remarkable pieces of sustained invention in any masque, full of touches of comic pretence, yet finally hieratic, fashioning a mouthpiece for an earnestly didactic poet.

The more public aspects of the Welsh gubernatorial situation must also be considered. The three young aristocrats, reflecting their parents, show the kind of pious education on which good governance is based. When the spirit of degenerate luxury is driven from the place, a new spirit can be called in to exercise her powers of chaste influence, thus allowing, as I have said, a vision of pious prosperity in the land around a river. In the triumph of this ritual action, one could say that resources of great visitors from

Introduction

court have been shown and also that a strength has been drawn from the region and its people. There is a complex combination of resources of persons and place, a coming together in hopeful augury.

Such a combination reflects the inaugural occasion of the masque, performed on a symbolic day on the new President's first visitation to Wales. Milton's text refers to the occasion as a feast of gratulation. With that and other considerations in mind I have offered to set the whole Michaelmas occasion into context by describing the tour of the Earl of Bridgewater as President of Wales in 1634. Evidence comes from several sets of documents, some of them not fully exploited before or not known to Milton scholarship. Various household records, for example, and some sets of correspondence concerning Bridgewater and Henry Lawes, give one a sense of the President's movements, activities and attitudes during this summer visitation, showing not only the journeys to and from Wales, but also the travelling that was done in the Welsh Marches, North Wales and Cheshire. The various entertainments offered to Bridgewater and his family at large houses in the summer of 1634 included another dramatic one, a banquet entertainment at Chirk Castle, in August. That text, like much of this information, allows one to see how persons and place, President and principality, came together in celebration.

With Milton's two aristocratic entertainments, then, an idealistic, reforming authorial intent, on the one hand, and a complex relationship to particular occasions, on the other, add up to a very special, teasing case for literary texts of this kind, and it is made all the more special by the unusually rich textual resources. For both entertainments the priceless record of Milton's autograph Trinity manuscript gives us ample evidence of textual development both before and after performance. In both cases, the first printings came some while after performance – three years after with *Comus*, some thirteen years after with *Arcades* – so that the occasion of publication was more than usually distanced from performance, thus bringing new perspectives into view. And the textual records are particularly rich for *Comus*, because as well as the authorially controlled manuscript and printed texts we have a presentation manuscript, the Bridgewater manuscript, given to Bridgewater as a memento after performance, and this manu-

Introduction

script seems to reflect something like what actually happened on the performance night. There can be no more telling story of the development of texts for an aristocratic festivity and subsequent publication than this one; the tracing of this development is a running theme throughout the book.

My first account of these texts keeps in constant view some of the evidence of Milton's revisions before performance and therefore aims at a sense of Milton's design for performance rather than for print. Initially most of my quotations are from the Trinity manuscript text at the relevant stage of development. At the same time, for the Ludlow masque I have noted instances of the more considerable cuts and alterations effected in the Bridgewater manuscript, usually illustrating damage done to Milton's design. Then, mainly in Chapter 6, I have tried to analyse, somewhat selectively, the drift of the '1637' changes made by Milton in preparation for the text being published to the nation at large. Even the smaller *Arcades* text shows characteristic changes in preparation for the new occasion of publication. My intention throughout is not to repeat the exercise of a detailed analysis of all textual changes, of the kind set out in the evidence of S. E. Sprott in his edition of the early *Comus* texts, but rather to highlight the issues underlying the chief textual changes, with regard to Milton's addresses to his occasion of performance and print. It is from the evidence of the changes for the *1637* text of *Comus* and the *1645* text of *Arcades* that I develop the last section of the book, concerning the development of Milton's sense of vocation in the period of the 1630s. The alterations made for publication are visibly in the spirit of the poet of *Lycidas*: they show a growing determination to take opportunities to speak out to the nation, in something approaching prophetic address. Intricate though the evidence is, I believe that it tells a story of considerable importance for the understanding of Milton's career in these years before the Civil War.

Milton's art in these texts, as in the 1645 volume at large, is the art of occasional writing, relatable, as Helgerson has said, to other volumes being published at that time.[5] With the entertainments Milton's address to his original occasions, for performance, was always complicated and displayed to an unusual degree the kinds of tension endemic to such texts.[6] In particular, there are tensions

Introduction

to be observed between the pastorly impulse, characteristically rigorous about the ways of men, and a sense of decorum for the happy, celebratory occasion, in the development of the Trinity manuscript text of these entertainments. But it would seem that some of the many difficulties of critical understanding in the twentieth century have connected with readers taking too little care to grasp the particular nature of occasional address present in whatever text was being used. Despite that amateur disclaimer on the title page, Milton seems to have taken the opportunity of publication of the masque not only to immortalise a celebratory occasion but also to realise a *new* occasion, in an address to a more general readership in the nation. When one is discussing the intricacies of tone in the parts of the children, for example, it makes some difference whether one reads Trinity manuscript in a state before performance or whether one reads the printed text of 1637, in which perceptible damage was done to the nice judgement of the children's parts. By 1637, the fine touch with individual parts mattered rather less. Or, to give a more blatant example, it is important to realise that Milton's problematically extended epilogue in *1637* speaks out as to a general readership, through the Attendant Spirit, in a way which would have been somewhat disruptive to the original performance, in which masquers and audience at Ludlow were sent in piety to their beds. There are other examples. It also matters, I believe, to realise that the sense of decorum in relation to occasion is different in the Bridgewater manuscript, because that text seems to embody the priorities of some other party or parties (which I have called the 'censor' in the Appendix) than Milton to the demands of occasion. In whichever version we read either entertainment, we discover a continuing story of constantly shifting, sometimes urgent dialogue with occasion. For that reason, in one way or another, with differing degrees of emphasis, each major stage of both entertainments has been considered against a sense of the occasion to which it belongs.

In the closing chapter of the book, which picks up from the rather hortatory post-performance changes in the text of *Comus*, I have not offered a comprehensive account of *Lycidas*, but have suggested, in a tentative spirit, a main device by which its prophetic address to the nation might be realised. Although the

Introduction

prophetic element in Milton's sense of his role as a writer has quite often been considered, especially in recent years, mainly in relation to *Lycidas* and to the later career, as far as I know this prophetic gesture, reading the death of the righteous man as a sign to the nation, has not been documented before. To debate the relative importance of the prophetic element in Milton's elegy for King, no easy matter, is also to bring into question another instance of changing functions of a text in two different occasions of publication, first in the Cambridge memorial volume, another celebratory occasion, then in yet darker times in a volume addressed to the nation at large. As with the masque text, the prophetic dimension took on new importance in the retrospective publication. A full discussion of the relationship of different versions of the *Lycidas* text to their occasions is however beyond the scope of this book. I am chiefly concerned to bring *Lycidas* into the discussion to relate it to the increasingly prophetic element in the masque text, and in that way to document something of the development of Milton's sense of vocation through the 1630s. Milton's sense of vocation is the factor which gives clearest indication of the peculiarities of the programmes of his major occasional poems in this period.

A last word about interpretative arguments. Anyone working in close detail on these early poems of Milton is uncomfortably aware that he is picking a way through a minefield of debate. The difficulties of Miltonic masquing apart, *Lycidas* notoriously shares with *Comus* a history of confusion about the meaning and method of certain passages of Miltonic pastoral. There is doubtless a book to be written in analysis of the source of difficulty in the Miltonic pastoral. Although the present book is not chiefly devoted to questions of academic polemic, certain views about the two entertainments (and even about *Lycidas*) have, openly or tacitly, been challenged, especially where those views are or have been prevalent. It has sometimes proved convenient for the sake of clarity of definition to make an argument by offering an adjustment to some usually recent theory. Specialists will note that I have not been exhaustive or even-handed in my references to scholarly opinion, but selective: there is no intention to offer here another attempt at the Variorum Commentary. This may however be the place to mention, finally, one book, Maryann Gale

Introduction

McGuire's *Milton's Puritan Masque,* which arrived after the present book was completed but which I must acknowledge here, because its main argument about the reforming nature of Milton's masque runs parallel to parts of my own. The present book differs a good deal from *Milton's Puritan Masque* in the range of materials adduced and in quite a number of points of interpretation, but I should like to say that I find it most encouraging to read another account of the Protestant radicalism of Milton's writing for the aristocracy. The approach McGuire makes from the debate surrounding the 1633 Book of Sports (also mentioned below) is similar to that I have made from the *kōmos* itself.

In that method, and leaving aside the major arguments of the book already mentioned, I have entered debate on such as the following: a review of common misunderstandings about the staging and form of *Arcades*; a placement of some of the many interpretations of Haemony and the shepherd lad in the Ludlow masque, whilst putting forward my own (a matter of great importance for the understanding of the whole text); an examination of the rather hoary but influential debate initiated by A. S. P. Woodhouse about the role of grace in the masque; and an argument against Sprott about the responsibility for the cuts in the Bridgewater manuscript. Examples of realignments of recent statements are the adjustments offered to the arguments of John D. Cox about the 'provisional' nature of Milton's compliment to Bridgewater and the challenge to the account of John Spencer Hill on certain aspects of Milton's sense of vocation in the 1630s, as manifested in literary texts. There are various other passing debates, as with Georgia B. Christopher on the 'word' in the masque text and Leah S. Marcus on the relationship of the presidency to the role of Sabrina, as mirrored in Drayton's *Polyolbion*. All these, and more, are offered, I hope, in the spirit of constructiveness and in the pursuit of clarification. Also I should say that they are not presented in the manner of the wholly specialist discourse, but rather as accessibly as possible, and contained within something like a progressive account of the texts. I trust that the discourse will be, as Sir Kenelm Digby said so blithely of allegory in *The Faerie Queene*, obvious to any ordinary capacity.[7]

1 · CONTEXTS AND OCCASIONS

MILTON wrote his two aristocratic entertainments for branches of the same family. It would seem probable that the one commission was connected with the other. However, there is as yet no firm evidence to indicate that Milton's link with the family was particularly close, or even to tell us whether he actually went to either place of entertainment, Harefield or Ludlow. Harefield, in Middlesex, was of course within easy reach of his father's home west of London at Hammersmith. A visit to Harefield, to see those elms and the hillside mentioned in *Arcades*, seems far more likely than one to Ludlow, in the Welsh marches. But the fact is that we simply do not know how or how far the young Cambridge scholar was introduced into this circle of nobility in the early 1630s.

A conjecture has been that it may have come about from mutual acquaintances amongst musicians in London. Milton's father, a London scrivener who had nobility amongst his clients,[1] was a keen amateur musician, who would have known other musicians in the city, and the young poet himself spent some time with music, amongst his other studies, after he finally came down from Cambridge, aged twenty-four, in 1632. His poetry of the 1630s offers many connections with music and song, seeking the ancient ideal of the marriage of the arts. *At a Solemn Music* follows *Arcades* in the Trinity manuscript.

If by this time Milton's musical connection included the Lawes brothers, William and Henry, the link with the aristocratic group for which he wrote would be easier to imagine. Henry Lawes, the royal musician, taught singing to Lady Alice Egerton, the Lady of *Comus*, as he had previously to one of her older sisters, Lady Mary. Lawes (plate 1) was publicly to acknowledge a close connection with the family of the Earl of Bridgewater, for whom the Ludlow masque was written.² His brother William operated on the fringes of the royal music at this time. His occupations are not clear, except that we know that he wrote music for the theatre, for the King's Men.³ It is just possible that he had some connection with Ludlow.⁴ The three Egerton children who performed in the Ludlow masque all had some masquing experience at court in the early 1630s, when they would have been in contact with the royal music, as did George Brydges, Lord Chandos, a boy who lived at Harefield when *Arcades* was performed.⁵ We know from household accounts that the Lawes brothers visited Harefield during December 1634.⁶ We do not know whether they had been visitors before.

But we cannot assume that we know how the personal connections were made,⁷ and with regard to Henry Lawes, although it is plain from later documents⁸ that Milton knew him quite well, and although the poet's treatment of him in his role at Ludlow might suggest affection, one still cannot dismiss the possibility that the friendship developed as a consequence of joint enterprise in entertainment, rather than that it caused the enterprise. In particular, it seems less than necessary to regard Henry as a central participant in *Arcades*, as is sometimes assumed.⁹ Nothing from a Harefield entertainment survives in the Henry Lawes Manuscript, which records music from several masques.¹⁰ One could easily speculate about other kinds of connection with this large aristocratic family.

It could be, for example, that the Dowager Countess of Derby, at Harefield, one of Spenser's circle of good Protestant patronage back in Elizabethan times, was seeking to patronise a young scholar, just down from Cambridge apparently without a position and destined for the ministry, seemingly, or even to be a tutor or secretary, a gentleman–servant.¹¹ Everything about Milton's entertainment texts advertises the author as distinctly pastorly in attitude, amidst all the other social gestures for the occasions. Indeed no such texts are more pastorly than young Milton's, and few are as sophisticated in their display of learning. If such were being looked for, good religion and good learning were being displayed by the young scholar. Vocational interests are at least as likely as connections through music. The so-called Letter to a

Friend, in which Milton justifies his delay in entering orders, comes next but one to the text of *Arcades* in the Trinity manuscript.[12]

However the connection came about, the poet needed to know something of the families and situations for which he wrote, and to show that he knew. Aristocratic entertainments of this kind are built about known persons, present in the room or actually participating in the show. And they may be built about specific occasions.

Yet even here one must not assume too much. The technique of the better writers of masques and entertainments involved as much generalisation as particularity. Milton's audiences were invited to think beyond, or through, the specifics of the occasion towards exemplary ideas of fitness and conduct, even towards the fit subjects for a cultivated elite among whom serious poetry might flourish. Since the programmes of his entertainments are not merely constructed from personal allusion, general notions of the education of the nobility and their role in the nation are as relevant as particular private circumstances.

It is probably a mistake, too, to assume that the socially inferior young poet would have wished to allude too privately to the lives of his patrons. The point will become crucial in assessing the importance of the infamous Castlehaven scandal of 1631 to both occasions. As far as *Arcades* is concerned, apparently a private family entertainment including some of those directly affected by the scandal, all the poet needed to allude to were the general outlines of the family situation and the kinds of familial gesture that were to be made to the dowager countess. Of course he would have known about the scandal – everyone did – but he would hardly have wished to bring it to fresh notice in family festivities, either at Harefield, a year or two later, or more distantly at Ludlow in 1634.

With such reservations in mind, this chapter seeks to provide some immediate relevant contexts for both entertainments. There is much to appreciate. I shall suggest that *Arcades* makes a good deal of sense if understood in some particular contexts of life at Harefield in the 1630s. After some study of the position of members of the family at that time, one may begin to sense why some of them may have wished to dress as Arcadians to pay ritual

Contexts and occasions

tribute to the dowager countess. The Ludlow masque is of course a larger and more public affair, for a specific celebratory occasion, and presents greater variety of possible interactions with occasion. But here too considerations of the known actors and of the nature and circumstances of the Welsh presidential occasion enhance appreciation of the entertainment as entertainment, and also as exemplary statement. Through the Ludlow occasion Milton gave patterns not merely to nobility, in their festivity, but also of the well-being of nations.

Harefield in the 1630s

In *Arcades* a group of noble persons, mainly younger members of her family, bring courtly festivity, song and dance and music, to the Dowager Countess of Derby as she sits in her own house. It is a tribute of respect and affection, 'honour & devotion'. As a girl, as Alice Spenser, she had been brought up in a very prosperous country house in the Midlands. It was for her father's house, Althorp, that Ben Jonson was to write his first entertainment for royalty in 1603. (Milton seems to have known the text.) Her first husband, Ferdinando Stanley, Lord Strange, who became Earl of Derby in 1593, inherited also the ancient title of King of Man. By marriage Alice became, as in Milton's text, a kind of queen (plate 2). Stanley himself was a poet of some charm,[13] and he and his family, who were of the Leicester circle in Elizabeth's court, had well-established connections with literature and theatre, and also a lavish social life, especially at the 'Northern Court' of the Stanleys at Knowsley in Lancashire.[14] Ferdinando seems to be the 'Amyntas' mourned in Spenser's *Colin Clout's Come Home Again*, whilst Alice herself is celebrated as 'Amaryllis'. This is the family which gave patronage to Lord Strange's and Lord Derby's Men. At court Alice had participated in at least two Jacobean masques – Daniel's *Vision of the Twelve Goddesses* (1604) and Jonson's *Masque of Beauty* (1608)[15] – and had seen various country-house entertainments before. As Derby's wife, from 1579 to 1594, and as wife of Lord Keeper Egerton, from 1600 until his death in 1617, she had been celebrated by poets or named as patron.[16] She and Egerton had put on an entertainment at Harefield for the visit of Queen

Milton's Aristocratic entertainments

Elizabeth on the last summer progress in 1602. Sir John Davies had provided that text.[17] The countess herself had been welcomed in a royal-style entertainment at Ashby de la Zouch by her daughter and son-in-law, the Earl of Huntingdon, in 1607. For that occasion John Marston wrote the verses.[18] She had moved in the world of courtly and aristocratic ritual. By the time of *Arcades* she was in her seventies and did not stir from Harefield so far as to go to court, but younger members of her family were attending and participating in court masques. So a taste of Arcadian court fashion in entertainment is brought by them to her.

The dowager was a lively, determined character. Like most nobility of her time, especially perhaps the newer aristocracy, she cared a good deal about family status and style. Her father, Sir John Spenser, was an influential man in the Midlands, whose family had made its wealth out of sheep farming. Her first marriage had brought her into the highest circles at court. Her husband died, however, only nine months after inheriting the earldom. Egerton, her second husband, was a very important self-made man at court and he knew the Stanley estates in his capacity as legal adviser. Since she and Derby had no male issue but only three daughters, the earldom passed to Ferdinando's younger brother William. Much of the estate had been willed to her. The new earl tried to keep as much land as he could with the title. In the legal wrangles over Ferdinando's estate, Egerton acted for the countess. The dispute came to be of celebrated proportions, both parties being fighters, and lasted sixteen years until finished by an act of parliament in 1609. In all this, the dowager, aided by Egerton, proved, as Fogle says, a 'sturdy and tenacious defender of her interests'. Those same tenacious qualities can be seen in her in the 1630s.

Egerton, however, had found his wife too independent and self-interested for his tastes, after he had married her. They had a notoriously bad relationship. There was personal antipathy and a clash of wills. According to sad and embittered notes which Egerton left for his only surviving son, John (the future Earl of Bridgewater), the troubles began early, after John had been married to Frances, one of the countess' daughters, in 1601. Egerton accused the mother of resisting delivering the dowry out of the Stanley estates and of grasping at his own wealth. Disputed inheritances can hardly have helped, but both were holding and trying to better what they had.

Important man though he was, Egerton was the countess' social inferior. Whether for this reason, or for sheer distaste, her funeral monument in Harefield church did not mention her second marriage, until later generations added to the inscription. It featured her first marriage and the noble unions of her three daughters. The same omission and the same emphasis on noble unions, for her and her daughters, is evident in the engraved portrait of the countess, evidently made in 1624 or after (plate 3). But, preoccupied with family status though she was, hers was far from being a crude mind. She was a woman of some sophistication and high principle.

Harefield had been bought by Egerton after his marriage to the dowager at the beginning of the century. As an elderly woman she lived on there until her death on 26 January 1636/7. The estate itself at Harefield was of moderate size and comprised the manors of Harefield and Moor Hall. The Moor Hall manor house, by her time probably little more than a farm, stood in the valley by an old Knights Templar chapel apparently used as a stone barn.[19] The manor house of Harefield, surrounded by its park, stood on rising ground above the church and commanded a view over the river Colne and across towards Windsor Forest. The site (actually of a later house) is still visible, though unattractively kept and engulfed in suburbia. Almshouses built by the countess still stand along the road below.

By about 1630 she had rather a diminished household. For her station, she was not conspicuously prosperous. Her style was dignified – never less than that – but not lavish. On 14 June 1630, for example, she wrote to her daughter Frances, Countess of Bridgewater, that

> If you here any more speech of my Lady Killigray coming to see me I pray send me word with all speed it may be, that I may send to London for provision because I am not so well furnished in mine owne house as I could wish. Besides, I am sometimes from home at the house which I am building to set it forward; that if it should please God to call me, I might have a place to lay my stuffe in, out of my Lord of Castlehaven's fingering.[20]

The building of a house elsewhere was no extravagance but rather a measure of prudent opposition to the Earl of Castlehaven, to whom we shall return. He had married her eldest daughter, Lady Anne, widow of Lord Chandos, in 1624.[21] As one of the three daughters Anne was co-heir to the estate.

In order to understand the position at Harefield at the time that *Arcades* was performed, we must first understand the position of the dowager's three daughters and of her grandchildren. Her three middle-aged daughters were in differing circumstances, but had married earls. The second daughter was the most happily placed. As I have mentioned, Frances had married her step-brother Sir John Egerton, later Earl of Bridgewater, the only surviving son of the Lord Keeper. The Egerton estates, built up by the canny old lawyer, were considerable. Bridgewater was also a privy councillor and in 1631 he was selected to become President of Wales, the vacancy having occurred with the death of the Earl of Northampton. However, thus far he had married off nothing but daughters, which must have called heavily on his resources. By 1634, when the three youngest and only unmarried children, Alice (b. 1619), John (b. 1623), and Thomas (b. 1625), performed in the Ludlow masque, he had given away seven daughters in marriage.[22] This branch was prosperous, but not unembarrassed by financial concern. In fact Bridgewater ran seriously into debt by the late 1630s, and his son struggled with the debts for a lifetime. The problems arose largely because of the failure of the East Indies venture of the Courteens. Bridgewater had made large investments in them.[23]

The Countess of Derby's eldest daughter Anne had, to begin with, made a rich and prestigious match with Grey Brydges, fifth Baron Chandos, the so-called King of the Cotswolds, who died in 1621. This was an alliance with older nobility and a life of some style. Her second marriage, at Harefield in 1624, to Mervyn Touchet, Lord Audley, Earl of Castlehaven, proved a bane, when the family discovered that it had disposed of estates to a man who was untrustworthy and an infamous sexual pervert. This marriage to an earl is also unmentioned on the funeral monument (plate 4) in Harefield church. There were no children born of the alliance of Lady Anne and Castlehaven, but both had children by their previous marriages. Anne's children were two boys, George, Lord Chandos (b. 1620), and William (b. 1621), and two girls,

Contexts and occasions

Elizabeth (b. 1616?) and another daughter probably named Frances.²⁴

The Countess of Derby's third daughter, Elizabeth, (plate 5) for whom Donne had written verse, had married Henry Hastings in 1603. Hastings was heir to the earldom of Huntingdon, to which he soon succeeded in December 1604. This also was a prestigious match. The Hastings, like the Stanleys, had connections with the blood royal, and their wealth had once been very large. Henry still fulfilled some offices consonant with his station – he was Lord Lieutenant of Leicestershire and Rutland. But his great-uncle, the famous open-handed 'Puritan Earl', the greatest benefactor of reformers in the Elizabethan period, had been compelled to sell off or mortgage most of his lands, and his estates were left in ruins at his death in 1595. Neither George, the fourth earl, nor Henry, the fifth, could recover from the enormous burden of inherited debts. One single schedule of debts for 1621 shows that at that time he raised loans to the amount of £11,662 and that he also owed £600 further to the crown.²⁵ By 1630 he was living in sadly reduced circumstances at Donnington Park, Leicestershire, ill and oppressed, seldom coming to court – his life was one long string of excuses to the king – and repeatedly failing to pay his subsidies. His wife often did his business for him, when she was in London. In his own words, this is how he stood:

all my lands as y^r Lo. knowes are in extent to his Matie for my Ancestors debt, my land intayled, three of my yonger Children unprovided for, and my self in many Thowsand pounds debts, & the lands I have reserved for the payment therof being but sufficient for that end; therefore I hope by y^r Lps favourable information unto his Matie of these just reasons, I shalbe excused for lending seing I cannot doe it unlesse I take it upon use and plunge my self further into debt.²⁶

By 1631 his wife, when in London, is trying to recover pawned beds and bedhangings.²⁷ The Hastings finances were dire. The dowager gave assistance to this branch of her family, to which she was close, and in which she had four grandchildren: Ferdinand, Lord Hastings (b. 1608), married in 1623 to Lucy, only daughter of Sir John Davies, when she was still a child but brought a good dowry; Henry (b. 1609); Alice (b. 1606); and Elizabeth (b. 1612).²⁸

Milton's Aristocratic entertainments

To understand Harefield in the 1630s it is necessary also to rehearse the disasters of 1631. In that year, when the dowager was seventy-two, the pattern of life in the house changed after the behaviour of Castlehaven was brought to public notice by his son and heir, James Touchet, Lord Audley, as soon as he came of age. The Castlehaven affair was a scandal through the land, and there are several contemporary accounts of it.[29] Recently it has been described again in connection with Milton's Ludlow masque. The concentration on the ideal of chastity in *Comus* and what look like cuts in passages connected with sexual mores in the Bridgewater manuscript text have been associated with it, so that the masque has been seen as a kind of public purgation for the family.[30] It seems to me unlikely that the scandal did very much to determine the masque thematically, at least in such a pointed way. The evils countered in the masque can be accounted for otherwise. (The nature of the cuts in the Bridgewater text is discussed in the Appendix below.) What might be noticed, however, is the relevance of the Castlehaven affair to the familial situation out of which *Arcades* grew. It is quite possible that there would have been no *Arcades* had the upheavals caused by the affair not taken place.

Briefly, the events were these. Soon after his marriage to Lady Anne, Castlehaven submitted her to all sorts of sexual insults and outrages. He had some of his favourite servants assault her sexually, while he watched, and made others display their sexual organs in front of her. He himself seems to have had homosexual relations with a number of his servants and to have kept a common prostitute in the house. So much was alleged. He contrived a marriage between his elder son and Anne's elder daughter, Elizabeth, in 1628. The girl was then about twelve. Having married her to his son, Castlehaven reputedly had her forced by one of his servants, while he watched, and his servants often sleep with her, hoping, it was alleged, to beget a further heir and to disinherit his own son. To complete his case, he was suspected of popery. For his sexual misdemeanours he was tried by his peers, and his execution took place in May 1631. In July two of his servants were hanged at Tyburn, talking to the last. Castlehaven always protested his innocence, as did his deranged sister, the prophetess Lady Eleanor Douglas (the former wife of Sir John

Contexts and occasions

Davies), but few can have believed him, and certainly none of his wife's family.

Much of the aftermath was reaped by the Countess of Derby, whose daughter and granddaughter were the injured or tainted parties. She took in Lady Castlehaven's children and undertook their proper education. She would not at first welcome Lady Castlehaven herself or the ruined granddaughter Elizabeth. She wrote to Secretary Dorchester:

> And that my daughter and she [Elizabeth] may be so happie to receive their pardon from the King. and till such time I shall never willinglie yeeld to see either of them. for the sight of them would but Increase my griefs, whose hart is almost wounded to death already wth thinking of so fowle a businesse.[31]

Furthermore, she was frightened lest 'there should be some sparkes of my Grandchilde Awdlies misbehaviour remaining, wch might give ill example to ye young ones wch are wth me'. For she had in her house at Harefield 'two of her young Brothers, & sister, whoe as yet, (I humbly thanke God) are both hopefull & vertuous'. She was going to do her best to 'govern' these young ones and to re-establish them in respectable circles. Quite realistically, she was taking no further chances with the damaged name of the family.

Money also concerned her. During the summer of 1631 she entered into negotiations with the crown for help in maintaining her new dependants. Without help from the king, she said, her daughter and granddaughter

> are lefte most miserable in deed: destitute of all other meanes to mayntaine either of them, but that myselfe out of my poore estate am faine to releeve them, and all the children of my daughters besides.[32]

In 1631, then, the dowager gained five noble dependants in desperate straits. Two of these she helped to support away from her own home, and three of the children she maintained within her own household at Harefield. I have no evidence that the two ever came to reside at Harefield on a long-term basis, although the desired pardons were granted in November of the same year.[33] By 1634, a year for which household accounts survive, Elizabeth does not seem to be in the house, and Lady Castlehaven certainly was living elsewhere, for money is dispatched to her by servant for her to give away in charity.³⁴ Nor can I find any mention of the other Brydges girl about the house in 1634. Although of course she continued to bear some responsibility for this whole stricken branch of the family (and with the girls this may have lasted until they could be married off), it may be that in 1634 she had chiefly to watch over the boys in her house. On Lord Chandos, of course (plate 6), the future dignity of the line would depend. When they came to her in 1631, George Lord Chandos was eleven, and William his brother ten. Masson (1 562) suggested that the Brydges children might have been among the 'Noble members of her family' who appeared as Arcadians in the entertainment. This seems very likely, as all were dependent on her to some extent, and two or three permanent residents of the house. It was to Lord Chandos that she bequeathed the Harefield and Moor Hall estates in her will.³⁵

The Brydges children were far from being the dowager's only juvenile care. At least two of her other grandchildren were resident at Harefield. Living with her grandmother through this period was Lady Alice Hastings, called 'Ayels' by her family, the elder daughter of the impoverished and world-worn Earl of Huntingdon. When her Brydges cousins arrived in the house, she was already a mature spinster of twenty-five. She had been taken over and brought up by her grandmother and became her constant companion for the rest of the dowager's lifetime. It is to Lady Alice Hastings alone that Ralph Codrington, writer of tedious and precious elegies, addresses his piece on the dowager's death.³⁶ She is regularly referred to in accounts as 'lady Alice', and some further measure of her permanence, if such is needed, may be gained from the fact that she had become a copyholder of some valley land in the manor.³⁷ Back in 1626, when Alice had reached twenty, her grandmother had proposed to her parents that she should be married and that she herself would furnish a dowry of £3,000 for her.³⁸ Her parents plainly could raise no worthy dowry. Alice was to be shown to various families who might be interested in the match. Nothing came of these schemes, which put Huntingdon and his wife under even greater sense of obligation to the countess, but one should note how even the Countess of Huntingdon expressed herself to the earl: 'my la[dy] dothe not mean ever to part wth her but to a husband'.

Contexts and occasions

Alice's younger sister Elizabeth, 'Bess', seems also to have been brought up at Harefield at her grandmother's expense. Her mother visited Harefield in most years, on her London trips, and her lively letters back to Huntingdon sometimes report how their two girls are doing. My lady is well, she reports in 1626, 'my children so to[o] . . . Bess sings very fynely' and 'is something fatter wch well becomes her'.[39] The girl was about fourteen at the time. Elizabeth left her adopted home when in the spring of 1634, aged twenty-two, she was married to Hugh Calverley. The wedding was at Harefield and her grandmother bore the cost of the festivity.[40] I do not know where the dowry came from.[41] There was a family gathering, to which various of the Hastings (even including Huntingdon himself) and Egertons came.[42]

The mention of Bess' singing probably indicates that the countess provided musical tuition for her charges. When she undertook something, she did it in the proper way. Grandchildren in her care were brought up to fulfil their true station in life. Though we have no record of Alice's musicality, it may be symptomatic of her musical education also that we find her giving authority to Mr Jones for the payment for new strings for the viols in 1634.[43] All in all, Hastings' debts of gratitude to the dowager for the care of the two girls were almost as great as those of the two Brydges boys, and stretched back much further.

The Countess of Derby was in fact a vigorous manager of the lives of those in her family who needed support. She was the sort of benefactor who knew what she wanted for the wellbeing and honour of the family. One tried not to offend her.[44] Everywhere one meets signs of her most practical care for all these people, as in her tactful if down-to-earth attempt, in 1635, to persuade her son-in-law Huntingdon to remarry, his beloved wife having died in January 1633/4,[45] in order to help his estate and the fortunes of his children;[46] or in little things like the purchase of Quarles' *Emblems*, good instructive fare, for William Brydges, then aged twelve, at Christmas 1634.[47] She took an active interest, too, in the education of Lord Hastings' child-bride, commending her in a letter of 1625 for the improvement of her letter-writing.[48] Protestantism was at its most positive in this imperious old lady, whom Milton was not unaptly to celebrate as aristocrat and to call a rural queen.

Milton's Aristocratic entertainments

There can be little doubt that this group of people, especially the grandchildren she had taken into her care, was at the centre of that group of nobles presenting 'honour & devotion'. The general situation in the family in this the last portion of the dowager's life suggests that the entertainment of which *Arcades* was a part might have been dedicated to her out of a sense of obligation and grateful recognition for the way in which she had served as centre to the family in a difficult time. This would seem to be part of the social or familial gesture behind the ordering of the text. Milton's verses celebrated her as the head of an ideal household, a 'shrine' of virtue around which nature is blessed back into health and prosperity each night, and where a spirit of rural innocence can demonstrate the presence of virtue by listening to the music of the spheres.

The relationship with the Egerton branch of the family should be considered too, all the more so, since communication between the houses was frequent. Ashridge, the country seat of the Earl of Bridgewater, is only some sixteen miles from Harefield. There were frequent messages and visits from Ashridge. Communications with the Egertons were also regular when they were in London, and, perhaps most significant of all, since the distance is large, letters went to and fro many times when the earl and his family went down to Wales on the presidential visit of 1634. Doubtless the dowager was keen to hear of those events. Unfortunately, little of all this correspondence has survived.

Of course the countess stood rather differently against this branch of her family, so much the most prosperous at this time. It has been said that the wealthier Bridgewater offered no help to her during the crisis,[49] but there is evidence to the contrary. For example, he paid Lady Castlehaven's livery fees in October 1631.[50] Perhaps it was considered prudent for him not to appear to get involved too publicly; the prestige of the family depended largely on him. But he certainly gave help, for which she was grateful. The following is the beginning of a letter dating from before those troubles, but it gives an idea of the cordial relationship between the dowager and the Egertons. She writes to her daughter –

how much I think my selfe beholding to my Lo: and yo^u for both yor caers, & readynes to doe me all the Courtesies y^t may be in my businese's, theis lines cannot witnes. but I hope ere longe to see my Lo: & yo^w heere where I may in some sort expresse my thankfull heart to his Lo:^{sh}.[51]

Worth noting, too, is the fact that on his visit to Harefield in the summer of 1634, his farewell visit before departure to Ludlow, Bridgewater seems to have had with him in his party young Lord Castlehaven.[52]

In a sense, the countess was trying to achieve for her new dependants, especially the Brydges boys, the same sort of station which her Egerton grandchildren had already gained at court. She must have taken some satisfaction in this branch of the family, which was upholding the sort of position she herself had known as a younger woman. In connection with *Arcades* the place of all her grandchildren at court may be of some relevance, since another function of the entertainment would seem to be to set the Harefield festivity against courtly festivities such as some of the younger members of the family had been participating in.

By the winter festive season of 1633/4 Harefield itself was contributing to royal masque. On Shrove Tuesday young Lord Chandos joined his two Egerton cousins, the two brothers of Milton's masque, as one of the pages performing in Carew's *Coelum Britannicum*. The boys danced with torches in their hands as a prelude to the entry of the king and other main masquers. Chandos was then about thirteen and a half. In the summer of 1634, after his fourteenth birthday, he went up to Oxford for a term, returning in mid December. After that Christmas he spent further time in London, staying at Bridgewater House, attending a legal hearing, and moving again in court circles, this time as spectator in the latest masque, *The Temple of Love*.[53] He was being prepared for his role in life and coming out into the world. A few years later his younger brother was also to be entered at Oxford.

The year 1634 was also of course the auspicious one of Bridgewater's presidential visit to Wales and of the impressive parts of her three youngest Egerton grandchildren in the Ludlow masque. But Egertons had been appearing in court masque for some years before. The queen's Shrove Tuesday masque of 1631/2, *Tempe Restored*, for example, had given masquing roles to two Egerton girls and one boy. And of course the Egerton family regularly attended masque nights, even when they hadn't masquing parts.

Milton's Aristocratic entertainments

The exact date of the *Arcades* entertainment is not known. It presents a problem not without interest for Milton's career, because it also marks the start of Milton's use of the Trinity manuscript book. Whatever its precise occasion, *Arcades* comes between the troubled times of the Castlehaven crisis in 1631, presumably a comfortable time after the spring of that year, and the festive highpoint for the family in 1634. It seems to pay tribute to the dowager, as well as to entertain her, during a period in which she had been more than ever active for the welfare of her family, especially for the interests of its youngest generation, its masquing generation. The celebration of her in *Arcades* as unrivalled centre to the family spoke well enough to the real situation.

Ludlow and the presidential feast

Lord Keeper Egerton, finally Lord Chancellor Egerton under James, had died before receiving a major peerage for his many services to the crown. James had created him Baron Ellesmere in 1603. He became Viscount Brackley in 1616 and died in 1617. The honour of an earldom was bestowed, at a price, on his son John, who was created first Earl of Bridgewater in 1617. In the same year Bridgewater became a member of the Council of Wales, as his father had been before him.

The Council consisted formally of many peers and gentlemen, but the working part of it, for most purposes, was a group of judges and attendant officers who were resident in Wales and centred at Ludlow in Shropshire.[54] The castle served as court and as main official residence of the president.

Bridgewater (plate 7), the patron of Milton's Ludlow masque of 1634, was a man of principle. As a twenty-year-old he had briefly sought fame by going on Essex's Irish expedition, but since then his experience had been parliamentary and administrative. By the time of the masque he was fifty-five, somewhat delicate in health, and gout-ridden. Much quieter, much less forceful than his father, apt to play the part of being overburdened, he took all his duties seriously. The Margery Evans case, discussed by Marcus,[55] is just one instance of his general conscientiousness. He had become a

Contexts and occasions

privy councillor in 1626. In June 1631 he had been nominated to be President of the Council in Wales and in the same year was made Lord Lieutenant of the Welsh and border counties, as was usual with Lords President. These were honours a good deal more than nominal. Some of the Ellesmere estates were in the marches. Bridgewater had well-established connections there.

The Instructions issued on behalf of the king to the new president followed a pattern set in the previous century.[56] As Lord President, Bridgewater was to be the direct representative of the crown in one of the outlying regions of the kingdom, responsible for the due order of justice and civil peace in those parts. An equivalent position was that of Lord President of the North, whose court sat at York. One of Bridgewater's predecessors as President of Wales, Lord Zouch, had been referred to, laconically, as playing 'rex in Wales'.[57]

There had been considerable objection in Jacobean times to the extent of the court's jurisdiction, especially with regard to the four English counties, Shropshire, Gloucestershire, Herefordshire and Worcestershire. The Privy Council of the 1630s, however, seems to have been determined to uphold the dignity of the court, seeing in it something of a parallel case with that of Star Chamber. It may be symptomatic of this resolve to support the court that the list of councillors in the 1633 Instructions is much longer than any before, numbering in excess of eighty-four, including twenty-four peers and eleven bishops.

At this time Sir Thomas Wentworth, later Earl of Strafford, held the positions of Lord President of the North and of Lord Deputy of Ireland. He was vigorous enough on behalf of the authority of the king. Bridgewater would have begun his duties with a consciousness that a certain effort was required on his part to maintain or better the standing of his court. His responsibilities, especially those as Lord Lieutenant, were to become pretty unpleasant by the late 1630s, in the deteriorating political climate and with his worsening finances.

Presidents were not expected to be continuously resident at Ludlow or to travel everywhere with the court when it was held elsewhere. The routine business was seen to by a system of deputies.[58] The celebrated early president, Bishop Lee, who took up his duties in 1534, had travelled extensively about Wales and the marches, seeking out enormities to redress: 'sythens that tyme ... there hath not succeded such stowte travelling Presidentes', remarked Gerard later that century.[59] In the early seventeenth century presidents were only sporadically resident at Ludlow. But it was clearly regarded as necessary that a president should spend some time with his court. There must have been some pressure on Bridgewater, to which he would have been responsive, to put in an appearance as soon as he reasonably could.

In fact, he began on some of his duties immediately in 1631. The many letters about the vexatious business of nominating sheriffs and escheators, for example, begin at this time. An interchange of letters also took place between Bridgewater's London and Hertfordshire homes and the officer in charge at Ludlow, Capt. Betts, to establish the condition of the castle and its grounds. The place needed some refurbishing. Bridgewater sent a man down to inspect it in the summer of 1631.[60] Preparations were beginning. Yet the first period of residence was not to begin for three years, not until the summer of 1634. In a letter to the council the earl apologised for the delay and pleaded 'extraordinary occasions preventing my coming to Ludlow'.[61] Circumstances evidently prevented the first residence in the summers of 1631, 1632 and 1633.

What was happening in this interim is not entirely clear, although several factors emerge. Some household accounts tell us that Bridgewater was away for a while 'towards the North', leaving in October 1630.[62] I do not know what business took him there, or where he went. He was back in London only in June 1631, having not been among the peers trying Castlehaven in April of that year. He seems to have been absent from Privy Council, in fact, from February 1630 to 10 June 1631.[63] That he had been away so recently may at least explain why he did not make the journey to Ludlow in the summer of 1631.

The difficulties of 1632 probably connect with money. In a letter to her husband that summer, Lady Huntingdon reported that complications had arisen about the grant of land which was to furnish the expenses for the president. The same lands had been granted to someone else.[64] It would seem likely that the crown itself had not been properly organised to allow residence in 1632.

Contexts and occasions

The new Instructions were issued on 8 May 1633, shortly before the king's Scottish journey. The issue of the Instructions would seem to indicate that Bridgewater had finally been expected to go to Ludlow during the summer of 1633. Exactly what went wrong with 1633 one can only guess. It may have been something to do with illness. The earl was quite ill in February, as he had been at various other times.[65] It has also been conjectured, for the whole period of the delay, that it had to do with the arrangement of three marriages for daughters.[66] It may even be to do with the pressure of other court business. Whatever it was, in the summer of 1633 Bridgewater was one of the privy councillors left in London whilst the king was in Scotland, and he was in the thick of court business at that time, as the records show. In the previous two years he had followed the practice of leaving the court in early August and returning in early November, presumably to spend most of that time in the country at Ashridge. The summer of 1633 seems to have been particularly busy for him at court.

All this delay can only have added to the sense of expectancy for the ceremonial visit, on which Bridgewater eventually set out from Ashridge on 1 July 1634.[67] We know also that it added to the pile of work awaiting him in Wales.[68] He attended his last Privy Council on 27 June. Preparations for Ludlow and the tying up of other business gave him plenty to do. He refused an invitation to stay at supper at Sir William Courteen's house in Fenchurch Street one evening at this time, because he was too busy.[69] Presumably he moved from London to Ashridge, where the journey proper was to begin. Then, as we have seen, he came across from Ashridge to Harefield at the very end of June for farewells, and quite a company of people assembled there.[70] Young William Courteen, his son-in-law, seems to have been propositioning him about some venture even as the earl was leaving in his coach.[71]

The journey from Ashridge to Ludlow lasted four days, with overnight stops at Bicester, Moreton-in-Marsh and Worcester. There were at least one coach (later a 'best' one is mentioned), a cart and many packhorses. Bells were rung in Worcester. The Courteens, always attentive, delivered some trout for the earl's supper in Moreton-in-Marsh, and the servant of the younger Courteen who had delivered the trout, together with a chaplain and various servants and tenants of the elder Courteen, met

Bridgewater on the road at Pershore and gave him company into Worcester.[72] They also saw him out of town the next morning. Such courtesies attended the journey. Money was dispensed to the poor. The party came into Ludlow in the evening of 4 July.

Bridgewater was back in London again before the end of October.[73] This was no long residence at Ludlow, but a first official visitation, marked with some ceremony. There were to be later visits, some of them protracted. The visitation was also not simply of the court at Ludlow, but of Wales, or at least of the marches, and of the area of some of the Ellesmere estates. Bridgewater was not even continuously resident in Ludlow after his arrival in early July. Fragments of accounts in the Ellesmere papers,[74] and other sources, show that he left Ludlow probably after the end of the Midsummer term of the court, at the end of July, and travelled up the marches and into Cheshire, before making an extended stay – a kind of holiday, I think – of some three weeks at Lyme Park, north of Macclesfield and at the foot of the Pennines. He had arrived at Lyme by 24 August. When he left again, it was on the morning of 15 September, to travel to Congleton (where bells were rung) for the first night, and then to Market Drayton (where he lodged at the Talbot), to arrive back in Ludlow on the evening of the 17th. His family was with him at Lyme, as was Henry Lawes.

There were, then, in fact, two stays at Ludlow in 1634, the first period of nearly a month from 4 July, and the second in the latter part of September and the first part of October. The return itinerary from Ludlow to Ashridge is not known, except that it ran further east than the journey there and went through Towcester.

As for the journeys from Ludlow to Lyme and back, they were quite different from one another. The three-day return to Ludlow was as fast and as straightforward as could be expected. The journey up to Lyme is the one of greater interest, a little more like a progress. It took the first three weeks of August and involved staying in a series of great houses with the influential families of the region. The first entertainment we can be sure of on this tour was at Chirk Castle, some two days' journey north of Ludlow. The host at Chirk was Sir Thomas Middleton. The intermediate stopping-place between Ludlow and Chirk, seems to have been Eyton Hall, the mansion of the Newport family, relatives of the Herberts, thence kinsmen of Bridgewater, on the banks of the

Severn southeast of Shrewsbury. Bridgewater may have stayed at Eyton for two days.

The stay at Chirk was short. Scraps of accounts for the journey from Chirk to Lyme, beginning on 3 August, giving tantalising hints of the itinerary. They went into Denbighshire, into the Clwyd valley, coming through Ruthin on 5 August, as Peter Roberts noted in his chronicle. On the following day, a Wednesday, the earl reappeared in Ruthin for a muster. In that area the houses he stayed in were probably Bachymbyd and Plas Coch. Next the party seems to have gone north, to the coast at Mostyn, where they probably stayed in the Hall and the countess gave alms to a poor boy. Then, proceeding eastwards, they stayed at Bretton Hall, just west of Chester, before coming across, southeast, to Cholmondley Hall, north of Whitchurch. From that area (from Ridley – 'Rdy'?) they travelled to Dunham Massey Hall, by Altrincham. The last leg was from Dunham to Lyme. It had been a substantial, looping journey, lasting more than three weeks and including many activities.[75]

Lyme Park, the destination, was the home of Sir Peter Legh, a relative and friend of Bridgewater.[76] The Leghs were an old Cheshire family, part of a circle to which Egertons were allied. Sir Peter had married as his second wife Dorothy Brereton, née Egerton, a half-sister of Sir Thomas Egerton. By 1634 Legh was an old man; he was to die two years later. Though he could be a tyrant – Bridgewater had once interceded on behalf of one of the Legh sons in disgrace with an unforgiving father – it would seem that Lyme could be a jocular place. Its master was quite cultured, liked books and music, and his large household had once included a jester.

The following letter to Sir Peter is a belated thank-you for the hospitality at Lyme in the summer of 1634, not from Bridgewater himself, who had seen to it at parting that the household had its gifts, but from the musician Henry Lawes.[77] It is, I believe, the only concrete evidence we have of Lawes' presence with the family on the Welsh tour, apart from the printed masque text, and it proves that he had accompanied the family at Lyme as well as at Ludlow for the time of the masque. The letter was written on 5 February 1634/5, some six months after the visit, and begins by apologising for the delay in rendering thanks, but the sev'rall Objects And diversity of unlookd for Occasions (y^t Enterpose, And that I daily met wth where I Move And have my beinge) doe soe Often divert me from my best Intentions, that I must of for[c]e be liable to much Censure, And in perticular [beg] yor pardon, that I have not let loose my respects, & [hu]mble thankfullness to you Longe since for ye good welcome & many favors I receavd from you when I was at Lyme. but you have A Noble way to Oblige all y^t make Adress unto you. I must Ingeniously Confess, I never went more willingly to Schoole, Or Ever found better Conversation in a Dog-keñell then at Lyme. whyther I could more willingly retorne (if my fate would guide me) then to Any part of ye principallitye. I shall be bound for this Sūmer. but I will not dispaire to visitt you Once More at Lyme, & greet you wth the second part of my Lord said to Sr Edward &c or somthinge as ridiculous to make sport wth, though nothinge can be thought on soe Contemptible as Sr Edward or his Lor[?] wch is the Only thinge y^t now remaines of Either of them.

S^r I dare not trouble you wth much protestation, nor will I sprinkle you wth Court holy water, yet give me leave, hastily, to wish you all ye happines A Good Man can Expect or desire in this world. that you may longe Enjoy yor Health And Abillitys both of body & Mynde, to ye good of many y^t subsist by you, And to ye Generall Joy of those Numerous ffriends you have whoe Really Love you. as for me that Am Scarce worthy of yor knowledge, I shall In what I can whylst I Am, Ever remaine

yor ffaithful Servant
Henry Lawes

S^r if I Appear not too Rashe[?], I shall desire you to present my service to yor Good Lady, for the Rest, I shall Convay my respects to them by A second Hand.

London this 5th of ffeb.
1634.

These pieces of information about the presidential activities and journeyings in the summer of 1634 have not been known or at least assembled for Miltonists before, and they help to suggest some contexts and functions for the whole tour as well as for Milton's Ludlow masque. As far as Bridgewater himself was concerned, he was showing himself, and in response various places were honouring him as president, privy councillor and influential landowner. He had plenty to do, at first especially, in administrative work at Ludlow. Correspondence shows that for him the first period of stay at Ludlow was wholly taken up with business. That year the Midsummer term of the court was between 27 June, just before he arrived, and 23 July.[78] During term time everyone would be present in town. Still by 28 July, after the end of the term and presumably just prior to departure towards the north, Bridgewater excuses the brevity of one letter for the 'dispatch of my Businesse' and complains mildly in another that he is 'ful of Businesse as I could wish & pr^{haps} more'.[79] On 19 July he had written to his son-in-law Courteen about 'recreations':

> I wish y^o more plenty than I have had yet founde since my comming hether; having not yet had leasure to goe out of the Castle Gate since I first entered therin, save onely that on Sunday last I went to the Church, in the Towne here, forenoone & afternoone, whereof I give yo^u notice not to make any bragges of my devotions, but to lett y^o knowe how close I am kept to my work, wch lyeth the heavier upon me both in respect of my long absence hence, & Sr Jno Brygeman's [the Chief Justice of Chester] employm^{nt} in the Justice seate at Glost^r.[80]

It was the second period of stay at Ludlow, from mid September to mid October, which had more of the sense of recreations about it. The Michaelmas term of the court did not begin until 3 November, after the president had returned to Hertfordshire and London. Milton's masque was of course performed on Michaelmas night, 29 September, during this second period of stay.

Disappointingly, there is no mention of the Michaelmas festivity of which the masque was a part either in the patchy Bridgewater correspondence or in the fragmentary household papers of the period. The masque would as usual have followed a banquet; Milton's text assumes as much and creates its adversary, Comus, accordingly. But it might have been too much to hope that mention of masquing would have come through in the earl's correspondence, even supposing that we had it all. Not that he was uninterested in cultural things – he had a large library, took an interest in the education of his children, and the copy he made as a youth of Coprario's book of musical composition still survives[81] – but rather that he always gave the air of being busily preoccupied with his various duties, even before the visit to Ludlow. It might have been in the papers of Lady Bridgewater (plate 8), very few of which have survived, that more active involvement with these things would have appeared. The catalogue of her own books proves that she was well-read, and, like her sister Lady Huntingdon, she kept abreast of literature, theatrical, historical, devotional. Acquisitions of 1633 included Herbert's *The Temple* and Jonson's *The New Inn*.[82]

Milton's Aristocratic entertainments

In fact, the Ludlow masque was not the only dramatic presentation during Bridgewater's presidential tour. The earl, his wife and the three youngest children, the group of *Comus*, were given songs and speeches at a banquet entertainment at Chirk Castle at the beginning of August.[83] The presentation copy, once in the Bridgewater Library, is now, somewhat disguised by Payne Collier, in the British Library. In this text, hastily written for the occasion, probably by Sir Thomas Salusbury, the region is made to honour its great visitors from court, alluding to Bridgewater's presidential function. Provinciality touches its forelock and offers what riches it can. This poet, like Milton though far more simply, is concerned to define a right relationship between President and region, and to take a certain auspiciousness from the occasion of their coming together.

As for Milton's masque, there is the intriguing question of just how and where the performance was prepared for. Staging may have been simple by comparison with court masques, but some scenic effects were required. Moreover, Milton's text was hardly simple to learn, the whole style being much more dramatic than was usual and all the parts of some length, especially considering the young age of the two boys. The strenuousness of the itinerary between the beginning of July and 29 September might give us pause to wonder. More specifically, between the return from Lyme and the day of performance there were only eleven days.

We do not know when the masque was first planned or when and for how long Milton was writing it. If one believes that Michaelmas themes were integral from the start, then the date of conception is not likely to have been too long in advance: would they have been aiming precisely for 29 September many months before? On the other hand, the ambitious nature of the text might suggest that Bridgewater's family had a version of it with them in Wales for some time prior to performance, that it must have been planned some while in advance, and that Milton would have been working on it in the early summer at the latest. Henry Lawes and perhaps others must have consulted with Milton during the composition. It may be that some of these consultative developments are visible in alterations in the 1634 Trinity manuscript text. At some point Lawes himself must have left London for Wales, probably at the beginning of July with Bridgewater, but possibly at a slightly later time, taking with him a text, perhaps. For reasons which I argue later in the book,[84] I think that the modifications in the text as represented by the Bridgewater manuscript were made after it had left Milton's hands and had departed to its destiny at Ludlow. As for the Egerton children themselves, it seems likely that they would have had their parts with them at Lyme, in all likelihood before, during the first spell at Ludlow, and that the rehearsal of this most literary, sophisticated entertainment was as it were their educational vacation project. Various tutors may have been involved. The masque has its urgent public symbolism, but as a familial gesture it seems like a cultured offering of three children to their parents, in recognition of the education they were receiving, 'so goodly growne'. Lyme would have been a fit place for preparation of the children's dramatic and musical parts. It could have been that Lawes composed his songs for the masque whilst at Lyme, and that other parties left behind in Ludlow arranged the other music which we do not have, only Lawes' contribution having survived.[85]

Questions have been raised about the parties actually present at the masque and participants in it. Whilst we do not know the full composition of Bridgewater's own party in Wales, both *Comus* and the Chirk entertainment indicate that only the president, his wife and the three youngest, unmarried children, of the immediate family, went to Wales. At this time Lady Alice was 15, John, Lord Brackley, the earl's elder son, 11, and Thomas, the younger, 9 (plates 9–14). Milton fitted the ages of the three young masquers with intelligence, in both realistic and exemplary fashion, and built much on considerations of godly education and noble conduct; *daemon iuvenis*, a spirit of youth, one book dubbed Comus the adversary, in its index.[86] Amongst various guesses in the past about other participants, the idea has sometimes been put forward that the role of Sabrina was taken by one of the older Egerton daughters.[87] These, however, were by now all married, and if any other member of the family, or any other high-born person, had featured in the masque, the name would have joined those of Alice, John and Thomas in the list of masquers at the end of *1637*. The matter is of some interpretative importance, for there was reason for Sabrina to be distinct from the family: the pretence is that she is a resource from the region itself.

Milton's Aristocratic entertainments

Certainly a number of the household travelled. Lawes, or whoever was organising the masque, would have needed help of various kinds from within the household or from the establishment resident in Ludlow. Musicians, actors for Sabrina, her attendants, Comus, and his rout (of young people, presumably), men who could see to the staging and seating accommodation, people who could do the costumes, however few, all these and more had to be assembled for the September performance.

The establishment at Ludlow was of some size. Richard Baxter gives a brief, entirely disapproving picture in his autobiography. He spent some time there as an impressionable young man, as servitor to the chaplain of the council. He left the town in 1633. Far more simply than Milton, Baxter offered Comus as an enemy of the place:

> The House was great, there being four judges, the king's attorney, the secretary, the clerk of the fines, with all their servants, and all the Lord President's servants, and many more; and the town was full of temptation, through the multitude of persons, counsellors, attorneys, officers and clerks, and much given to tippling and excess.[88]

On the occasion of a festivity of semi-official kind, such as the Michaelmas masque of 1634, we must imagine the presence of a fair number of people connected with the president and court. We know, too, that some townspeople were invited.[89] The coming together of administrative officers and local population, selectively represented, for the presidential feast is suggested in fact by the idea of a 'gratulation' and in the last 'scene' of the masque.

To think of the parties present at the masque is to invite another contentious question of just how the whole festivity was fitted into its most likely place of performance, the great hall of the castle. This served as the room for the court. The chamber seems to have measured about fifty-eight feet by thirty feet, a confined space for a masque, if one thinks of the full-blown performances at Whitehall. Because of this small space, the suggestion has been made again, recently, that Milton's masque must have been played not in the great hall but outside.[90]

As Demaray rightly observed,[91] for all sorts of reasons of practicality and custom, it is most unlikely that the masque would have been performed out of doors. (It is not even likely that *Arcades* was performed out of doors.) In any case, *Comus* is not a full-blown masque. It has a peculiarly small number of masquers, only three children. Their dance figure, whether or not it was augmented, would have been small. The dance of the rustics need not have involved many people either. A big royal masque needed room for the large groups of masquers, first on the elaborate stage set, then on the central floor area between stage and state, to which the main masquers descended and around which on three sides the sought-after seating was arranged. This central space was then used for the social dancing, the revels, which followed the dramatic performance. There are no indication of revels in the texts of *Comus*. By normal – that is to say, court – standards, dancing elements, like elements of spectacle, were much abbreviated.

It would seem likely that Milton was aware to some extent from the start that the Ludlow masque was not to share all the opulent emphases of the great royal masques. Hence he provided a text which elaborated the dramatic at the expense of the choreographic, and suited a small number of participants. His text asked for three 'scenes' to be managed, presumably by shutter and backcloth. A mechanism was also needed to make Sabrina 'rise' through the stage on her chariot. These seem to have been provided. Textual evidence suggests that Milton first assumed a machine as well to lower and raise the 'spirit' Henry Lawes, but it is not clear that one was actually constructed.[92] In this connection one of the features of the room still traceable in the ruins may be of relevance: there was a gallery at one end. Tradition often placed musicians in galleries of great halls. Lawes may have been intended to use, or may have actually used, a gallery as his 'heavens', a place already associated with heavenly harmonies.

Since dance is small in Milton's masque, the better analogy as regards staging might be not the grand court masques in the Banqueting Hall but special performances of plays for royalty in private theatres, where scenic and spectacular effects were also sometimes used. The Cockpit-in-Court, for example, measured only fifty-eight feet square on the outside, and its interior measurements were further restricted by its octagonal configuration.[93] At the best of times masques were uncomfortably cramped, but we have to imagine at Ludlow a particularly intimate kind of presentation packed by an audience doubtless carefully selected from the relevant parties and institutions, and having only some tokens of the lavishness of spectacle and dance associated with the great masques.[94] Nevertheless, it functioned, within these special conditions, as a kind of masque.

A review of the presidential visitation of 1634 would not be complete without a consideration of the choice of day on which the masque was to be performed. The gratulation came not near the beginning of the period in the principality but rather near the end, during the second stay in Ludlow. Recent scholarship has made much of the possible significances of Michaelmas, with relation to presidential occasion and Milton's text.[95]

The role of a guardian spirit in the Ludlow masque may have come about as a consequence of thinking of how a part could be made around Henry Lawes, servant to the family and heavenly singer. So ingenious is Milton's writing for Lawes, and so expressive of the whole tone of the masque, that one assumes the role to have been at the very centre of Milton's invention from the start. But the idea of a guardian spirit could have come about also as a result of thinking of the significances of the day of performance, the feast of St Michael and All Angels. A dominant role was allowed to a guardian spirit on the one day of the year in which the meditations of the church were turned to the guardianship of angels.

So promising have Michaelmas associations seemed to scholars, that it may appear churlish to offer hints of doubt. Was it mere forgetfulness, of the actual day of performance, of the significance of the day, or just temporary indifference to both, that made Henry Lawes put 1 October, not 29 September, on the *Comus* music in his manuscript book? Is it not the case that protective spirits, which occur in both *Arcades* and *Comus*, are a stock constituent of Milton's pastoral vocabulary at this period? They may be an index to his constant preoccupation of relating human actions to the divine plan. And, as I have said, how certain can one be that the date of performance was known at the very inception of planning?

Yet there can be little doubt that Michaelmas night was chosen as the performance night for reasons of tradition, even if we have to admit that we cannot be quite sure by whom it was chosen or

Contexts and occasions

exactly when the decision was made. Michaelmas day was associated with the election of new magistrates and governors. Bridgewater's presidential feast at Ludlow, though it came towards the end of his first summer visitation, and despite the delays since 1631, approximated to the situation of presenting a new magistrate and governor. The secular customs of the day are, though, only part of its significance as a religious festival. There is a possibility – one might call it no more than that – that those organising the whole occasion were primarily following secular traditions, whereas Milton, if he thought of the issue at all, chose to emphasise the significance of the day in a more directly religious way. The distinctions are worth rehearsing.

At the more secular level, some of the expected range of associations can be neatly shown through the analogy of the Lord Mayor's festivities in London.[96] The following passage is from a Jacobean mayoral entertainment called *The Triumphes of re-united Britannia*, written by the hack Anthony Munday. Neptune is speaking. The play with Holyday arises because the new mayor was Sir Leonard Holyday:

> Bethink thee how on that high Holyday,
> Which beares Gods champion, th'Arch-angels name,
> When conquering Sathan in a glorious fray,
> Michael Hels-monster nobly overcame,
> And now a sacred Sabaoth being the same,
> A free and full election on all parts,
> Made choice of thee, both with their hands and hearts.
>
> Albeit this day is usuall every yeare,
> For new election of a Magistrate,
> Yet, now to me some instance doth appeare,
> Worth note, which to my selfe I thus relate,
> Holyday, cald on Holyday to state.
> Requiers methinks a yeare of Holydayes.
> To be disposd in good and vertuous wayes.
>
> For I account tis a Lord Holyday,
> When Iustice shines in perfect Majesty[97]

The parallels are easy to see: the election of a new magistrate is set in the context of the heavenly overthrow of the forces of evil. Traditions for the day saw earthly governance as parallel to the guardianship of men, perhaps even of nations by angels. ('Look homeward, angel, now ...') Thus the collect prays for the protection of angels on earth to match the service of angels to God in heaven.[98]

The gospel for the day, however, is a famous passage from Matthew 18, linking angels with children in spiritual instruction: 'Take heed that yee despise not one of these little ones; for I say unto you, that in heaven their Angels doe alwayes behold the face of my Father which is in heaven.' Milton's Attendant Spirit is sent from heaven by Jove for the 'defence, & guard' of those of 'tender age' who are caught in a trial of faith. Again, one may compare other pious authors. This is the busy George Wither writing about Michaelmas in his popular *Hymns and Songs of the Church*:

> This Day we glorifie God for the victory of S. *Michael*, and his *Angels* obtained over the *Dragon*, and his Angels; Whereby the *Church* is freed from being prevailed against by the furious attempts, or malitious accusations of the Devill. This *Commemoration* is appointed also, to minde us thankfully to acknowledge *God's* mercy towards us, in the daily ministry of his *Angels*, who are said to pitch their Tents about his Children, and to defend them from the temptations and mischievous practises of evil Spirits, watching every moment for advantage to destroy them: Which, if we oftner considered, and how there be armies of *Angels* and *Devils*, night and day fighting for us, and round about us, we would become more carefull how wee grieved those good *Spirits*, (who attend us for our safety) to the reioicing of them that seeke our destruction.[99]

It is the evil spirit Comus' confident rejoicings that are banished by faith in the masque, and, as well as a spirit who defends real children against temptation and mischief, we have the Elder Brother himself remembering the armies of angels who 'lackey' the virtuous soul by night. If he seems too breezily optimistic (forgetting the devils perhaps), his faith is born out of godly training, those considerations of providence recommended by Wither. And the masque is certainly mindful of God's mercy.

It seems remarkable, not to say providential, that Michaelmas day offered government and angels and children of the faith, whilst the familial commission meant writing for children and a musical tutor easily turned into guardian and angelic singer. Something of this remarkable conjunction of occasional opportunities Milton presumably realised, though, again, just in what order they presented themselves to him is very hard to know.

2 · THE ARCADIANS

THERE IS a main structural device in common between Milton's two aristocratic entertainments, which expresses something of the situations outlined in the last chapter. I am referring to the idea of the journey. In each case, the device of the journey both defines a set of values for the occasion and articulates a relationship between those who travel to the place and the quality of the place itself, with its festivity.

Although there are clearly differences between a brief dedica-tory gesture, in *Arcades*, and an extended masque action, in *Comus*, Milton exploits the same fundamental movement in each, of the masquers to the chair of estate. This movement, ending in a presentation, is basic to many masques; in Milton's texts it is an obviously expressive device.

In *Arcades* the action is based on a conjunction of resources meeting in the festivity: the notable aristocratic 'visitors', Arcadians, come to meet with the notable resources of place, Harefield. Spirit of place, though it is expounded by Genius, is defined by the most important person in the celebration, the dowager countess herself. In this ritual coming together of persons and place, therefore, here a quest to her chair of estate, Arcadianism finds its proper nature and its truest home.

The Ludlow masque also presents a unique conjunction of resources of 'arriving' persons with resources of place. The journey of the children is an echo of the Odyssean journey, creating moral definition by adaptation of familiar allegorical myth. At the same time the children are said to be coming to Ludlow to enable them to participate like everyone else in the region in the gratulation of their father's 'new entrusted scepter', the public occasion of the festivity. The children are the exemplary participants in the festivity. So the journey *to* the feast also defines virtue *in* the feast. It is a self-defining action. The fiction suggests that aristocratic virtue in the form of hopeful youth is being brought to Ludlow, and such a device reflects on the president himself, to whose state the children are taken across the floor and presented as his own. The courtesies are deft enough and indirect enough to be interesting. But here too associations of place are important. Not only is the last 'scene' that of Ludlow itself, town and castle together, court and community assembled, but also the final means of aid providentially provided for the journeying children is a power drawn from the Welsh region itself, through literary tradition, through the legendary nymph Sabrina. In the vision of Sabrina, nymph of the river Severn, Milton raised thoughts to the health and well-being of a whole people along her banks, imaged in the pious heroism of pastoral ideals. In this masque ritual both 'arriving' persons, of the president's family, and place, Ludlow and Wales, take cognisance of the potentialities of the other. Even the slight Chirk entertainment had found ways of relating place to great visitors in instructive augury.

In the end, this conjunction seems to me one of the most difficult things to understand about the Ludlow masque. Yet to appreciate the masque fully in its Welsh-presidential context, to think of the auguries that could be made on the much-delayed, rather ceremonial visitation of 1634, one might give full weight to all considerations of persons and place relevant to the gathering of the gratulation. By contrast, the gathering of persons to place at Harefield in *Arcades*, to which we now turn in detail, is a rather simpler matter to understand.

Seemingly slight, problematically called 'Part of an Entertainment', *Arcades* has touched the heart of a few admirers for its grace, but has usually been misunderstood in its dramatic form, wrongly reconstructed in its staging, and has been somewhat under-investigated as a piece of occasional writing. Aspects of it are conventional, it is low-keyed. It was originally intended for a private aristocratic audience, though *1645* offered it to a more general audience and as a major example of occasional writing in the early career of the poet, one of the three English works set apart at the end of the volume. To appreciate the art of the piece as occasional writing one must sense first and foremost not an

The Arcadians

allegory[1] so much as a familial gesture, which Milton produced with deftness and, most of all, with seriousness of intent.

Arcades consists of an action designed in 'honour & devotion'[2] for the Countess Dowager of Derby at her seat at Harefield. The gesture is evidently the responsibility of members of her family, who dress up as shepherds and shepherdesses together, probably, with one or more musicians. Pretending that they have come from Arcadia, they are told that they should dance no more there, but rather come and live at Harefield, to serve the lady of that place. She creates a new Arcadia about her. She is the centre of a place of blessedness, of innocent virtue and piety, a place pitied of God. Here, as in the prologue added to Guarini's famous pastoral drama, *Il Pastor Fido*, the device is the transference of Arcadianism to a new locality. Like Guarini, Milton expresses such transference by means of the analogy of the well-worn tale of Alpheus and Arethusa.

Pan is god-king of Arcadians. By the 1630s in England literary Arcadians are likely to be aristocratic or courtly, as for example in Jonson's *Pan's Anniversarie* written for the birthday of James I in 1620, where the scene is Arcadia and it is the shepherds' holiday. In Milton's verses even Syrinx would have to yield to the lady of Harefield, for she outshines all Arcadian queens whatever.

The Countess sits in a 'state' either really or imaginarily illuminated, and the Arcadians are drawn to her by radiant light. This is the familiar divinity of courtly compliment, 'too divine to be mistooke'. More precisely, in one verse of the opening song, she is celebrated as like Latona, *magna mater* and *mater deorum*, 'mother of a hundred gods'; and as like Juno, *matrona* and *regina*, heavenly queen. For Juno Milton had once written Ceres in the Trinity manuscript, and Ceres is another matron, *quasi* γῆ μήτηρ.[3] The terms suit the mother and grandmother of many noble offspring.[4] As portrait and monument make clear, she delighted in having her aristocratic connections displayed. The headnote of *1645* points to 'som Noble persons of her Family', and, as we have seen, some of her grandchildren were amongst her festive celebrators.

The Genius of the Wood, a servant and musician who is part of the establishment, acts as guide through the park, and he adds to the celebration by describing his protective and healing activities. This is an aspect of Jove's general providence –

Milton's Aristocratic entertainments

> For know by lot from *Jove* I am the powr
> Of this fair Wood, and live in Oak'n bowr,
> To nurse the Saplings tall (*1645*)

but particularly to be marked at Harefield. Genius listens to the music of the spheres, as only the purely spiritual or chastely virtuous can. This reference he turns into further compliment by bringing heavenly harmony to earth for her: 'and yet such musick worthiest were to blaze / the peerlesse height of her immortall praise'. As the Arcadians move across to the state, so that the nobles among them may kiss the hem of the lady's garment, they complete a gesture which is intended to celebrate her and her residence and which is, above all, to be heard by her.

At the same time the device brings courtly entertainment to her house. Arcadians bring song and dance. Thus an 'entertainment' is brought to her and her house. The rest of the entertainment we do not have, but it would be a reasonable guess that *Arcades* was the presentation which opened 'this nights glad solemnitie' as a kind of dedication.[5]

With the familial context in mind, let us look more closely at some of the leading characteristics of Milton's invention in *Arcades*. The text furnishes quite a few indications of function.

First, the whole household and demesne of Harefield is celebrated as fortunate in its mistress. The action leads to a gesture of honour, the kissing of the garment, but with this greeting there is also the invitation to 'bring yor flocks & live with us. / heere yee shall have greater grace / to serve the Ladie of this place'. Not merely a ritual visitation but also a residence seems to be proposed. Younger members of her family dress up and *pretend* to be aliens to the place with which they are familiar. Whichever branches of the family participated, at least two, if not three, of the Brydges children came among shepherds and shepherdesses, and presumably Alice and Elizabeth Hastings, and these grandchildren were actually resident in the house. A fiction which suggested 'greater grace' in coming to live at Harefield would have been an apt way in which some of the family could have acknowledged the happiness of their coming to a new home, under the care and influence of the countess. Any in the party who were actual visitors, like the Egertons, if they were there, could at the same time express the happiness of a visit and thanks to their host.

The Arcadians

The party of 'visiting' Arcadians also evidently included some who were not 'Noble persons of her Family'. Only those 'that are of noble stemme' may approach the state and kiss the garment. One explanation of the inclusion of lesser mortals in the train of approaching Arcadians might be that one or more persons who sang well were needed to help in the singing of the opening songs. Or might it merely be that the numbers betwen the sexes needed to be made even, as for the purposes of later dance? Rather oddly, with regard to singing, the Trinity manuscript does not label the opening verses as a song, though it does label Genius' closing verses 'Song' and '2 Song'. As I have argued elsewhere,[6] the Trinity text began as a text before performance. Though he knew that family and servants were to be involved, Milton may have been in doubt about the exact make-up of the Arcadian group. Of the noble residents at Harefield, both Hastings girls seem to have had some interest in music,[7] whilst at least three of the servants of the house had their musical instruments kept up at the expense of the countess.[8] Amongst obvious visitors, we know of course that Lady Alice Egerton was an accomplished singer. The only one of her elder sisters that we know for certain to have been similarly capable, Lady Mary, had married in 1627 and is unlikely as a visitor to Harefield at this time.

Milton was always more certain of the musical gifts of Genius. The piece is made partly around him. Genius was also not of the nobility: he is one of the 'lesser gods' offering 'helpful service' to the Arcadians and sharing with them a respect for the lady of the house: 'low reverence' and a wondering gaze. He is evidently noted as a musician. Each night, his work done, he listens to the music of the spheres, and he sings the final two songs of Milton's 'part'. Rather like Henry Lawes at Ludlow, he acts as a kind of presenter. His holding a brief from Jove to look after the estate probably means that he was actually employed in the household. His sitting 'full oft' in the estate indicates regular attendance, more regular, I would have thought, than would fit Henry Lawes.

In any case, it would have been more satisfying if the 'visiting' Arcadians could have been met and guided by someone primarily associated with the place. He addresses them with due respect but also as if he were well acquainted with them and with their intentions:

Milton's Aristocratic entertainments

> I know this quest of yo^{rs} & free intent
> was all in honour & devotion ment
> To the great mistresse of yon princely shrine
> whome wth low reverence I adore as mine

He may have been someone like Messrs Jones, Allen or Cotton, that is to say, someone employed in the household who could also act as musician. His work suggests responsibility and care, whilst his music establishes Arcadian arts as already in the place.

The idea of the quest also suggests the nature of the festivity. Masquing skills are being brought to the house, to delight the grand old lady of the family. The third song says that Arcadians have been dancing somewhere else, in Arcadia proper. There may be a literal quality to the pretence. Could the Arcadia they have come from allude to a place at which a queen reigns, who delights above all in masque and pastoral celebration?

The Arcadians feign surprise that 'this clime' should hold 'a deity so unparallel'd'. The transference of Arcadian excellence to this location is justified during the action, so that at the end Genius, being local, being partisan, can resort to a touch of triumphant mischief: Arcadia itself is stony in comparison with these green lawns. Complete though the poetic pretences are – and the self-sufficiency of the poetic language is I think important – a reference to the court might give more point to the two lines which are marginal insertions in the Trinity manuscript and which have puzzled some commentators: 'though Syrinx yor Pans mistresse were / yet well might Syrinx wait on her'.[9] On this reckoning, Charles, like James before him, would be figured in Pan, and the upstaged mistress would be the queen. 'And the dame hath Syrinx grace!' Jonson had written of James' queen in the pastoral entertainment at Althorp.[10]

From this possible connection with court masquing one might also speculate as to how Milton's verses were only a part of an evening's entertainment, in the words of *1645*, 'Part of an entertainment presented to the Countess Dowager of *Darby* at *Harefield*, by som Noble persons of her Family . . .' In the cancelled start of the manuscript text, Milton seems first to have called the piece 'Part of a maske'. That he flirted with the term masque would imply that some kind of dancing was to take place during

The Arcadians

the evening. This the invitation in the third song would also imply: 'dance no more / by sandie Ladons lillied bancks / On old Lycaeus or Cyllene hoare / trip no more in twilight rancks . . .' If the intention was to present to the dowager some sample of the kinds of skills in masquing that her grandchildren were acquiring at court, then it is easy to imagine that the 'entertainment' might have been made up of some of recapitulations or adaptations of previous dance, or song, or dramatic presentation. The other parts of the festivity the poet would then have no need to write.

Recollections need not have been very precise. The resident grandchildren and other visitors could have joined young Egertons in presenting samples of masquing skills. The Brydges boys were not so far in age from their Egerton boy cousins, and the Hastings daughters could presumably have joined Katherine and young Alice. Something could have been improvised, as country-house entertainments often were, to involve as many of the family as possible, whilst still recalling activities at court.

Such an idea would suggest that *Arcades* might have come close in time to some court theatricals in which members of the family had participated. On the basis of an extended study of family records, the chronology of the Trinity manuscript text, and various other factors, I have suggested that the most likely time for performance is the summer vacation period of 1632 perhaps the late summer, between about mid August and the beginning of October.[11]

Whether or not allusions to the court were intended, the gesture of Milton's verses for Harefield articulated an evaluative idea as well as a familial offering. Within the family, kinship, respect and obligation are suggested, as also a determination on this day to make a country house display its qualities in a truly regal way. But the underlying general idea is an evaluation of the quality of true nobility itself. Things of Pan and Syrinx have found greater regality and truer pastoralism with this 'rurall Queene'. A true, or truer, Arcadianism is established.

Milton seems to have found this evaluative idea congenial, because he worked variations on it for Ludlow. It is an idea of some importance, because it prescribes the qualities of those who are truly aristocratic, truly exemplary governors in a nation. I shall be suggesting that this idea took on a new urgency when the texts of Milton's aristocratic entertainments were published for a general audience in the nation.

Matters of form have been a problem in the appreciation of *Arcades* in the past, and assumptions about staging continue to be very dubious.[12] Misunderstandings on these issues have sometimes led to critical prejudice, judging the piece by the standards of what it is not.

In form *Arcades* is difficult to describe. On the one hand, although its main questing device is masque-like, the entertainment is not actually a masque, even a 'little masque'.[13] On the other, although it seems to recall some elements of the country-house welcome, it is not actually that either. The fact is that *Arcades* is shaped like nothing else that survives from the period. Its uniqueness arises out of the particularities of occasion and function.

The heading in the manuscript may have read, at first, before performance, 'Part of a maske', but in the end, in print, Milton did not call his part a masque or even part of a masque. But he gave it masque-like features, to recall the world of masquing. The performing nobility assume disguise symbolic of their own being in a questing fiction appropriate to the occasion. (Rather curiously, in this respect *Arcades* is more masque-like than *Comus*, in which the chief masquers are limited to three children, who assume virtually no disguise, act rather as in a play, and are not 'discovered' in any fashion, though they do dance at the end.) The fiction of the quest itself is masque-like. The idea of the quest, as often in court masque, is an extension of the coming of the disguised figures to serve a person seated in the state. For all this, Milton's piece lacks the one feature most essential to masque proper: the action does not lead into dance or revels within the compass of the text, although critics have often tried to make out that dances feature somewhere in it. As I have argued at greater length elsewhere, dancing may have belonged to some later parts of the evening's entertainment, not to this dedicatory opening which Milton wrote. Nothing in the text of the second song actually suggests dance at that point,[14] and there is no reason to think that prose directions signifying dance are missing from the text,[15] either in the Trinity manuscript or the text of *1645*; or that the text of *Arcades* is any more defective in this regard than that of the Ludlow masque, in either case. Attempts to establish dancing within the compass of Milton's text connect with the mistaken assumption that it is, formally, a masque.

Confusion of similar order has arisen in assuming a likeness between *Arcades* and parts of country-house entertainments. I am referring to the kind of event put on at country-houses for the visit of some great personage, usually though not solely of royalty.[16] It has been an analogy with the first, welcoming parts of these entertainments that has taken the minds of Milton's commentators. Usually, proceedings began out of doors, frequently at the entrance to the park enclosure or at some convenient point within the park, where the visiting party could be intercepted. The speeches were generally spoken by someone playing local rustic or deity, or several such people. Place met visitor. Sometimes apparent rudeness or ignorance was contrived to begin with, feigning absence of welcome or lack of decorum, so that this could be superseded by more courtly, more fitting welcomes as the party was conducted towards the house. Thus a sense of progression was created, leading in a dramatic way to a proper act of celebration.

There are several ways in which one might compare *Arcades*, as the opening of some kind of entertainment, with the welcomes of these entertainments.[17] Some of the figures of compliment are similar, though commonplace; the function of both extends to the encouragement of a state of mind in which the ensuing events might be enjoyed; both Milton's verses and these entertainments focus on the spirit of the particular place, hence use a local deity as mouthpiece. But one analogy, thought of especially in connection with the previous royal Harefield entertainment of 1602, has been assumed falsely, in my view, and it has caused considerable misunderstanding about the staging of *Arcades*: it has often been assumed that *Arcades* was staged out of doors.

Early scholars sensed some kinship between Milton's piece and country-house entertainments. Assumptions have passed through generations of commentary without proper examination. In his edition, Todd gave a long description of the Ashby entertainment for this same countess, which had not then been published, but he drew no specific conclusions about staging from the analogy.[18] It seems to have been Masson who gave currency to the idea of *Arcades* as an outdoor performance. He described it as 'a little open-air pastoral of songs and speeches' and imagined it, charmingly, in the following manner:

The time is evening. Harefield House is lit up; and, not far from it, on a throne of state so arranged as to glitter in the light, the aged countess is seated. . . . Suddenly torches are seen flickering amid the trees in the park; and up the long avenue of elms, as we fancy, – the identical avenue which had borne the name of 'the Queen's Walk' ever since Elizabeth had passed through it two-and-thirty years before – there advance torch-bearers, and with them a band of nymphs and shepherds, clad as Arcadians.[19]

In 1602 Elizabeth had been intercepted by a dairy farm out in the park, escorted down the avenue of elms, and directed to a chair placed on a stage specially built near the front steps of the house. Masson has re-created *Arcades* in the same way, except that the countess is seated on her state all through and the 'visitors' move towards her. Modern criticism has been seduced and reaches a cavalier unquestioning extreme in A. N. Wilson's picture of young people 'cavorting on the lawns'.[20]

To the notion of *Arcades* as outdoor performance there are serious objections, some of them practical. It would have been difficult for the countess to *hear* what was said by Arcadians and Genius at the opening of the action, across the length of lawns and woods. And yet all speeches are in her honour and must be heard by her. Critics have tried to slide round this difficulty.[21] Again, we may wonder about the fact that this is performed in the evening, being 'this nights glad solemnitie'. The 'blaze' of the state suggests some degree of darkness, and the elms are said to be 'starre proofe'. There are obvious difficulties in arranging something like a welcome outdoors in darkness. And if the state was *actually* illuminated, by torches and candles, could it really have been placed out of doors?[22]

Most crucially, *Arcades* simply is not the welcome of the familiar type. Though it remembers that tradition, its function is different. It is true that Genius pays compliment to the noble 'visitors' according to the pretence of the moment – 'Staye gentle Swayns . . . And yee . . . faire silver-buskin'd Nymphs' – but the piece is not primarily in honour of the 'visitors'. It honours throughout the resident lady, whose presence is the goal of their quest. From that

The Arcadians

point of view, the action is more like that of masque, moving towards the state; that seat, not the moving 'visitors', is the chief focus of the solemnity.

Arcades was surely played indoors, in whatever great chamber Harefield offered, in the evening after supper, perhaps making some use of carefully placed lights. The word 'scene' – 'who appear on the scene in pastoral habit, moving toward the seat of state' – might refer to a single standing set or at least playing place in the room.

It is reasonable to speculate about the arrangement in the room, since what immediately suggests itself is an organisation derived on a modest scale from the normal staging of masques. The chief dramatic action, such as it is – the song of the appearing Arcadians and the intercepting speech of Genius – take place on or in front of a 'scene' at one end of the room, facing the state, which is placed at, or toward, the other end. The Arcadians appear, speak or sing, gesturing across to the 'blaze' of the state, and offer to come forward across the room. Genius intercepts them, speaks his long speech, then conducts them across the intervening space of floor during the second song:

> Ore the smooth enameld greene
> where no print of step hath been
> > follow me as I sing

The third song marks the arrival to her presence, to 'kisse her sacred vestures hemme'.

The journey across the room is made to sound as if it were through the park, over lawns and 'under the shadie roofe / Of branching elme starre proofe', but this is I think the *pretence* that they are outside in the park, which is being celebrated. The 'smooth enameld greene' may in fact have been the customary green carpeting used for the central dance space in masques, set between stage and state. The general arrangement of 'scene' at one end of the room, state at the other, and an intervening floorspace for dancing, is in conscious imitation of the usual arrangement for court masques, deliberately reminding those present of masquing but adapted to the limitations of little spectacle and smaller scale.

It seems unlikely that there was much scenery, and there may

Milton's Aristocratic entertainments

have been none. For the three 'scenes' at Ludlow the salient features are described in the text. Nothing is mentioned for Harefield. Though the room had to be set up for whatever other parts there were of the evening's entertainment, the intention, as far as one can tell, was not for costly spectacle but rather to call up courtly show and then to establish the Arcadian superiority of this modest rural celebration, a truer Arcadianism resulting.

Milton's verses, then, are in no simple sense either masque or country-house entertainment, though they recall the conventions of both. Milton had no word for them except 'Part of an Entertainment', until finally, before publication, he gave them a poetic identity, 'the Arcadians'. In so far as that title invited the reader to dwell on the idea of Arcadianism, it was a well-considered choice.

Just how good is *Arcades*, judged according to its apparent functions? Clearly it is pointless to measure it against the full expectations of masque. It does not get us very far to have in mind all the potential public aspects of court masque, where all present were invited to see the court in the context of a mystique of virtuous power in king and nation, and where the images were likely to be drawn up on an historical, heroic, or schematically moral and philosophical basis. Despite its use of courtliness and the evidence of its moral tone, *Arcades* has little of these dimensions. It seems to me that it does not even bear the references to England that some seek to find, making 'this clime' a 'new homeland for pastoral poetry'.[23] The new Arcadia may give a pattern to the nation, but it is Harefield, not England. If *Arcades* is to be called 'a slight affair',[24] it must be because its function was private and rather limited.

Judged in the context of what it was apparently asked to do, Milton's 'part' is surely not unnoteworthy. Neither is the text devoid of the independent seriousness of thought and cultivated grace so evident in the Ludlow masque. In arguing for *Arcades* as a good example of Milton's achievements in occasional writing, I should like to begin by pointing to particular sources of delight in the pretences of the performance. In such epideictic modes delight, fitness for occasion, and moral exemplification ought to be hard to separate.

Plate 1. Henry Lawes. Portrait by unknown artist, School of Music, Oxford. Photograph by permission of the Heather Professor of Music.

Plate 2. The threequarter-length portrait is by Zucchero, painted before Ferdinando's death in 1594. There is stress on her lineage: the 'S's in the ruff stand for Spenser whilst in the tree beside her head are combined the arms of Stanley and Spenser, the Stanley arms quartering Lathom, Man, Warren, Lestrange, Widvile, Mohun, Monhast, Clifford, Brandon, Brune and Fitzwilliam, whilst the Spenser quarters Spenser ancient, Deverell, Badham, Dagworth and Rudlings. Painting in the collection of Lord Leigh of Stoneleigh; photograph courtesy of National Portrait Gallery.

ALICE, COUNTESS OF DERBY

Plate 3. The engraved image, showing her as widow, dates from the last part of her life, probably soon after 1624. Noble connections of herself and three daughters are shown at the base. There is no mention of her marriage to Sir Thomas Egerton. Also, for her daughter Anne, only the marriage to an earl rates mention, her first husband, Grey, Lord Brydges, being omitted. See Arthur M. Hind, *Engraving in England in the Sixteenth and Seventeenth Centuries*, II (1955), 370.

Plate 4. This nineteenth-century engraving of the Countess of Derby's monument, by Maximilian Colt, in Harefield church allows the original inscription to be seen. There is no mention of her marriage to Egerton and by now (1637) the noble alliance of her daughter Anne to the Earl of Castlehaven is not mentioned in the inscription. Photograph by courtesy of the National Portrait Gallery.

Plate 5. Elizabeth, Countess of Huntingdon, whose two daughters lived at Harefield and would have taken part in *Arcades*. The portrait is attributed to Paul van Somer. A related engraving by John Payne (Hind, III, plate 4c) bears an inscription to indicate that she is recently (*'nuper'*) Countess of Huntingdon. Huntingdon succeeded to the title in December 1604; the portrait is probably not long after 1605. Photograph by courtesy of the National Portrait Gallery and Christie's.

Plate 6. George Brydges, Lord Chandos. Living at Harefield at the time of *Arcades*, heir to the countess' estate, and a certain participant in the entertainment. Later known for his gallant appearance and his active part in the Civil War. The engraving is a nineteenth-century one from a portrait once at Sudeley and is taken from Emma Dent, *Annals of Winchcombe and Sudeley* (1877).

Plate 7. John, Earl of Bridgewater. Portrait is said to be a copy, after Honthorst (?) of the original in the Ellesmere collection. In Tatton Park collection; photograph by courtesy of the Courtauld Institute and the National Trust.

Plate 8. Frances, Countess of Bridgewater. Artist unknown. Photograph, by courtesy of the Ellesmere 1939 Settlement and Mr Cyril Egerton, from Lady Alix Egerton I (ed.), *Milton's Comus*, (London, 1910).

THE THREE YOUNG MASQUERS AS INFANTS

Plate 9. John, Lord Brackley, the Elder Brother.
Plate 10. Thomas Egerton, the Younger Brother.
Plate 11. Lady Alice Egerton, the Lady.

From a set of portraits of the children of the first earl now at Mertoun in the house of the Duke of Sutherland. Painter unknown.
Photographs by courtesy of the National Portrait Gallery of Scotland and the duke.

Plate 12. John, Lord Brackley, the Elder Brother.

THE BROTHERS AS YOUNG MEN

Plate 13. Thomas Egerton, the Younger Brother.

Photographs by courtesy of the Duke of Sutherland and the National Portrait Gallery of Scotland.

Plate 14. The Golden Grove portrait. Traditionally assumed to be Lady Alice Egerton. On the identification of subject and artist and the date of the painting, see the note at the end of the book. Photograph provided by Lord Cawdor.

The Arcadians

The first source of pleasure is the delight in dramatic pretence itself, a delight which binds together all those concerned in the festivity. The countess sees those she knows dressed as shepherds and shepherdesses and hears that they are pretending to be strange to her: she is drawn into imaginative participation, asked to have the device discovered to her. She is asked to imagine, with them, that they could mistake this 'she' or only guess at her identity or be informed of her only by Fame.

The particular Arcadian disguise adds to these pleasures. It is an identity rich with literary association, Virgilian, Sidneian, yet conceivable in the present country place. In fact Genius' opening words exploit pretence in more ways than one. It is plain that he is privy to the whole affair, yet he asserts that he can recognise them *despite* their disguise, 'though in this disguise'. The delight of such pieces, which Milton fully realised, was always in the curious interplay between real and fictional identities.

The role of Genius has its own delights of pretence. There is a touch of comic portentousness in his announcement: 'For know by lot from *Jove* I am the powr' (*1645*). At the same time he registers the self-sufficiency of the poetic language, in which God is figured as Jove. His identity reinforces the sense of the whole scene as a wood, and it plays further with the delights of holding together in the mind the real identities of servant–musician and the fictional identity of guardian divinity of the wood. The sport with identity is given a twist, when, in the persona of deity, though with reference to his actual musicality, he states that he hears the music of the spheres 'wch none can heare / of humaine mould wth grosse unpurged eare'. The momentary supra-human pride does not sort with a musician's subservient station. Then he becomes less divinely arrogant:

> if my inferior hand or voice could hit
> inimitable sounds yet as wee goe
> what ere the skill of lesser gods can show
> I will assay her worth to celebrate.

The social reality has reasserted itself. Although the delights here anticipate those produced by the other servant–musician–spirit of the Ludlow masque, Genius' self-deprecation about his musical abilities sounds rather unlike the self-celebration which Milton wove into the Attendant Spirit's part; another sign, perhaps, that Genius was not Lawes or some notable musician from court.

The consistency of the whole figure of Genius' speech supports the praise. There was no better strategy, in praise, than evident poetic integrity. By the logic of the application of the music of the spheres, 'worthiest' to 'blaze' her eminence, the countess is now raised to all-heavenly goddess, so that it is no wonder that a lower earth-bound spirit might hesitate to express her. Rhetorical assertion, delight in pretence, a kind of intimate comedy, all these work inextricably together.

There is nothing slight in the conception of Genius' speech. It is sustained and confident. Fifteen lines go to the description of plant doctoring. Ten lines play out 'the caelestiall sirens harmonie'. And each balances the other in a 'puritan' rhythm: a kind of work, followed by a kind of pious rest. The sustained inventiveness of the speech is in itself offered as a source of delight. There is also pleasure in the picturesque detail. Figures of pastoral healing can be met elsewhere, from Virgil to *A Midsummer Night's Dream* to *The Faithful Shepherdess*, but no one does these things with such resourcefulness as Milton, here and in the Ludlow masque. At the same time, these figures of pastoral healing and of the music of the spheres convey a moral force. Didacticism is inseparable from poetic play.

The whole fiction, however short, is satisfyingly complete in its articulation. The names and features of the third song bear the marks of a true literary Arcadia of Virgilian pedigree. The care for the style and consistency of the poetic language is important not merely for the pleasure it gives but also because if the poetic language does not satisfy, in this kind of epideictic writing, the hyperbole becomes too blatantly apparent. Then its terms are *seen* to be dependent on actuality duly magnified in praise. In these situations the best art of courtesy is to make the poetic fiction seem to generate all. The peculiar chemistry of this kind of writing depends upon such a degree of self-sufficiency in the poetic language, that actualities can always be fused into or separated out from the fictional, according to the decorous demands of each moment. There is a finely calculated pleasure in the courtesies of praise.

The spirit of intimate play in language and action has

The Arcadians

sometimes eluded those commentators who have bothered with the piece. Too often the pretences have been taken with inflexible literalness or converted, for easier handling, into the more sombre mode of schematic allegory.[25] Allegorisations of the piece have not been able to cope with the elusive and shifting effects of intimate disguise, or to account for the structure of its rhetorical procedures. Similar problems have arisen in commentary on the Ludlow masque. *Comus* has some of the firmer symbolism and more programmatic idealisations and exhortations for a public occasion, but at the same time it also delights and teases with pretence and depends for its effects upon the shared enjoyments of a poetic fiction.

A touch of extravagance or irreverence is also important. My suggestion that Syrinx makes a hit at court can only be conjectural, but there is other evidence in the speech and final song of Genius of an edge of extravagance in comic pretence. Milton understood that in various kinds of celebratory composition some licence of bold play is understood and appreciated; else, the praise is apt to become a burden, and dull, and if dull indecorous. Donne provides examples of the technique in an extreme way in his addresses to noblewomen, in which there is a deliberately precarious balance between high idealisation and impudent amusement. Country-house entertainments often used irreverent risk as a means by which to create the proper gesture. One thinks of the easy spirit of Sidney in his much-reprinted *Lady of May*. Masque itself did similar things. That 'comic' risks are taken in *Arcades*, however restrained in their provocation in this case, is another mark of its success. As usual, the irreverence cannot be disjoined from the means of compliment.

As to the moral seriousness of *Arcades*, this quality its commentators have been quicker to describe. Many have noted the insistence on the figure of the music of the spheres, and with knowledge of Milton's other writings the modern critic can see far better than the Countess of Derby the signs of a favourite Miltonic figure of high ethical import. Critical responses to implications of salvation or redemption do not seem altogether wide of the mark,[26] though, again, the context is one of an aristocratic ideal. Like his brother spirit in *Comus* Genius in effect issues a challenge to his audience to consider whether their ears are 'grosse' and 'unpurged'. Dressed as spirits, musician–servants may evidently remind their noble patrons of the priority of religious virtue during these rituals of self-definition. The peculiar insistence of Milton's entertainments for nobility is in this juxtaposition of nobility with a spiritual elite.

What seems so remarkable about this religious part of Genius' speech is that it is so much contained within the demands of decorum. It would be too simple to say that the earnest young poet was impatient of the language of aristocratic celebration and therefore sought to point the conventions in a new direction. The distinctive seriousness is not achieved at the expense of the aristocratic gesture. The moral integrity of the passage actually contributes to its art of compliment. The opening verses of the Arcadians had set the social gesture: the guiding speech of the spirit leads into the parallel religious definition.

There is in fact a particular integrity about the whole of Genius' speech which amounts to a scrupulousness both aristocratic and religious. The praises which had been offered in the first expressions of the Arcadians had been commonplace, not unfittingly. The seeking of a divinity, the guessing at a goddess' name, these are readily acceptable gestures, because they announce the pretences and recollect the kind of courtly aesthetic to which the grandchildren had been introduced. What Genius offers is both more elaborate and more serious, since it relates this aesthetic to considerations of moral purity and of God's providence. And of course the figure of healing, quietly but firmly, assumes the fallen nature of the world. We know that it is a part of a large strategy of praise, that special protective powers ordained by God should be associated with the countess' estate. But a lesser poet than Milton would have *said* that it was because of her presence that such prosperous benediction reigned. This is not simply the case of a poet stopping one short of idolatry in praise, acknowledging Fall and Grace, and pointing his art a new way. It should have been a compliment and a delight to her, that the poet expected in the chief beholder that degree of acuteness in shared judgement. The integrity of the poet in celebration is projected on to the chief recipient of the entertainment. That is the mark of a truly aristocratic entertainment.

3 · 'KŌMOS' – THE ADVERSARY FOR THE OCCASION

IN BOTH ENTERTAINMENTS of Milton there is stress on providence. In both, a protective spirit sent by Jove comes to the aid of travellers and counters evils which accompany darkness. If the Fall is felt briefly, by implication, in Genius' nightly care over mundane evils on the estate, it will be felt more directly, often, in the Ludlow masque. If one senses that Milton was being rather precise in the way he related a providential agent to the lady of the house, then a similar precision is on view in the more complex invention for Ludlow, where the idea of providence was made to engage the history both of individuals and of a people. The sense of darkness, which is moral realism, shows more determinedly through the pastoral at Ludlow.

In the idea of establishing true Arcadianism, too, the two entertainments occupy common ground. At Ludlow the pastoral was also used, finally, as a means of depicting an ideal order centred on piety. In the Sabrina section of *Comus* there is a celebration of happy prosperity, blessed with the merciful virtues of the river itself, and here held up as a pattern for a whole land. True Arcadianism at Ludlow extended to the model of a nation blessed by God.

The radical Arcadianism is of course a mark of Milton's earnest educational and political idealism. In his hands the pastoral becomes a means by which young aristocrats could prescribe to themselves, within the delights of their dramatic festivities, the kind of godliness which could be exemplary to a nation.

Such reformist sentiment may underlie one further feature of the *Arcades* text which it shares with the *Comus* text, that is, an interesting history of textual change. The significance of some of the textual emendations in *Arcades* has not been fully appreciated. As I have argued elsewhere,[1] the Trinity manuscript text of *Arcades* presents in brief form some of the same characteristics as the Trinity text of the masque: it shows Milton at work over a considerable span of time, from before performance right through to a time some good while after performance, when he seems to have been preparing for publication. The title 'Arcades' is a change of the kind of some of the '1637' changes in the masque text, a readjustment in the light of a new perceived occasion, an address to the nation at large. By *1645* Milton had encapsulated the essential reformist point of his verses in that one word 'Arcades', seeming to ask any who read them, at that less happy time, to test the qualities of the nobility they knew. This is a theme I shall resume, for the masque, later in the book. Here, however, I would like to turn to the earnestly conceived, reformist programme of *Comus*, in particular to the challenge of the specific darkness in its pastoral ritual to the occasion of the masque.

The heart of the action in the Ludlow masque is the confrontation between the President's children and the enchanter Comus. Young nobility is tested in ritual against the evils appropriate to the occasion. Milton wished to provoke thoughts about aristocratic youth and festivity at large, all the more when he augmented the text for publication. Yet as usual in masque the terms were also specific, celebratory and auspicious.

If we isolate the encounter between Comus and the Lady, the drift of the debate is, as was intended, easy to see. It is the maintenance of chaste temperance in the face of devilish persuasions to luxury. In such a context Comus himself can readily be grasped as 'son' of Circe, the most common of all Renaissance figures for seductive intemperance, and of Bacchus, god of wine and excess. His name is the usual Latin transliteration of *kōmos*, the Greek word for revelry. He is the deceptive spirit of that kind of luxurious feasting which habitually perverts its company. Yet I do not think that the full power of his name has often been appreciated. By that I mean the associations of the *kōmos* for the literary but pious Protestant mind. Comus is in fact an urgent indication of Milton's continuing social thought. There is his proper challenge to occasion.

Kōmos – the adversary for the occasion

One might well begin to describe the action by examining the offered figure of evil. Milton's art shows his vigilant Protestantism in nothing so clearly as in his dynamic, detailed presentation of deceptive evils, in all the major poems. Evil delights in perverting 'God's dearest benefits', he noted out of Tertullian.[2] It seeks out its best occasions. A masque defines its occasion as best. The significance of Comus is to be seen against the very benefits of the occasion for which he is produced, the gratulatory feast at Ludlow, with its masque of children, its ritualistic display of nobility, its context of government, in an area of Britain associated in myth with an heroic race.

The poet seems to invite some such approach. The Attendant Spirit's 'task' is to explain the conjunction of forces gathering at Ludlow Castle. Milton gathers his presences with marked elaboration, as if fond of playing with fictions. The authority of the President is derived from the sovereignty of Neptune over seas and islands. This touches familiar celebrations of the nation: *megalon nēson*, the great island; *Britannia insularum optima*, Britain the best of islands – 'this isle / the greatest & the best of all the maine'.[3] Then another encomium, of Wales as home of a race from Troy: *hinc populum . . . belloque superbum* – 'an old and haughtie nation proud in armes'.[4] To this place, invested with these tokens of authority and greatness, the children are imagined to be travelling, 'to attend thire fathers state / and new entrusted scepter'.

The Spirit then begins to introduce the nature of the evil seeking to spoil the congregation. The revelation of Comus in the opening speech is not factual or even complete. Instead, Milton chooses this moment to make the first large, open invitation to the audience for new myth and story: 'and listen why, for I will tell you now / what never yet was heard in tale or song'. He feigns a cumulative progress westwards from the lands of Greek myth. Combining elements of Ovidian metamorphosis, he produces a parentage and a 'roaving' towards western parts which look satanically ominous:

> Bacchus, that first from out of the purple grape
> crush't the sweet poyson of mis-used wine
> after the Tuscaine mariners transform'd
> coasting the Tyrrhene shore, as ye winds listed
> on Circe's Island fell (who knows not Circe

59

Milton's Aristocratic entertainments

>   the Daughter of ye sun, whose charmed cup
>   whoever tasted lost his upright shape
>   & downeward fell into a groveling swine)
>   this nymph that gaz'd upon his clustring locks
>   wth ivie berries wreath'd, & his blith youth
>   had by him ere he parted thence, a son
>   much like his father, but his mother more
>   wch therfore she brought up and Comus nam'd
>   who ripe and frolick of his full growne age
>   roaving the Celtick, & Iberian feilds
>   at last betaks him to this ominous wood
>   & in thick shelter of black shade imbour'd
>   excells his mother at her mightie art

The incident of Bacchus turning the sailors into dolphins seems to perform two functions. By putting the god on a ship, the poet has him in motion and likely to run into Circe's island, Aeaea. Milton is deliberately vague about where the transformation of the mariners took place, so that it is easy to suggest that the winds drifted the god westwards, west of Italy, in the Tyrrhenian sea, where Aeaea was to be found. At the same time, the story associates Bacchus with an act of transforming men and therefore makes easier the conjunction of his powers with those of Circe, better known for changing men into beasts.

Sharply relevant details of the power of Comus are being anticipated. Exact weight falls on key words like 'upright' and 'downeward fell', terms of moral definition, and a way has been found of joining Circe's degrading magic with 'blith youth'. The result of this union is a power perniciously adapted to youth in festivity by night.

The latter parts of the figure, in which Comus, having been trained by his mother in her arts, travels further westward over France and Spain until 'at last' he arrives in Ludlow, look forward to another passage about ominous westward progress, in *Paradise Lost*:

>   or who with *Saturn* old
>   Fled over *Adria* to th'*Hesperian* Fields,
>   And ore the *Celtic* roam'd the utmost Isles.   (*PL* 1.519–522)

There the flight of Saturn westwards over Greece and Italy and then through France to the isles at the edge of the ancient world

Kōmos – the adversary for the occasion

suggests also the spread of idolatrous evil into countries such as Britain. Protestant writers seem sometimes to have posited a westward progress of good and evil, shaping the history of church and world.[5] Milton's construction allows him one of those passing references to his own times, for which his epic is so remarkable. The roaming of this passage also resembles the roving of Comus. In the epics Satan is said to roam or rove through the earth, seeking occasion for evil.[6] It is the satanic walking about of I Peter 5.8 and the going to and fro and walking up and down in the earth of Job 1.7. Evil has the determination to seek out what best to pervert.

But the ominous if inevitable presence of a devilish agency at the Ludlow feast is conveyed with a playful casualness, as if the sequence were merely one of chance: 'as ye winds listed . . . fell . . . roaving . . . at last betaks him to this ominous wood'. For this disciple of Spenser, the way to moral definition is through the delights of fictive play.

The Spirit is informing the audience what to expect, an enchanter employing Circean arts, with cup and wand, and a palace in the wood. The audience can place immediately the animal-headed rout, which bursts in, and the whole journey of the children is being shaped by Odyssean myth. But in other ways, as I have said, the information remains provisional, or seems deliberately fictional. It makes strange sense to have 'every wearie travailer' crossing this particular wood and of these to have 'most' fall to intemperance. The unlikelihood of it, in relation to specific occasion, invites audience or reader to register some general symbolism. Curiosity is whetted. The precise, though generalised, nature of the dangers of the occasion, the workings of the adversary within the festivity, Milton will allow the action to reveal, by stages.

I would stress that method. The rituals of the action will resolve the doubt and complete the figures of the opening speech, by demonstrating how Britain, Wales, the President, his children and Comus the enchanter unite to give significance to the occasion. As for Comus himself, the audience's curiosity in his powers is met immediately, for the enchanter's first speech gives a dramatised definition to his name.

The opening speech of Comus has often been admired for its lively protean verse and its vivid self-revelation. In an early state of the Trinity manuscript the Attendant Spirit had been made to begin his prologue by speaking about his heavenly abode, pictured as Hesperian gardens eternally bright and peaceful, in contrast to the present mundane darkness.[7] In this way the evening hour of the masque had been moralised at the outset. Comus' speech, welcoming the darkness of night, stands partly as false prologue to that earlier version of the Spirit's true prologue. The Spirit had presented virtuous festivity 'as in the day', with an eye to eternity; Comus presents vice in festivity, 'works of darkness'.[8]

His first words are not immediately ominous. They have a quick relish to them, little more:

> The starre that bids ye shepheard fold
> now the top of heav'n doth hold
> and the gilded carre of day
> his glowing axle doth allay
> in the steepe Atlantick streame

Only in the following lines does he begin to advertise the dangers that are the consequence of the mood of carefree excess. A process is being imitated. Provocation begins with 'midnight shout' and 'tipsie dance'. The tone becomes darker, the language wilder. In Comus' thoughts, joy and feast lead to the obscene rites of Cotytto. Revelry becomes riot. The decision to delete the moralised 'Hesperian' section of the Attendant Spirit's prologue allowed the poet to re-use some of the ideas in the epilogue; it also allowed him to hold back until the beginning of Comus' speech the full exploitation of the evening hour, therefore to exploit it more dramatically. The audience is being drawn into understanding a dark design behind the light Teian strain.

Comus' mirth is not all innocence, however, even at the beginning, for the moral signposts already given in the prologue are plain, and visual display enforces the point. The audience would see rather more readily than the reader. The appearance of the rout, with grotesque animal heads and 'riotous and unruly noise' (*1637*), was meant as constant index to understanding. Young people are visibly bestialised, the divine image of reason

Kōmos – the adversary for the occasion

defaced. The audience is not deceived (to adopt an idea familiar to critics of *Paradise Lost*) but is made to understand how men are deceived by devilish illusion.

The self-revelation of the speech amounts to quite a full definition of the traditional idea of the *kōmos*. His cue is the expectation of mirth in the masque night, *hilaritas festi*:[9]

> mean while welcome Joy & feast
> midnight shout & revelry
> tipsie dance & jollity.

The infectious verse measure fits. It may be an English version of the Anacreontic line, associated with carefree mirth, wine and love.[10] The next lines seem to suggest that, like some of the 'Cavalier' poets, he is actually imitating the *Anacreontea*: 'Braid yor locks wth rosie twine / dropping odours, dropping wine'. The call is for the spirit of youth – 'what youth and pleasure prompts us to'[11] – and the restraints of sober age are to be resisted. Nevertheless, the President and other elders of the judicial council sit in the hall, watching and listening. This is amusement by provocation; they have not 'gon to bed':

> Rigor is gon to bed
> & Advice wth scrupulous head
> Strict age, & sowre severity
> wth thire grave saws in slumber lie.

Apparently picking up a phrase, 'of purer fire', from Milton's courtly-fashionable contemporary Thomas Randolph,[12] Comus celebrates dance by night, citing the motions of the heavenly bodies and moon-drawn seas, fairies and nymphs. The disparity between these pastoral images of delicate harmony and the heavy-moving, grotesque and noisy rout, must have made the boast all the more obvious:

> wee that are of purer fire
> imitate the starrie quire
> who in thire nightly watchfull spheares
> lead in swift round the months & yeares
> the sounds & seas wth all thire finnie drove
> now to the moone in wavering morrice move
> and on the tawnie sands & shelves
> trip the pert fayries, & the dapper elves.

Milton's Aristocratic entertainments

>by dimpled brooke & fountayne brim
>the wood nymphs deck't wth daysies trim
>thire merrie wakes & pastimes keepe
>what hath night to doe wth sleepe.

This is a mind of literary, theatrical fancy: like Randolph's, only better. And like Bacchus *nuktelios* ('nightly'), it becomes active with the dark. Comus watches for Venus, evening star, to waken love: 'night has better sweets to prove / Venus now wakes, & wakens Love.' But love turns into sports of obscenity, the shamelessness of *dea impudentiae*. Her darkness is hellish, 'Stygian'. When Cotytto is named, the unstable verse becomes for four lines theatrical decasyllabics (to which it also returns in two later lines):

>Come let us our rights begin
>tis only daylight that makes sin
>wch these dun shades will ne'er report
>Haile goddesse of nocturnall sport
>Dark-vaild Cotytto, to whome the secret flame
>of midnight torches burnes, mysterious Dame
>that neere are call'd but when the dragon womb
>Of Stygian darknesse spitts her thickest gloome
>and makes one blot of all ye aire
>stay thy clowdie ebon chaire
>wherein thou rid'st wth Hecate & befriend
>us thy vow'd preists till utmost end
>of all thy dues bee done & none left out

'Rights', 'dues', 'preists' and 'sin' and the association with Hecate, witch goddess, ensure (if such is needed) the galling of nice pious sensibilities. The speech ends in the full display of devilish perversion in a 'conceal'd sollemnity' exposed to the audience: Comus' sense of privacy, like Satan's, is a delusion –

>ere the blabbing easterne scout
>the nice morne on th'Indian steepe
>from her cabin'd loopehole peepe
>and to ye telltale sun discry
>our conceal'd sollemnity.

The appeal is of boyish excitement, pitched against the telltale blab, but workers of darkness fear the day. The final opposition of day and darkness and the underlying sense of shame confirm the religious judgement. We are being shown the mind of a refined

Kōmos – the adversary for the occasion

dissolute, an image of 'effeminate' aristocracy, seen through the glass of a precise Protestant, who can imitate exactly. The best-known proof-text for *kōmos* in the Bible is Romans 13.12–13:

> The night is far spent, the day is at hand: let us therefore cast off the works of darkness, and let us put on the armour of light. Let us walk honestly, as in the day; not in riot and drunkenness [*mē kōmois kai methais*], not in chambering and wantonness

Comus' reversion to more innocent invitation now sounds more hollow than ever: the 'light fantastick round' is not in the mood of the 'light fantastic toe' of *L'Allegro*, despite the final recovery of the Anacreontic seven-syllable line: 'Come knit hands, & beate ye ground / in a light fantastick round.'

Other evidence of Comus' nature is revealed in the masque, of course, but his opening speech supplies the leading characteristics of the workings of the *kōmos* as Milton chose to present it in relation to the aristocratic occasion in his own times. Milton evidently knew a full range of associations of the word. He was a savourer of words, a poet of allusion. He was not, here or elsewhere, simply a worker from iconographical or mythographical handbooks. Of course he would have known about iconographical tradition and may well have remembered that the figure Comus was in Cartari's *Imagines* and elsewhere and that the figure was customarily derived from the description in Philostratus' *Icones*, a description which also appeared verbatim in Renaissance editions of Phornutus (L. Annaeus Cornutus) and which was constantly referred to in later glosses.[13] But there is no need to debate much, for example, whether Milton had read the masque of Ben Jonson, *Pleasure Reconciled to Virtue*, still in manuscript until 1640, in order to find 'influence' on his figure of Comus.[14] Nor, I suspect, though the parallel is much more suggestive in authorial attitude, can one be sure whether he had read Puteanus' satirical and moralistic dream–vision, *Comus*, of 1608 (reprinted in Oxford in 1634).[15] Puteanus offered some traditional characteristics and ready associations, in rather fuller fashion than usual. And the same is true of other 'sources'. Milton probably knew the figure Comus from a large number of texts, Greek, Latin and religious, too many perhaps to try to list, and, more importantly, he would have known the words *kōmos* (the revel), *kōmazein* (to revel, revelling), and *kōmazontes* and *kōmastes* (revellers), in texts as plentiful and contexts as suggestive as those mentions of the god. Glosses on these words often supplied the leading information about the *kōmos* as activity or *Kōmos* the god, as did glosses on the derived forms in Latin, *comessari, comessatio* and so on.

Milton's idea of the *kōmos*, conveyed in such lively fashion through his enchanter, is broadly consonant with that familiarly found in the writings of pious, educated men of his time. Rather than try to support his Comus from iconographical tradition, as has often been done before,[16] sometimes with little appropriateness, I would like to refer to a few literary allusions, scholarly glosses and commonplace usages to fill out the conception of the *kōmos* in a way which suggests something doctrinal to the nation.

First of all, we have evidence to show that Milton thought broadly in terms of the word, which he used twice in the Trinity manuscript, once in his list of possible subjects for tragedy, once in the masque itself. In both cases the form was *kōmazontes*, which he would probably have translated as rioters.

In the printed editions of the masque, Comus and his animal-headed rout are said in the stage direction to 'come in making a riotous and unruly noise, with torches in their hands'. In the Trinity manuscript this direction had ended (after several emendations): '. . . they come on in a wild & antick fashion / intrant *kōmazontes*'. Presumably Milton did not wish to leave the Greek word standing in the printed text, but he had given the sense of it: the transformed victims of Comus come in in the manner of nocturnal Bacchic revellers, riotously with torches in their hands.

In the list of subjects drawn from Old Testament history for possible use in a tragedy, Milton included this entry:

Comazontes or the Benjaminits Jud. 19.20 &c. or the Rioters.[17]

This refers to a vivid, chaotic piece of invective in the nineteenth and twentieth chapters of the book of Judges, made against the tribe of Benjamin. It is a story which puritan polemicists found useful and which Milton never forgot. It tells of a Levite who had taken a concubine out of Bethlehem-Judah. She 'played the harlot against him' and went back to her father's house. The Levite went

Kōmos – the adversary for the occasion

to fetch her, with a servant. Bringing her back, they came at night into Gibeah, a Benjaminite town. An Ephraimite put them up for the night, and they were making merry in his house, when certain 'sons of Belial', a band of local young men out on the street, clamoured at the door, demanding that the visiting Levite be delivered up to them, so that they could commit sodomy with him. They were fobbed off with the concubine, whom they raped until daybreak, leaving her dead on the threshold. The Levite divided her corpse into twelve pieces, sending them round the tribes of Israel as a protest against the Benjaminites, 'for they have committed lewdness and folly in Israel'. A war followed, in which thousands were said to be killed. This story, like others near it in Judges, is punctuated by repeated comments of the writer: 'In those days there was no king in Israel, but every man did which was right in his own eyes' (17.6; 21.25; cf. 28.1; 29.1) and 'there was no magistrate in the land, that might put them to shame in any thing' (18.7). The stories show the consequence of lack of leadership and unity. Presumably Milton's tragedy would have made some similar point, in the 1640s. In such a context the *kōmos*, the nocturnal riot of those youths, is a sign of national degeneracy and prelude to national disaster.

In the epics, when he had all history in mind, Milton enshrined his memories of this story in the fallen angel Belial, who is fair-seeming, voluptuous and gamesome, and in whom some readers have sensed invective against 'cavalier' degeneration:

> In Courts and Palaces he also Reigns
> And in luxurious Cities, where the noyse
> Of riot ascends about thir loftiest Towrs,
> And injury and outrage: And when Night
> Darkens the Streets, then wander forth the Sons
> Of *Belial*, flown with insolence and wine.
> Witness the Streets of *Sodom*, and that night
> In Gibeah, when th'hospitable door
> Expos'd a Matron to avoid worse rape.[18]   (*PL* 1.497–505)

That is the updated luxury, riot and outrage of the *kōmos*, to which rich courts and palaces are said to be prone. Then again, during the consultation of the fallen angels, Belial's arguments for ease and sloth are said to be 'clothed in reason's garb'; Comus' arguments to the Lady she calls 'pranck't in reasons garbe'. In

Milton's Aristocratic entertainments

Paradise Regained Belial argues that Christ might succumb to women, and the sons of Belial seduce or rape fair women in court and country to beget a 'race' (*PR* 2.181). Comus and Belial, perverters of the moral will, spoilers of the slackening aristocracy, come out of the same stable.

When he thought of giving a tragedy based on the story of the sons of Belial the title Comazontes or The Rioters, Milton was associating some of the features of the story with an idea of *kōmos* established in his mind. Groups of youths, especially at night, wine and drunken insolence at or after a banquet or party, outrage in the public streets, and manifestations of licentiousness are features that appear in other accounts of *kōmoi*.

From the beginning the *kōmos* was associated with night.[19] More characteristic uses of the word seem to come from the sixth and fifth centuries onwards, when it denotes processional revelling rites associated with Dionysia. *Kōmastes*, reveller, is one epithet for Dionysus. The *kōmos* is Bacchic and associated with unrestrained festive mirth. It was for the *kōmos* of these festivals that some authorities (falsely) derived the word comedy, and of course the processional and histrionic associations made the word, for Milton, even more appropriate for the occasion of a masque. Thereafter, the word came to stand in a general way for various festive and jocular habits, involving smaller or larger groups of people, not simply in the actual Dionysian festivals.[20]

There is the bursting of Alcibiades into Plato's *Symposium* (212C), for example. He is leader of a band of revellers. Late in the party he enters noisily, rather drunk, with his companions, seeking more drink, carrying a wreath for Agathon, with flute-girl, ivy, violets, ribands on his head. This is genial stuff, but here are some typical features: the nocturnal setting, a band of drunken young men, coming through the streets, breaking into a house, 'midnight shout', 'tipsie dance', flute-girls from eastern parts, erotic dancing to rhythmic music, festive crowns of flowers. This incident, like others, suggests that the *kōmos* had to do with the long continuance or the last stages of festivity: 'the after supper meetings of riotous persons', said a pious contemporary of Milton.[21] Masques, of course, usually took place after supper and went deep into the night. Many glosses cite the *Symposium*.

Another occasion is suggested by Euripides' *Alcestis* (918),

Kōmos – the adversary for the occasion

where revellers come in the train of Admetus' wedding. Or, a *kōmos* may be a rather more private affair, as when a young man, possibly accompanied by friends, servants or musicians, clamours at the door late at night for entry into a house, standing at the door of his beloved, perhaps offering a tipsy serenade. (The Judges story, also focussed on a street door, may have looked to Milton and others a darker version of this.) The young man may get in, break in or, more comically, sleep on the threshold until morning. Such is the result in Theocritus' third idyll, called in some manuscripts *Kōmastes* or *Kōmos*. Here the shepherd–singer intends to leave the care of his sheep: 'I'm off to serenade Amaryllis.' The sentence was often noticed in definitions, because it showed a Doric form of the verb: *kōmasdō*. Theocritus' poem is whimsical, putting a bucolic into the role of Alexandrian gallant, but it illustrates again the connections between the *kōmos* and the erotic. In fact, this kind of *kōmos*, at the door of the beloved, became a conventional subject for poems, a 'genre', as Milton would have known, and several variants of it appear in Theocritus and in the Roman elegists, Tibullus, Propertius and Ovid, as well as in Horace.[22] Some illustrations of Comus feature a door.[23]

As Milton would also have known, moral writers, like Plato, wrote how the *kōmos* might disable a whole community.[24] In Xenophon's *Cyropedia* (5.5.15) Cyrus takes the city of Babylon by night, with no resistance, because it has been having a *kōmos* and is boozed asleep. Such an example might be seen as a warning to peoples and nations about the consequences of effeminate ease and sloth, of Belial kind. Plato, in the *Republic* (573), names the *kōmos* with other festive habits of intemperate kind as part of the generation of tyrannical man. Plutarch, writing of the education of children, puts revels in the list of iniquities to which young blood is liable: unlimited gluttony, theft of parents' money, gambling, revels, drinking-bouts, love affairs with young girls and corruption of married women (*Moralia* 12B). In such a list the *kōmos* seems to have lost some of its specific associations with the Dionysia or other customs and has taken on the sense of generally riotous behaviour. In fact Plutarch uses the word in a fashion not dissimilar from the New Testament writers, who much influenced glosses of noun and god in Milton's time.

The use of *kōmos* in Romans 13 has been noted above, where 'riot and drunkenness' are named as shameful works of darkness. The text was very commonly referred to in discussions of *kōmos* and other kinds of luxury. In the fifth chapter of Galatians (v.21) *kōmos* appears in a list of works of the flesh. In the first epistle of Peter there is a passage which might almost serve as text for the debate in the masque about the use of the gifts of nature:

> For the time past of our life may suffice us to have wrought the will of the Gentiles, when we walked in lasciviousness, lusts, excess of wine, revellings, banquettings [*kōmois, potois*], and abominable idolatories. Wherein they think it strange that we walk not with them to the same excesses of riot.
> (4.3-4)

Commenting on Romans 13, the Tremellius Bible referred to the whole *luxus* of such lavish convivia as we read of in Amos 5 and Isaiah 6, in which music and every kind of delicacy are combined with the choicest food.[25]

Christian scholars were apt to recall Old Testament contexts, in which such luxurious feasting was often associated with the infection and degeneracy of nations. 'Therefore my people are gone into captivity', was the celebrated warning of Isaiah. When a nation degenerates in this way, it puts itself into bondage of oppressors; Milton knew the message well. 'Take example thereby', says Diodati, in paraphrase of Amos, 'not to grow in carnall security.'[26] This kind of Christian placement of feasting and the *kōmos* in high places is inevitably behind Milton's godly masque for the children of a magistrate.

The iconographical record of Comus has been traced several times before, from Philostratus through to reference books of near Milton's own time, like Caseneuve's *Hieroglyphica*.[27] In fact the more sumptuously produced iconographical books carried as much information about *kōmos* in their scholarly apparatus as in the description of the god, and much information about Comus the god was often given in explanations of the common noun in scholarly editions of various Greek texts. This set of sources is probably more important for Milton than iconographical handbooks. Translators and annotators often assumed that the word was personified in literary texts, when it probably was not. Whenever the history of Comus as daemon or god begins, the definition in some sixteenth-century dictionaries merely said *Deus apud veteres habitus*, a god recognised in the writings of the ancients.

Kōmos – the adversary for the occasion

Given a context which could bear personification, they frequently pushed back the history of the god to coincide with that of the common noun. Godly students of the gods were only too willing to find opportunities for tracing all demons back beyond Greek culture, to see them as fallen angels if possible.

The annotations of Vigenère in the French edition of Philostratus refer to a good example of this kind of unhistorical scholarship, which was so common that Milton must have felt its effects. In a full gloss of *kōmos*, Vigenère remembered (as did other scholars) one occurrence in the *Anacreontea*, at the end of the poem sometimes entitled *Kōmos*. Vigenère noted dissent between two translators on the word *kōmos*, 'one of them translating Comus as a dance . . . and the other as the daemon of which Philostratus speaks'. It was in fact Henri Estienne who put the dance and Elie André who put the god.[28] André was the less correct. Nevertheless, we have a scholar translating from Greek into Latin in the middle of the sixteenth century, who assumed that the legendary Anacreon would have heard of the god Comus in the sixth century BC.

There must be dozens of similar instances in editions of other Greek texts. Thomas Stanley, for example, was prepared to read Comus into the *Agamemnon* of Aeschylus in 1663.[29] The future Madame Dacier was happy to follow André in the Anacreontic ode in 1681, and Addison followed suit in 1735, as did Tom Moore as late as 1800.[30]

Most bizarre and amusing of all piously learned but fallacious, unhistorical appearances of Comus the god is the guise in which he is said to feature in the Old Testament as Chemosh/Baal-Peor, 'the obscene dread of Moab's sons'. This god was often identified with Bacchus or Priapus and it was associated with saturnalia. For example, in an early-seventeenth-century treatise devoted to convivia among the ancients, Johann Wilhelm Stuck has a chapter on nocturnal convivia, in which he gives much of the usual material on *kōmos* and then says

> There are some who wish to derive the Greek *kōmos* (from which word take their meaning the god of drunkenness, the wanton convivium, the singing and the lascivious dancing) from Cemosh, which is the name of the god or idol of the Moabites . . . The Seventy translate *Chamas* . . . Perhaps this god is named from CAMAS, that is, to hide or conceal, as Bacchus is *nuktelios*.[31]

Just how many scholars are included in the 'some' I do not know, but the conjecture was current in Milton's time, as its mention in Drusius' biblical commentary shows.³² Robert Gell, one of the fellows of Christ's College when Milton was there, in a Christmas sermon, names Chemosh as 'God of riot and drunkenness', implying though not stating the connection the *kōmos*, with the same kind of brief familiarity as that with which he referred to Mammon as god of riches in the same sentence.³³ There was evidently nothing rare about the idea. The conjecture is also in Edward Leigh's derivative *Critica Sacra* (1639, 1641), where it is put in a tone rather firmer than speculative. After discussing the *kōmos* of Romans 13, he says:

> From hence the heathen called their god of wantonness and revelling, *Kōmos*, and hereby was signified those pastimes that they used in their festivities, as Saturnalia, in honour of the heathen gods; like to which be our Whitsun ales, mummings, etc. This was likewise that abominable Idol of Moab, Chemosh, so called from some filthy behaviour used, or seen in the worship of the Idol.³⁴

When he glosses the idol, he goes straight from Chemosh to comedy: 'Camos, nomen idol, quod Moabitae colebant . . . Hinc *kōmos* et *kōmazein*, & comoedia. Rom. 13.13.' These were the godly connections common in Milton's time.

Clement of Alexandria had begun one of the chapters of his *Paedagogus*, written for the instruction of youth, with the sentence: 'Let the *kōmos* be absent from our rational banquet.'³⁵ That same exhortation is being made by dramatic example in Ludlow in 1634. The nub of the matter is the quality of aristocratic festivity itself, which is being seen as subject to the same pernicious dangers as had haunted the halls of princes from Old Testament times. An augury is being taken from the control that the young nobility manifest over luxury in the feast.

Masques commonly enacted virtue appropriate to their occasions. Comus was a richly appropriate choice for adversary. He engaged the chief delights of masque festivity with his infectious evil. Masques, the most lavish of nocturnal festivities of the contemporary court, concerned wealth and influence of 'some few', those castigated by the Lady, and their splendours followed a banquet. In no period in England had masques at court been made with more conspicuous lavishness than in the 1630s. Never

Kōmos – the adversary for the occasion

had the outcry against them in puritan quarters been louder. Writing in 1634, Milton cannot have been unaware, for example, of Prynne's notorious *Histriomastix*, written against the stage in general but construed to be against the court, published and prosecuted the year before. Calling upon the figure of Comus enabled Milton to frame an action in distant Ludlow which debated the nature of princely festivity itself, though with finer discrimination than Prynne had used against the stage. No masque ever examined the moral bases of its own rituals more directly than this.

The moral realism of the writing, even in this early, occasional text, makes one wonder how much the more political consequences of the *kōmos* may have been uppermost in Milton's mind at the time. By the time he thought of using Comazontes or The Rioters as a tragedy, in the late 1630s or early 1640s, he was clearly drawing on the full political significance of the *kōmos*. The dire words of the story in Judges might fit the Ludlow occasion of the presidency, if one cared to remember them, as well as the England Milton would have alluded to by type in the tragedy: 'there was no magistrate in the land'.

However this may be, the idea of the failure of civil and spiritual leadership through moral degeneration was to become a fixed part of his thought. In the poetry it is seen in the present reign of Belial in courts and palaces (*PL* 1.497ff), in the casual fruition, mixed dance, wanton mask, midnight ball, and serenade of the starved lover (4.767ff), and in the special relish of the catastrophe of *Samson Agonistes*, where providence orders that the flower of Philistia, nobility and youth, be cut down in the moment of drunken idolatrous festivity. Just such a phase of history, too, is that which ends with Noah, who preaches to warn the people at 'assemblies', 'triumphs' and 'festivities':

> All now was turn'd to jollitie and game,
> To luxurie and riot, feast and dance,
> Marrying or prostituting, as befell,
> Rape or Adulterie, where passing faire
> Allurd them; thence from Cups to civil Broiles.   (*PL* 10.710–714)

When he wrote that, Milton was sure he had also lived through such a phase of history at home.

Milton's Aristocratic entertainments

Thinking of the strictures of more radical Protestants, one might remember not only Prynne but also the infamous 'Book of Sports' of the year before the masque. In *Of Reformation*, admittedly in belligerent mood of national remembrancer, Milton wrote this of the authorities who gave that licence for Sunday pastimes in 1633:

so have they hamstrung the valour of the Subject by seeking to effeminate us all at home. Well knows every wise Nation that their Liberty consists in manly and honest labours, in sobriety and rigorous honour to the Marriage Bed, which in both Sexes should be bred up from chast hopes to loyall Enjoyments; and when the people slacken, and fall to loosenes, and riot, then doe they as much as is if they laid downe their necks for some wily Tyrant to get up and ride. Thus learnt *Cyrus* to tame the *Lydians*, whom by Armes he could not, whilst they kept themselves from Luxury; and with one easy Proclamation to set up *Stews*, dancing, feasting, & dicing he made them soone his slaves. I know not what drift the *Prelats* had, whose Brokers they were to prepare, and supple us either for a Forreigne Invasion or Domestick oppression; but this I am sure they took the ready way to despoile us both of *manhood* and *grace* at once, and that in the shamefullest and ungodliest manner upon that day which Gods Law, and even our own reason hath consecrated, that we might have one day at least of seven set apart wherein to examin and encrease our knowledge of God, to meditate, and commune of our Faith, our Hope, our eternall City in Heaven, and to quick'n, withall, the study, and exercise of Charity; at such a time that men should bee pluck't from their soberest and saddest thoughts, and by *Bishops* the pretended *Fathers of the Church* instigated by publique Edict, and with earnest indeavour push't forward to gaming, jigging, wasailing, and mixt dancing is a horror to think. Thus did the Reprobate hireling Preist *Balaam* seeke to subdue the Israelites to *Moab*, if not by force, then by this divellish *Pollicy*, to draw them from the Sanctuary of God to the luxurious, and ribald feast of *Baal-Peor*. Thus have they trespas't not onely against the *Monarchy* of *England*, but of Heaven also, as others, I doubt not, can prosecute against them.   (Yale I 588–589)

Context and function have changed, but this is *kōmos* on a Sunday, the insolence of the Lady's late wassailers, looseness and riot in the image of Chemosh/Baal-Peor, at work by devilish policy in the degeneration of a people. There is no absolute need to seek for sheer topicality in the design of *Comus*, but if one should do so and remember the loose unlettered hinds thanking the gods amiss, 'The Book of Sports' is probably of more relevance than the book of Prynne, and probably than the Castlehaven trial as well.[36]

In the second book *Of Reformation*, also, after rehearsing the

Kōmos – the adversary for the occasion

view that all political leadership depends upon godliness – 'this is the true florishing of a Land, other things follow as the shadow does the substance' – Milton lamented that modern political leaders served to enslave the people by allowing luxury and riot unchecked:

> To make men governable in this manner their precepts mainly tend to break a nationall spirit, and courage by count'nancing upon riot, luxury, and ignorance, till having disfigur'd and made men beneath men, as *Juno* in the fable of *Iö*, they deliver up the poor transformed heifer of the Commonwealth to be stung and vext with the breese, and goad of oppression under the custody of some *Argus* with a hundred eyes of jealousie.   (Yale I 572)

The choice of Comus for adversary carries with it the possibility of such analysis. Centring on the children of a magistrate, it engaged the education of those who lead. Without such leadership, men fall to cups, and thence to civil broils, or at least to bondage, a paralysis in the chair.

A last word about the dynamics of the presentation of Comus, concerning the Circean element in the pastoral fiction.

To the Lady Comus first conceals his identity within that of a rustic. In this typically Protestant way the beginning of the action resembles that of *Paradise Regained*, where the adversary also tries first a pastoral disguise. In the masque the second 'scene' reveals to all that Comus' true home is not the country but the luxurious palatial hall. Whatever the momentary distractions of the pastoral, attention is repeatedly directed to the behaviour of the privileged class. Hence the force of many asides, like the one already mentioned: 'Offring to every wearie travailer / his orient liquor in a crystall glasse'. It is an invitation to think of the way men commonly react to rich refreshment. The full delicacy of fine living is suggested, the drink sparkling like a precious eastern pearl, the glass being expensive ware from Venice. Into such rich living the easy-hearted man moves easily; and 'most doe tast'.[37]

Such censures are everywhere in Milton's text. Spirituality is rare in this 'sin-worn mould'; Comus gloats over the growing size of his herd; the world will not 'in a pet of temperance feed on pulse'. Pastoral covers the luxurious, the princely, by use of a Circean setting.

The myth of Circe offered special possibilities for the provincial

Ludlow occasion: a palace within a wood, a court in pastoral wilds, the significance of which travellers may discover. The discoveries which the children enact in the masque are therefore both of what is true and false in the princely and of what is true and false in the pastoral.

Many of the characteristics of Milton's Comus and his rout are Bacchic, others both Bacchic and Circean, others again relating to the literary tradition of the *kōmos*. Conscious of the mixture, and sensing that critics had heretofore underplayed the Bacchic elements, John Steadman sought to redress the balance: 'They are characteristics not only of the god of wine, but also of his *son*, the Bacchic revel' (p. 110). Still, the words are 'much like his father, but his mother more'. Moreover, the myth of Circe provides a framework to be recognised by the audience. I do not think it satisfactory to call the myth the 'hinge' of the masque,[38] if by that is meant that it defines all the significances of the action – rather, it is a framing myth on which new variations are made – but in some way the spirit of Circe is being advertised as important.

There is a challenge to see something pervasive: 'who knows not Circe...' The recognition has much to do with common intemperance, but it is also of the prevalent powers of the influence of falsehood. Comus is referred to as sorcerer, necromancer, enchanter and damned magician. The dwelling on enchantment has a religious force. At the same time, it means that the fiction can freely exploit myth and especially romance, with its motifs of magic, the 'forest, and enchantments dear, / Where more is meant than meets the ear'. The poet offers symbols of satanic deception, whilst allowing his masquers to insist, in knowing innocence, that they are caught up in something merely fabulous.

Comus emerges as lively inheritor of Archimagan guile. Nothing is so suggestive of the influence of Spenser as this combination of a religious concern with a fiction, whilst pointing to religious truth:

> Ile tell you. Tis not vaine or fabulous
> (though so esteem'd by shallow ignorance)
> what the sage poets, taught by th'heav'nly Muse
> storied of old in high immortall verse
> of dire chimaera's and inchaunted Isles
> & rifted rocks whose entrance leads to hell
> for such there be, but unbeliefe is blind

Kōmos – the adversary for the occasion

Blind unbelief is a Pauline formulation.[39]

Details of the Circe story maintain pretence and make religious points at the same time, as in the idea of forgetting one's native home: '& all thire freinds, & native home forget'. This does not sort with specific occasion: the children have not come from a mundane Ithaca to which they are trying to return. One seeks other meaning. In fact, the phrase 'native home' recalls the biblical distinction between earthly and heavenly 'house' or 'country' (II Cor. 5.1; Heb. 11.16). In this idiom, to forget one's native home is to live according to the flesh, choosing not to keep in mind the home from which the Spirit descends.

Comus' particular likeness to Circe points, then, beyond intemperance, to the diabolical magic powers of perverting the truth by illusion and deceptive argument. That is the fatal enchantment, and it is a matter of right education to resist it. Comus' magic partakes of the satanic enmity, the hugging into snares, the blurring of godly truth. That is why, having heard the Lady's steps, he begins his campaign by hurling 'dazzling spells into the spungie aire / of power to cheate the eye wth bleare illusion / and give it false praesentments'. The Lady's first test with Comus, which she must partly fail, as all men do before such falsehood, is to detect the truth beneath the false image of pastoral humility. Romance magic is the intensifying vehicle for the expression of diabolical perversions of truth.

The gesture of sheer familiarity – who knows not Circe? – conveys the Protestant assumption that Duessa follows Una, from east to west, until the end of time. It is this gesture of sheer familiarity which ties the deceptive, Circean element in Comus to the Circean figure of false love in the celebrated personal passage in Milton's *Apology*, where there is mention of 'a certain Sorceresse the abuser of loves name' who cheats 'the rest'. In other words, nothing is more *common* than the perversion of love: Love, like Truth, is dogged with false images.

As we turn to the exemplary roles of the children in this most piously educational text, we shall see that the countering of the enchanter becomes, for both Lady and boys, most of all a matter of recognising relevant truth. The strength of the children against the enchanter is shown to depend upon their whole Christian education and upon spiritual virtues most of all.

4 · THE YOUNG HEROES – REALISM AND IDEALISM

THE sexes, ages and relevant accomplishments of the President's three youngest children set the conditions by which Milton had to work. He fitted them with seriousness, wit and delicacy. He displayed Lady Alice's ability to sing. He displayed the dancing of the children, such as they had already performed at court. He also provided long speaking parts, quite formidable for young people of 15, 11 and 9, even at a time when memories were highly trained. These children were to be the examples of aristocratic youth not seduced by the customary luxury in the feast.

One would dearly like to know how far Milton was allowed to establish procedures of his own. The decision to have the children perform full dramatic roles instead of merely making a spectacular entry as masquers was one that had repercussions on the display of their aristocratic talents and on the degree of realism it was possible to compass in the action. On the one hand, by showing declamatory and histrionic skill, they added to the delights of self-display. On the other, the dramatic realism revealed them as fallible mortals, who had to rehearse their own realisation that unaided their powers of virtue would not suffice. That one decision to make them act, whoever took it, opened the way for a sober religious realism, which may have showed the Protestant inheritance but which in masque, where mortals were made gods, came close to being subversive of the form. This was a situation which called for a blending of different techniques, requiring intricate control. The rigour, however, is characteristically Miltonic. One has to believe that the decision to go so far towards dramatic realism was his own, or that it was welcomed by him as if it were his own.

Milton designed separate actions for the Lady and the two boys.

The young heroes – realism and idealism

Somewhat different kinds of virtue are defined in each case – rather more different than is sometimes realised – and in each case there is a somewhat different technique. Only in the presentation of the three to their parents, and in the dance, do the virtues unite in a figure which suggests the whole Christian education behind their triumph, resulting from a trial of 'thire youth / thire faith, thire patience, & thire truth'.

One may see the division of roles as a signal variation on the pattern of the Circe episode. Comus' rout, presumably of young people, is like the collection of all those who have already succumbed to the Circean magic, and the President's offspring are to be like Odysseus himself, overcoming magic arts with divine aid. But Milton has separated out aspects of the Odyssean wisdom and has redistributed it between the Lady and the boys, whilst also investing some in Sabrina. The new partitions and suspensions of the myth are offered for delight and instruction.

'Thyrsis' himself draws attention to a delight in new pretence as he meets the boys. Arriving breathless and urgent, he puts the question which seems comically naive: 'but oh my virgin Ladie where is she / how chance she is not in yo[r] companie'. Then he tells how he himself heard her and saw her already in the clutches of the adversary: 'then downe the lawnes I ran wth headlong hast . . . soone I gues't / yee were the tow she meant . . . I found you heere / but furder know I not'. Such comedy is the mark of shared pretences between the participants, Lawes and the boys, joined by the audience. All agree that Hermes will not arrive in time, or will not be there with the expected means of help for one of the Odyssean parties; just as, after Comus is driven offstage, the boys pretend to have forgotten a part of the Odyssean task, so as to enable a new phase of definition to begin with Sabrina. Ways are being found for new virtues to be shown for each 'part' of the heroic endeavour.

The exemplary qualities of the Lady are expressed throughout the action. Her very first lines give assurance of social grace and piety. The exquisite echo song displays a grace acknowledged by Comus himself. The Lady's rejection of Comus' excessive praise and her rebuke at his unkindness give further assurance of her right-mindedness, whilst her acceptance of his offer of help, though showing an understandable failure to read hypocrisy, registers a pious innocence and a knowledge that court and courtesy are not the same. During the temptation scene she manifests trust in providence ('whilst heaven sees good'), asserts the freedom of the virtuous mind, and explains faultlessly by the puritan book the doctrine of temperance against smooth libertine arguments. One can hardly overstate the didactic and celebratory intentions in this presentation. The Lady is young, mortally frail, yet a model. Her role is not without its triumphantly assertive delights, but her frailty is I think never so close to drawing the patronising smile as do the parts of her little brothers.

In terms of dramatic technique her role involves the only too frequent use of irony. She walks into ominous situations already known by the audience. This is a device for pathos of sorts. When for example she reaches the spot from which the noise of riot came, she is struck by the empty blackness about her. Comus is watching in the wings. Her fearful thoughts – 'O thievish night / why shouldst thou, but for some fellonious end . . .' are only too justified in the event. There is a curious amalgam of 'tragic' method, expressive of moral realism, with a rather intimate mode of personal celebration, a mode which must ultimately deny the tragic.

The significance of the role of the Lady and the implications of some of the changes in the text may be seen more clearly if her trial is divided into its constituent parts. There are three pieces of action. The first is made up of her soliloquy, as she is discovered lost and alone in the dark wood. It leads into the singing of her echo song. The second part we might think of as the first encounter with Comus, during which she is deceived by his pastoral disguise. The third stage is represented by the second 'scene' of the masque, offering the picture of a palace feast. When the Lady becomes aware of what she faces, she meets the occasion heroically in argument, though unable to free herself from the bond of the customary chair. Previously her 'eyes' had been deceived; now her 'judgement' resists false argument.

In the soliloquy the situation is reminiscent of pastoral or romance, but the language is tipped specifically towards the religious. The Lady is in the country, in a wood, and imagining the nocturnal revelling of 'loose unlettr'd hinds' at the close of

The young heroes – realism and idealism

summer. She wishes to believe in the benevolence of nature about her: whilst in one breath she laments 'the blind mazes of this tangled wood', in the next she remembers 'such cooling fruit / as the kind hospitable woods provide'. Her present fear is set against a religious thought, an habitual trust in providence, and both fear and trust are expressed in pastoral terms. In a section cancelled early in the Trinity manuscript, the religious, perhaps rather heavy-handedly, broke through: she imagined 'this dusky hollow' as a 'paradise'.

The Lady also joins an apprehension of imminent danger with imaginings that derive from folklore or fabulous literature, in 'sands, & shoars, & desert wildernesses'. That sounds not unlike the semi-pastoral romance fiction of Shakespeare's *The Tempest*, for example. (A memory of that play, distinguishing mental images of guilty and clear consciences, might be appropriate.) However, when the Lady banishes her fear by meditating on Faith, Hope and Chastity, she uses a language which is more insistently religious than was usual in public plays, though conventional periphrases are still maintained:

> & now beleeve
> that he the supreme good to'whome all things ill
> are but the slavish officers of vengeance
> would send a glistering guardian if need were

The militancy of the language is in character, but several passages of religious expression were cut from the performance text as represented by the Bridgewater manuscript. As a result, the audience at Ludlow was not troubled by the triad:

> O welcome pure-eyd Faith, white-handed Hope
> thou flittering angell girt wth golden wings
> and thou unspotted forme of chastity
> I see yee visibly

For many modern readers expectation has been jarred by finding a familiar series finishes with anything other than charity. But in dramatic context this is not simply a case of substitution of chastity for charity.[1] Chastity is sharply appropriate to the occasion, where charity could not be. Chastity also links the religious imperatives with the literary conventions of pastoral and romance.

Milton's Aristocratic entertainments

To Milton, chastity, in all its forms, is a part of the discipline of the manly nation. We may see the appropriateness of chastity fully set out if we remember the nature of the evil prompted by Comus, an evil broadly represented by luxury, and think of the way Protestant thought of Milton's time defined chastity in action. The following comes from the popular *Medulla* of William Ames. Ames' chief definitions of chastity make it a part of justice respecting the purity of our neighbour. At the end of his discussion he makes further definition by means of opposites, giving wider examples of occasions on which it may be exercised:

> 44. Unto chastity luxury is opposed in a more strict sense, whereby it sets forth an unlawfull use of those things, which pertain to generation ...
> 45. Unto luxury are reckoned all the helping causes, effects, & signes of it as unchast lookes, Job. 31.1, Pro. 9.13. 2 Pet. 2.14. Mat. 5.28. Noddings, Kissings, Embracings, Touchings, Dancings, Showes, Songs, Gestures, and the like. Gal. 5.15.
> 46. Unto the helping causes of luxury are referred, Gluttony and Drunkennesse. Rom. 13.13. Eze. 16.49. Pro. 23.31–3.
> 47. Unto the effects, and signes of it are refered lasciviousness, and lascivious habit, Pro. 7.11. And obscene speech. Eph. 5.4.[2]

There are enough cross-references here in the 'helping causes, effects, and signs' of luxury to the usual biblical placement and moral definition of revellings and feasts to make one realise that any religiously determined work was likely at some point to oppose chastity to the luxury of the *kōmos*. Milton disagreed with hardline puritans about the uses of the arts in the education of a free people. The masque itself shows the power of words and music used to both good and evil effect. But the moral placement of luxury as an evil is absolutely the same as in any pious writer of the times, and the judgement of a people and its leaders by such discriminations remained always at the centre of his thought.

The Lady's calling on chastity, as on faith and hope, is appropriate to the danger in which she finds herself. Yet a further embarrassment may suggest itself, that her naming chastity at this point might imply a high degree of foreknowledge of the enchanter she has yet to meet, the spirit of luxury hidden in the wood. The dramatic difficulty links with the shared pretences of the masque and with questions of literary convention. Milton wished his audience to assume that it was watching a pastoral fiction,

The young heroes – realism and idealism

something relatable to *The Faithful Shepherdess* or *Il Pastor Fido* amongst dramas, or a kind of pastoral romance. In such an action one expects vice to take the form of unchastity. An audience conditioned by such fare, so popular at the Caroline court, might expect the action to be about nothing else but the display of kinds of vice and virtue in love and the final purification of all. The virgin Lady is, as it were, aware of the nature of the fiction in which she acts. Somehow one must grasp chastity as religiously exact and fictionally conventional at the same time.

Large cuts were made in this speech in the Bridgewater manuscript. Perhaps the combination of explicitly religious language with erotic suggestiveness was the problem, when it came from the mouth of the Lady. Faith, Hope and Chastity may have presented a difficulty to a 'censor' then, as much as to a modern critical audience.

However this may have been, Milton was aiming for a feeling of apprehension and pity in the audience for the 'hapless virgin', as he was setting up the central confrontation of the masque. The art of the echo song shows this was the case:

> Sweet Echo sweetest nymph that liv'st unseene
>   within thy ayrie shell
>   by slow Maeanders margent greene
> and in the violet-imbroider'd vale
>   where the love-lorne nightingale
> nightly to thee her sad song mourneth well
> Canst thou not tell me of a gentle paire
>   that likest thy Narcissus are?
>   Oh if thou have
>   hid them in some flowrie cave
>   tell me but where
> Sweet Queene of parlie, daughter of the sphaere
> So maist thou be translated to the skies
> And give resounding grace to all heavns harmonies.

The song expresses one who is solitary and lost in a wild country place. It prays to divinity for an answer. Milton makes the Lady call Echo, because Echo always gives an answer (as in the echo songs), because she fits the pastoral, and because her situation, as told in Ovid,[3] mirrors the Lady's own. Losing Narcissus, with whom she had fallen in love, Echo haunted lonely places, living in caves, hiding in woods, seeking her lost boy. The Lady has lost two boys in the dark wood.

There is a nice wit to the song. Echo is called 'sweet Queene of parlie' to give her courtly rank whilst also remembering her employment by Jove, to keep Juno talking whilst he entertained the nymphs. The singer imagines that Echo has actually found the brothers and hidden them in 'some flowrie cave' as substitutes for her lost boy. Furthermore, she is called 'daughter of the sphaere' to remind her of her mortality in the story. In this song, however, she has not died. The point is that she is being offered a reward, of being 'translated to the skies', if only she will produce those two boys. In heaven she would echo not sad nightingales but the celestial harmonies. Both versions of the last line in the manuscripts – 'And hold a counterpoint' and 'And give resounding grace' – offer musical sense to link Echo and the Lady in the idea of music or song. The touch of witty extravagance in this song makes it a charming, sophisticated vehicle for Lady Alice's singing.

There has been some puzzlement amongst Milton's commentators to account for Echo's presence on the banks of the Phrygian river Meander, for no myth puts her there.[4] The connections are expressive, not of mythical allusion. They arise from verbal reminiscences of Ovid and the dramatic situation of the singer. It is enough that in the terms of the myth Echo might plausibly hear the 'sad song' of the 'love-lorne nightingale' every night, a music to add affecting grace to her own sense of desolation. The Lady herself will be referred to as 'poor haplesse nightingale'. Echo might inhabit the 'vale' where the bird sings and also the banks of the Meander, because that river is always thought of in poetry as labyrinthine, as Ovid says, 'often returning upon her former course'.[5] The river provides another image of the irresolute movements of one who is lost. There are 'blind mazes' in the wood, also called 'leavie labyrinth'. It is the affecting power of these images which matters, in the witty unity of the poem.

Similarly with 'ayrie shell'. It is an image which suggests the intangibility of Echo, a sounding-board of mere air, not to be seen. It reinforces the sense of isolation in the dark. It suits the 'tragic' novelty of this echo song, in which there is no immediate answer, only the patience that providence requires and the savage irony of

The young heroes – realism and idealism

being overheard, answered, by the very evil she would avoid.

There is then a range of style in the modulations of this section of the soliloquy. Milton seems bent on marrying the dramatisations of an exemplary set of psychological reactions, determined religiously, to the performance of a song of such exemplary grace as to put to shame most courtly lyrics of the time. The Christian psychology needs further comment, perhaps.

I suspect that the use of the song bears an analogy to the use of the psalms. The point is made by the word 'enliven': 'such noise as I can make ... Ile venter, for my new-enliv'nd spirits / prompt me ...' The enlivening of the spirits is what she has achieved through her soliloquy by calling on the apposite virtues. Milton does not use the word 'enliven' elsewhere in his poetry, but the context suggests that it is a version of the 'quickening' often mentioned in the Psalms. It is the raising of the spirits, in trust of God. Milton's version of Psalm 80.75 runs: 'Quicken us thou, then gladly we shall call upon thy name.' Psalms 71, 80, and 119 ask for this quickening of the spirits, in order that the writer may sing songs of praise.

The idea of enlivening gives apt expression to the shape of the internal action during the soliloquy. The Lady's sadness is balanced by the assurance she has given of her mental strength, so that the song, so confident in its graceful wit, even in sadness, becomes an earnest of the happier gestures of charitable praise which are to follow in the masque. The large cuts in the Bridgewater manuscript, cuts beginning with the words 'O thievish night', ruined the demonstration of *how* her spirits had been enlivened by contemplation of religious virtue, whilst leaving the announcement that they *had* been enlivened. Such a cut cannot have been initiated by Milton himself.

The first confrontation between Comus and the Lady, so carefully prepared for, also depends somewhat on the deployment of images of pastoral innocence. Comus' address to her uses an old poetic formula current in romance and pastoral:

> Haile forreine wonder
> whome certaine these rough shades did never breed
> unlesse the goddesse that in rurall shrine
> dwell'st heere wth Pan or Silvan

Milton's Aristocratic entertainments

This is Odysseus to Nausicaa, craftily; Aeneas to Venus, in piety; Salmacis to Hermaphrodite, seductively; the Satyr to Clorin, in awed admiration; Ferdinand to Miranda, in delightful comic wonder.[6] And of course it is Satan's opening to Eve: 'Wonder not, sovran Mistress, if perhaps / Thou canst, who art sole Wonder...' (*PL* 9.532–533). This young Eve of Ludlow makes her mark by reading the gambit as flattery, false courtly stuff, where she was looking instead for solid help and sympathy.

Comus' figure about the magical effect of her song – 'by blest song / forbidding every bleake unkindly fogge / to touch the prosperous growth of this tall wood' – gains fuller effect if we register the perversion of a pastoral figure beloved of Milton, expressing providential blessings. It is reminiscent, for example, of the protection of the estate around the 'shrine' at Harefield: 'and all my plants I save from nightlie ill / of noysome winds, or blasting vapours chill...'

And of course Comus' disguise is also pastoral. He acts the false rustic, the Attendant Spirit the true shepherd. When the enchanter protests his skill as guide, the sense of perversion of pastoral innocence makes the speech richly ominous:

> I know each lane, & every alley greene
> dingle, or bushie dell of this wild wood
> & every bosky bourne from side, to side
> my dayly walks, & ancient neighbourhood
> and if yor stray attendance be yet lodg'd
> or shroud within these limits I shall know
> ere morrow wake or the low-roosted Larke
> from her thetch't pallat rowse...

Genius and satyr figures appear in other pastoral works offering an intimate knowledge of the country, as Satyr in *The Faithful Shepherdess*, wryly remembered perhaps by Shakespeare with his darker Caliban. Comus' 'I shall know' is of satanic professionalism.

Everything makes for dramatic irony. The audience is impressed with perversions of truth and simplicity not fully apparent to the Lady. Comus' speech from the wings – 'can any mortal mixture of earths mould' – a speech that is superbly actable, had already expressed a roué with a silver tongue. Now his language is also Ovidian in its eroticism and Shakespearian in

The young heroes – realism and idealism

its resourcefulness, and it manages to suggest long experience in the life of the senses taken to the point of satiety. When his exclamation resolves itself into 'but such a sacred, & home felt delight / such sober certainty of waking blisse / I never heard till now', the words become vividly simple, and the religious and the judicious, 'sacred' and 'sober certainty', have become part of the perversion, in the cause of erotic fantasy.

Prepared in this way, the audience is being primed to follow the quick revelations in the exchanges of stichomythia. This formal technique deriving from tragedy Milton used to dramatic effect. A relish at the Lady's isolation in the night, a cynical lack of feeling, and a constant guilty preoccupation with falsehood are revealed in Comus in a few lines. The technique in the whole interview ensures that the audience registers the full range of evil in Comus, whilst seeing that the Lady's right-minded reactions are fatally hampered by her inability to see the whole nature of the being before her.

That vulnerability matters. There is no fudging the case in the hyperboles of compliment in Milton's masque. The religious realism is such that the Lady's mistake in believing Comus is as inevitable as Uriel's in believing Satan, 'For neither Man nor Angel can discern / Hypocrisie, the only evil that walks / Invisible, except to God alone' (*PL* 3.682–684). Only in *Paradise Regained* do the old satanic disguisings fail.

Dynamic Protestantism apart, there are manifold ironies in the Lady's final acceptance of Comus' 'honest offer'd courtesie'. Her preference for pastoral honesty over courtly pretence ironically marks the frailty of the perceptions of simplicity in the face of diabolical falsehood, yet it also exposes Comus himself to judgement in the eyes of the audience. The judgement on Comus is understood by the actors, by the Lady Alice herself, even if 'the Lady' is not yet meant to recognise the luxurious spirit Comus is. In one sense the princely hall is more 'warranted' than the wilderness; in another, it is not.

Dramatic irony is most often the mark of realism, asking for the suspension of disbelief. The point of masque, on the other hand, is that the chief masquers are always themselves, in some way, and that the pretences of the action celebrate present place and occasion. Masques therefore seem limited in that kind of realism.

Milton's Aristocratic entertainments

But here the audience is being invited to a mixture of reactions unusual in the self-conscious devices of comedy or masque, for Milton's technique with the masque has a way of reasserting a realism, a moral realism, through the celebratory gestures. The moral definition is much more religiously exacting than usual, all the more so since the masquers act; and the effect of the pastoral pretences, in this section as elsewhere, is both to serve the idealised reality of the aristocratic participants and to prompt the audience to hold the seductions of the habitual rich spirit of festivity up to the proper standards of pious simplicity.

In the temptation scene, the confrontation takes place on a somewhat different footing. Now the context for luxury is on view. The impact of the 'scene' is important. Comus' first act is to proffer the intoxicating glass. Instantly recognising the danger, even in her imagined fatigue and hunger, the Lady tries to rise and leave the feast of excess. Forced to remain by the power of the wand, she is trapped into a situation symbolising a kind of participation, however unwilling. She sits as it were in the seat of the scorners and must behold the habitual means to riot.[7] That, one takes it, is the common position of godly persons in princely halls.

This crucial scene underwent considerable development in composition both before and after performance. The latter changes are discussed below, in Chapter 6. The focus here is on the leading features of the dramatic sequence in the scene.

As before, there is close interest in the enchanter's display. But the presentation of the Lady has shifted. Whereas previously the audience had been invited chiefly to feel pity for human frailty, setting her youthful innocence against Comus' long experience, now it is asked more to applaud the Lady's intellectual domination. She matches Comus' arguments point for point, achieving a dialectical triumph in a ritualised moral exposition against the lewdly pampered luxury of the few unmatched, or unlooked-for, elsewhere in the seventeenth-century masque. The mores of a class are openly scrutinised. The Lady's display fuses celebration of the speaker with instruction by ideal example.

The central interest is in the ritual debate. Nevertheless, Milton worked to improve the dramatic qualities of the exchange, in the development of the text up to the time of performance. A

The young heroes – realism and idealism

distinction is exploited between the Lady's physical bondage and her mental freedom. She asserts the freedom of her mind at the beginning; by the end the enchanter's verbal persuasions are exhausted. There is a progression, both because the audience can watch the process of Comus' resources becoming exhausted and because, having seen that, it expects him to resort to violence, which he threatens at the outset, in tyrannical style, and which he seems near at the end, when the boys interrupt him.

Beyond this pattern, there is further interest in seeing that Comus himself has become the subject of a kind of irony. Whereas in the earlier scene Milton worked largely for a compact between audience and the Lady of feeling, here there is another compact coming dominantly into play, one of shared knowledge and understanding. Comus no longer seems to be in possession of the most potent knowledge. And this is paradoxical, since we are now seeing in action some of his specialised powers, which habitually succeed.

As in the first encounter, the speeches are fully styled for dramatic performance. Comus' initial threat (a tactical error, like his mention of Daphne) is met by a strong riposte. He resorts to a coaxing, easily conveyed in the rhythm: 'Why are you vext, Ladie, why doe you frowne / heere dwell noe frowns, no anger . . .' He tries her supposed weak point, hunger and thirst:

> poore ladie thou hast need of some refreshing
> that have bin tir'd all day wthout repast
> & timely rest have wanted, but fair virgin
> this will restore all soone.

But this stage villainy is upstaged by the directness of the Lady, virtuous young spitfire, who accuses him of deception. She thrusts aside the bait of flattery, in his Nepenthes for Helen, with her 'were it a draft for Juno, when she banquets / I would not taste . . .'

The long response of Comus is written as a highly dramatised piece of hypocrisy. Its dialect is unstable. It begins with moral sententiousness – 'O foolishness of men' – quoting Proverbs (19.3). The language and argument, as has often been recognised, are intended to recall the conventions of literary justifications of libertinism. The speech is also well-paced, to suggest Comus' growing excitement of sensuous imagination, until he reaches 'to gaze upon the sun wth shameless browes'. After this he turns directly to the Lady – 'list Lady be not coy' – in an open appeal for an erotic response which was evidently too strong for a censoring hand, which removed it from the Bridgewater text. Roused into argument, the Lady preaches back to such effect that the enchanter seems to cut her off in sheer frustration, and more and more, as the debate progresses, the power of his appeal is seen to be vitiated not just by predictability but also by what would, in the eyes of a godly audience, seem manifest errors.

In Comus' second speech, especially, the audience is being prompted to judge.[8] The provocation is mainly by persistent misuses of the Bible, vice bolting its arguments. Apart from the proverbial 'O foolishness of men', the picture of Nature's fertility recalls Genesis, the 'corner' of earth may pick up Isaiah (11.12) and Revelation (7.1), the feeding on pulse seems, rather bizarrely, to remember the test of Daniel (1.12), and the distinction between bastards and sons, as Verity saw,[9] echoes Hebrews 12.8. At the same time, temperance is misrepresented as abstinence, as usual in libertine arguments, the creativity of nature is portrayed largely as the production of luxury goods, and a version of the argument about Nature's wanton growth is tried, which will appear in Eve's mistaken idea that the Creator made a world man could not look after. In no uncertain fashion the moral author is telling the audience that the speaker's mind is erroneously fixed on Cupid and Mammon.

Gathering momentum, Comus finally offers that wild version of overfertility which strains at its metrical constraints. I quote here from the 1637 printed text, simply because it is the clearest version:

> And live like Natures bastards, not her sons,
> Who would be quite surcharg'd with her own weight,
> And strangl'd with her wast fertilitie;
> Th'earth cumber'd, and the wing'd aire dark't with plumes,
> The heards would over-multitude their Lords,
> The sea ore-fraught would swell, and th'unsought diamonds
> Would so emblaze the forehead of the Deep,
> And so bestudde with starrs that they below
> Would grow inur'd to light, and come at last
> To gaze upon the Sun with shameless brows.

The young heroes – realism and idealism

This is perverse prophecy, and remarkable poetry, and the last section has proved difficult to follow. The basis of Comus' figure is fairly plain, however, if one takes it that he is again using a biblical formula. He is giving examples of 'every creature which is in heaven, and on the earth, and under the earth, and such as are in the sea' (Rev. 5.13). The deep, as twentieth-century critics have realised, is not the sea but the regions under the earth, the *abyssus* of Revelation 9.1. The early Trinity version was plainer, having 'center', meaning the centre of the earth. This subterranean region is pictured as a vaulted space, in which the gems are the equivalents of stars. The idea of propagation connects the gems to the earlier mention of fertility in birds, animals and fish. Gems were thought to reproduce themselves; uncollected by man, therefore, they would multiply. Comus' grand prophecy is meant to sound more tenuous, more fantastic, as he goes on. 'They below' – the inhabitants of the nether regions – would grow so used to the bright light of the gem-stars of the abyss, so privileged, as it were, with the gift of life, that they would grow brazen and come to the surface to face the real sun. The scale of nature would be upturned. Comus is made to use this figure as the ultimate proof of disorder deriving from the wrong use of nature. The language is patently self-referential. The brazenness attributed to denizens of hell is the boldness and shamelessness of Comus' own display. It is what derives from custom in vice, of becoming 'inur'd'. This splendid climax is yet another authorial device for exposing hypocrisy to the ears of a well-trained audience.

The Lady's arguments for temperance are also familiar, but quite apart from their Protestant solidity they gain effectiveness dramatically in other ways. For one thing, this is the first time in the masque that the argument against luxury has been squarely set out. It has been reserved for this crucial moment. The spirited expression of the Lady is also remarkable. The authoritatively disdainful rhythms are surprising, yet right, in the speech of a young woman of fifteen. The proper effect of the Lady's age can only be felt if the role is given to a girl of the right age. Her arguments are exactly focussed on the issue of luxury seen in context, the true social context for Comus. After her copybook statement of the appropriateness of Nature's provisions to the temperate society, she dismisses the whole of Comus' elaborate picture of overfertility in a single line: 'and she no whit encumberd wth her store'. Evidently Truth has a simple rhetoric. Not merely does she place Comus as the expression of degenerate luxury among the rich, she also sees the social consequences for the poor. The directness of the critique of riches is I think unique in the masque of the period. She also voices the thought to which good Protestant minds were being provoked by Comus' speech, that the use of God's gifts needs recognition of thanks, of charity to God: 'and then the giver would be better thankt / his praise due paid'.

In an earlier state of the text, which was several times emended at this point, and in the Bridgewater text, the Lady's speech was ended by a brief interruption from the enchanter: 'Come no more / this is meere morall babble, and direct / against the canon laws of our foundation.' In those lines Milton had wryly placed the mind of Comus as like that of a dead order of superstitious monks. The Lady, however, has acted out a foreshadowing of the ultimate victory of Truth. Comus can only restate what he said at the beginning of the scene, that the cup, which he offers a second time, will like the Homeric *nepenthes*, remove sorrow and offer joy.[10]

Although the Elder Brother talks idealistically about the powers of chastity, and although the two boys share in some of the same spiritual trials as their sister, they remind the audience of other virtues in what they say and do, more traditionally masculine virtues of heroic fortitude. And each of them relates to fortitude in a different way.

What Milton wittily offers in the masque is, in fact, a version of something expected in aristocratic and courtly celebration, which in itself reflected literary tradition. The ladies enacted chaste goddesses, the gentlemen martial heroes. In Caroline masque this expectation was fulfilled to the point of tedium. The fact that Milton was using children instead of adults allowed him a certain distance from the usual mode of idolatry. He also made use of their full acting parts to delineate differences of character related to age.

There is typical contrast in the speeches of the two boys. The eleven-year-old tries to correct the fears of the nine-year-old by remembering the heroism of knights of romance, fictional ideals of antiquity, and finally the militant language of apocalypse. He shows an aspiring virtue and his education. He attempts a stirring

The young heroes – realism and idealism

idealism, presumably exemplary for a young aristocrat and curiously like Milton's own, if we are to believe the *Apology*. The Attendant Spirit admires his 'bold emprise' but also issues reminders of the harder facts of experience in the real world of evil.

There has been an unnecessary radicalisation of critical attitudes towards the Elder Brother's part. The Brooks and Hardy edition caused a good deal of the trouble by offering a reading which showed the author as heavily, clumsily ironic at the boy's expense. For a good many years afterwards commentators tried to eschew irony by offering the simply complimentary. The mixture is I think more intelligent than these radicalised readings tend to suggest. C. L. Barber did not elaborate on the scheme of values engaged in the roles of the boys, but I find myself in agreement with his instinctive judgement: 'we are intended', he said of the Elder Brother, 'to feel a youthful idealism, not unlike Milton's own as a boy reading romances'.[11]

The dramatic sequence is managed for comic effect and exemplary demonstration at the same time. After the Elder Brother has overcome the fears of the Younger, he is confronted with new grounds for fear by 'Thyrsis' and has to listen to the dangers of Comus described at length. His little brother immediately rounds on him: 'is this the confidence / you gave me brother?' But Lord Brackley rallies by reasserting his courage, until he is prepared to storm off-stage as antique hero:

> but for y^t damn'd magician, let him be girt
> wth all the greisly legions that troope
> under the sootie flag of Acheron
> harpyes and Hydra's or all the monstrous buggs
> twixt Africa and Inde. Ile find him out
> and force him to restore his purchase back
> or drag him by the curls & cleave his scalpe
> downe to the hips.

The Spirit's explanation of the need for other religious preparations is studiously polite, but he himself, only a mortal servant in disguise, is not allowed unembarrassed authority: '... why prethee shep[herd] / how durst thou then thy selfe approach so neere / as to make this relation'. After the Spirit's explanations, the Elder Brother rephrases his endeavour so as to give fuller acknowledgement of the power of God. The first draft of the

Milton's Aristocratic entertainments

Trinity manuscript ran: 'Thyrsis lead on apace I follow thee / & good heaven cast his best regard upon us.' This became, after performance, 'and some good angell beare a shield before us'. The comedy of the boys feigning not to know that Thyrsis is also guardian spirit leaves the audience with suitably mixed reactions to the whole scene. The earl's son has finally phrased himself correctly, whilst still not knowing exactly what Providence has provided. All the better that the boy himself speaks the lines that allow the smile, as if he himself was granting his auditors the right to be amused. With these things Milton had a fine touch.

We can point up the differences in the virtues engaged in the parts of the Lady and the boys by drawing parallels with Randolph's *The Muses Looking-Glass*, played in London in 1630. This is not to suggest specific allusion (though the possibilities here are interesting) but to show familiar expressions used in definition of familiar virtues on an Aristotelian frame of temperance. Todd and several later commentators sensed a similarity between Comus' picture of nature's libertinism and a speech of Colax flattering Acolastus in Act 2 Scene 3 of Randolph's academic 'entertainment', an analogy particularly close in expression to Milton.[12] A further similarity between the two works, concerning the two boys, occurs in the previous scene of Randolph's play. Again, both Cambridge authors are taking up Aristotelian distinctions.

In Act 2 Scene 2 the two contrasting characters are Aphobus, 'one that out of an impious confidence fears nothing', and Deilus, 'that from an atheistical distrust shakes at the motions of a reed'. 'These', says Randolph, 'are the extremes of Fortitude, that steers an even course between overmuch daring and overmuch fearing.' Aphobus' boldest assertion is this:

> Why should we think there be such things as dangers?
> Scylla, Charybdis, Python, are but fables;
> Medea's bull and dragon very tales;
> Sea-monsters, serpents, all poetical figments;
> Nay, Hell itself and Acheron mere inventions.
> Or were they true, as they are false, should I be
> So timorous as to fear these bugbear Harpies,
> Medusas, Centaurs, Gorgons?

The young heroes – realism and idealism

This is not unlike the Elder Brother's 'sootie flag of Acheron' and 'all the monstrous buggs / twixt Africa and Inde'. Neither brother goes to Randolph's atheistical extremes, of course: both are hopeful scions of the earl, brought up in godliness. The one strives, comically and splendidly for a boy of eleven, to show too little fear, whilst obviously being frightened; the other tends to show overmuch fear, whilst nevertheless having a soberer apprehension of evil than his older brother will admit to. Each manifests a propensity to virtue, whilst their errors can be laid at the door of their youth. Between them they have all the makings of true fortitude. The scene acts out their induction into a proper apprehension of evil in the world.

The Elder Brother's entry is dramatic in the grand manner: 'unmuffle ye faint starres, & thou faire moone / that wont'st to love the travailers benizon . . .' He speaks an elevated language full of literary allusions, well-informed in familiar figures ultimately derived from Latin poetry.[13] The Younger Brother's opening speech is based on a more homely version of the pastoral, of 'folded flocks' and 'reed wth oaten stopps'. His more ambitious comparison of his sister with Proserpina, which was in the earlier Trinity and Bridgewater versions, was deleted for *1637*.

In the Elder Brother's reply to the Younger's fears for their sister, his hope is based on the known virtue of the Lady. He sounds more sure of this than secure in his own fearlessness:

> I doe not think my sister soe to seeke
> or so unprincipl'd in vertues booke
> and the sweet peace y^t goodnesse bosomes ever
> as that the single want of light & noise
> (not beeing in danger, as I trust she is not)
> could stirre the constant mood of her calme thought
> & put them into misbecomming plight.

The construction sounds reasonable, but for the overinsistent aside. But the next assertion calls his tutored judgement more obviously in question, by its blithe overstatement: 'Vertue could see to doe what vertue would / by her own radiant light though sun & moone / were in the flat sea sunke . . .' Had he not himself complained about the muffled moon? The sun and moon figure, recalling portentous biblical prophecy, gives spurious weight to the proposition about self-sufficient virtue, which commentators have often, aptly, compared to Redcross' words to Una near the beginning of *The Faerie Queene*:

> Ah Ladie (said he) shame were to revoke
> The forward footing for an hidden shade:
> Vertue gives her selfe light, through darknesse for to wade (1 i 12)

Redcross is too rashly confident in his own powers, or takes too slight a view of the real powers of darkness in the world. He is a young man full of idealistic courage. This may be one model for the grand romantic optimism of the boy.

As for his rehearsal of the benefits of solitude for contemplation, one assumes that the audience was meant to attribute this to the hopeful learning of a young nobleman and be amused at its lack of relevance to the situation. The contemplative hermit is no analogy for his sister in distress, as Thomas immediately points out:

> tis most true
> that musing meditation most affects
> the pensive secrecie of desert cell . . .
>
> but beautie like the faire Hesperian tree
> laden wth blooming gold had need the guard
> of dragon watch wth unenchaunted eye

As it hears this, the audience knows that Comus has already lured the Lady to his palace. But for all its telling, down-to-earth commonsense, the role of the Younger Brother is likewise tinged with comedy deriving from circumstance and from his own habits of mind. His sister is already in danger, but she is also in fact in 'a senate house', the council chamber at Ludlow. This the boy-actor feigns not to know. And to him each wood by night turns into a landscape of romance, in which maidens get into distress. Each boy tries to apply some sober sense to the fancies of the other, whilst still pursuing fancies of his own. The masque has its ways of justifying sober sense and romantic fiction at the same time.

The embarrassment of the Elder Brother is beautifully suggested in the rhythm of his response: insecurity is covered by pomposity:

> I doe not brother
> inferre, as if I thought my sisters state
> secure, wthout all doubt or question, no . . .

The young heroes – realism and idealism

> but where an equall poise of hopes & feares
> dos arbitrate the event my nature is
> that I incline to hope, rather then feare
> and gladly banish squint suspicion.

The Trinity and Bridgewater texts have five lines which were omitted from the middle of this passage in *1637*. They made a comic intent rather blatant:

> I could be willing though now i'the darke to trie
> a tough encounter wth the shaggiest ruffian
> that lurks by hedge or lane of this dead circuit
> to have her by my side, though I were sure
> she might be free from perill where she is.

Earlier drafts were still more stagey: 'I could be willing' was originally 'beshrew me but I would' and 'tough encounter' began as 'tough passado'.

Too often apparently didactic passages of the Elder Brother have been taken as straight Miltonic statement. The next part of the scene, in which Lord Brackley expounds the 'hidden strength' of chastity in so charming a fashion as to convince little Thomas, is also determined by the age of the speaker and presents, if rather more problematically, a mixture of exemplary thought and comedy. The question of tone is delicate in this speech. It may be the issue has been made harder for readers by one of the additions to the text for publication, the Lady's own celebration of chastity in the temptation scene.

The Elder Brother seems to assert that virginity itself has an essential force. He attributes a 'virtue' to it in a similar way to that in which Satan, giving the cue to idolators and our general mother, attributed virtue to the fatal tree.

> tis chastitie, my brother, chastitie
> she that has that is clad in compleate steele
> and like a quiverd nymph wth arrows keene
> may trace huge forests, & unharbour'd heaths
> infamous hills, & sandie perilous wilds
> where through the sacred rays of chastitie
> no salvage fierce, bandite, or mountaneere
> will dare to soile her virgin puritie
> yea even where very desolation dwells
> by grots, and cavern's shag'd wth horrid shads

> she may passe on wth unblensh't majestie
> bee it not don in pride or in praesumption.

The reservation about pride and presumption sounds scrupulous enough. The assurance of the preacher and the words of the prophet are in 'yea even where very desolation dwells'. This is a kind of hope, based on a kind of faith. But the Lady, he says, passes on with the 'majesty' or royalty celebrated in the famous forty-fifth psalm: 'in this majesty ride prosperously because of truth and meekness and righteousness' (2–4). The majesty of that passage was usually understood to signify Christ. In the masque the Lady does not quite 'passe on wth unblensh't majestie', except in righteous debate. To Comus her virginity merely made her mettle more attractive: 'Some virgin sure . . . benighted in these woods; now to my charms . . .' Not even Una, who carries far more religious symbolism about her, and 'sacred rays', is saved from lawless rape by her virginity. What saves her is what saves the Lady, that is, 'Eternal Providence'. A gentle but precise authorial irony registers youthful presumption about the self-sufficiency of man in the boy's stirring speech.

The question of self-sufficiency had been begged at the beginning of the speech, in the reiterations of 'hidden strength':

> my sister is not so defencelesse left
> as you imagine brother she has a hidden strength
> wch you remember not   2 bro. what hidden strenth
> unlesse the strength of heaven, if you meane that
> 1 bro. I meane that too, but yet a hidden strength
> w^{ch}, if heaven gave it, may be term'd her owne

The boys recognise the idea of man's insufficiency, but their grasp of this doctrine is put to the test as the exposition of the powers of chastity proceeds. The explanation of chastity in this speech leads into Platonic imagery, in a similar mixture to that which appears in Milton's protestations of personal purity in the *Apology*. Milton himself seems to have read Plato with appreciation and put great weight on ideals of chastity. The question at issue is the *attitude* which the boy takes up towards chastity, an attitude which is not quite mature Protestant sense. The taste of a promising eleven-year-old boy in the masque corresponds to the taste Milton says he had, when he was virtuously inclined, but immature, in his

The young heroes – realism and idealism

reading. Youthful idealism awaits experience in the real world. Literary fashion may also be relevant. *The Faithful Shepherdess*, Fletcher's old yet eternally youthful play, had been revived as a spectacular entertainment at court shortly before *Comus* was written. The mixture of sentimentality and sensationalism in the play suited a Caroline fashion, as Milton would have realised. Clorin, the virgin shepherdess retired into the woods as a kind of eremite, rather like the Younger Brother's solitary hermit, says this of her magic powers as virgin, as she sees a rough satyr kneel before her:

>   my feare saies I am mortall:
> Yet I have heard (my mother told it me)
> And now I doe believe it, if I keepe
> My virgin flower uncropt, pure, chast, and faire,
> No goblin, wood-god, Faiery, Elfe, or Feind,
> Satyr or other powers that haunts these groaves,
> Shall hurt my body, or by vain illusion,
> Draw me to wander after idle fiers,
> Or voices calling me in dead of night,
> To make me follow, and so tole me on,
> Through mores and standing pooles: . . .
>   sure there is a power
> In that great name of virgin, that bindes fast
> All rude uncivill bloods, all appetites
> That break their confines: then strong chastity,
> Be thou my strongest guarde, for heere Il'e dwell
> In opposition against Fate and Hell.   (I i 110–129)

The play seems to justify her surmise. However much Milton may have remembered it as he was writing the masque, he would not have taken its artifices simply as serious thought. Rather, he may have delighted in placing such pastoralism within the proper framework of religious doctrine, relishing a judgement of courtly affectation. In TMS² the Lady herself says nothing quite like that; nor are those the terms of her new passage about chastity in *1637*.

The Elder Brother's 'some day' is rather like Clorin's 'my mother told me'. His nocturnal spirits, goblins and swart fairies of the mine are not dissimilar to Fletcher's fairies, fauns, fiends and *igni fatui*. The fanciful quality of the speech was more marked in the early version of Trinity and Bridgewater, which included the line '& yawning dens where glaring monsters house'. As with 'shaggiest ruffian', Milton took out some of the broader comic element in *1637*.

The Elder Brother concludes, like an aspiring disputant, by calling on what authorities he can, the wisdom of the ancients and religion, though he then turns to the fabulous rather than the philosophic: 'hence had the huntresse Dian her dred bow . . . what was that snakie-headed Gorgon sheild . . .' 'It is Plato's method', remarked Verity (p. 136). But the control is in context. Diana may have tamed passionate beasts, counteracted frivolous Cupid and have been feared 'Q[ueen] o'the woods'; his sister is more ominously designed for Comus' 'queene'. In court masque a lady may personate Diana or Minerva in ritual triumph of chastity; at Ludlow the claims of divine immunity are made with dramatic irony. Thus point is added to pastoral ritual and the precocious playfulness of an academic exercise.

It has often been observed that the last part of the speech is close to the *Phaedo* (81 B–D), even to the details of the 'earthy' souls haunting tombs and sepulchres. The good man ascends, the bad descends, degrades, progressively. The Younger Brother is charmed by the 'divine philosophy', as earlier humanists had frequently been charmed by the Platonic metaphors in the Renaissance. A common placement of Plato was that he was the most 'divine' of philosophers, whilst sometimes speaking more ideal fiction than sober truth. I see no reason for believing that Milton did not share this view. It is a matter of some importance in assessing the influence of Platonism on him.

The noble actors must not be forgotten. In comparing her with Diana and Minerva, Lord Brackley issues a compliment to his sister, just as he compliments himself through his idealism and by matching an undergraduate, for the delight of his parents and others gathered in the Council Chamber. His lack of complete apprehension of the 'real' world of moral evil is easily forgiven, and, what is more, as his language turns more to the religious, it may also be felt to be more affecting. That is to say, dramatic irony is felt more as it was in his sister's speeches, as the audience tests an ardent, innocent idealism against its own greater knowledge of the peril:

The young heroes – realism and idealism

> So deare to heaven is sainctly chastitie
> that when a soul is found sincerely so
> a thousand liveried angells lackey her
> and in cleare dream & sollemne vision
> tell her of things that no grosse eare can heare
> till oft converse wth heavnly habitants
> begins to cast a beame on th'outward shape
> the unpolluted temple of the mind
> and turnes it by degrees to the souls essence
> till all be made immortall.

It is an ennobling thought, placed with affecting irony. At an early stage in the Trinity manuscript there was another line after 'lackey her', which made the placement more obvious: 'driving farre off each thing of sin & guilt'. A thousand angels have not yet driven Comus off. The rich trappings of the imagery – 'liveried', 'lackey' – are in tune with the grand optimism.

The last part of the speech also has a significant analogy in the speech of Raphael in Book Five of *Paradise Lost* (468–505). After describing the scale of nature, from spirit to matter, the archangel describes to the unfallen Adam how embodied men may eventually become spiritual enough to share the heavenly paradise of angels. Both speeches are controlled by context and avert the reader to a similar theological point, placing premature idealism. Living in the era of Christian history and aware of the Fall impending, the reader of Raphael's speech is asked to feel the sense of loss emphasised by conjectures of what might have been 'if ye be found obedient'. It is a false surmise. So, too, the audience at Ludlow is being reminded of impending evil, as it listens to the Elder Brother. The Platonic doctrine of ascent – 'his fine conception of self-perfectibility', as Verity nicely called it – glosses over what were for Milton the facts of man's position in a world still dominated by the fight against active evil. Young minds may be tempted to use Plato as a means of jumping present evil to reach the world to come.

The Younger Brother's response is, as usual, right, without his knowing exactly why. 'Charming' is the word. It is at this precariously innocent moment of comfort and assurance that the boys hear someone, must once more show their fortitude, and, after the relief of finding their visitor to be Henry Lawes, must listen to the real plight of their sister, caught in a deceptive magic only too familiar.

Before turning to aspects of the Attendant Spirit's further instructions, let me review the remarkable success, as I think it is, of Milton's writing for the three young masquers. To have three main masquers as young people, two of one sex, one of the other, and to have them play full dramatic parts, created a situation most unusual in masques. Milton exploited that situation with intelligence. These masquers are exposed to appraisal by techniques of dramatic realism, whilst still performing, to their own praise, exemplary functions for the occasion. Dramatic realism, in this case, entailed the proper placement of the children according to sex and age, and also the proper religious placement of them as young people trying to understand and cope with evil.

The young Milton's problems were complex; the touch he needed was delicate. His adequate sense of the exemplary, adequate to religious realism, that is, was harder to attain than Spenser's, in so far as his characters were real nobility who were to act themselves in some complimentary way, not figures drawn in the relative safety of a fiction of an antique time. Just how delicate the task was may be illustrated from changes in the text, as I hope to show. Excisions in the Bridgewater text show that someone else thought that greater tactfulness was required at several points. Changes made by Milton himself for the printed version of 1637 show that relatively slight alterations, made to underline the moral and religious exposition, nevertheless upset the fine balance of some of the characterisation.

Critics have not very often tried to recover the delicacies of tone and function in the writing for children. One notices how rare it is in staged revivals of the masque for children to take the children's roles, let alone children of the right ages. That surely must be the first step in sympathetic imaginative reconstruction, not merely that the complexities of tone may be judged but also in trying to define with accuracy the moral seriousness of the masque, which bears upon the ages of its masquers.

One must realise how very personal to Milton the idealism of the children probably was, how very revealing of his own

The young heroes – realism and idealism

rationalisations of an educative process in which he had shared. If much of his career was concerned with the definitions and redefinitions of heroic endeavour, personal and national, in the context of growing difficulty and growing isolation, the strident repudiations of literary models of heroism sometimes betraying difficulties of orientation, then in his writing for the President's children he was already engaged on that life-long pursuit. His was an idealism constantly modified by experience. Ideals of chaste manliness and militant heroism informed the pattern of his life. But it is only by seeing the intelligent, sophisticated presentation of the tensions between youthful idealism and hard-won realism in the text of the masque that we can see in it the proper beginning of that lifelong series of rationalisations.

5 · SPIRITUAL INSTRUCTIONS

FROM THE MOMENT that the Attendant Spirit stops the Elder Brother's rash heroism with a warning that special preparations are necessary, in Haemony, for an encounter with Comus, the burden of instruction shifts largely to the part of the Spirit himself. His voice, the didactic medium for the poet, orders for the rest of the masque. In this chapter I wish to examine the range of instruction comprised in Haemony and Sabrina.[1]

Haemony stems from the moly of the Circe story, the divine talismanic gift conveyed by Hermes, best known in Homer and Ovid but recalled many times since. However, Milton insists – 'more med'cinall is it then that Moly' – that it has a significance distinct from that, or those many, of the mythical herb of tradition. There are many signs of fresh definition in a new invention.

There is a distinct allegory in Haemony. No other passage in the masque is written in quite this way. Haemony takes its chief definition in the allegory from biblical pastoral, though mythical and poetic decorum are kept as scrupulously as possible. The problem of its significance is compounded by more contextual difficulties than that of the two-handed engine in *Lycidas*, and the shepherd lad who supplies the herb to 'Thyrsis' in the Spirit's little story of explanation is a main part of those contextual difficulties, which engage a web of personal, celebratory references in the masque.

What the Lady lacked when she first met the enchanter, what anyone including the boys might need, was a means of perceiving the full nature of the deceptive evil she was encountering. Temperance itself she did not need. What is given to the boys is precisely a means of knowing, which exposes and renders ineffective the pernicious deceptions of evil. It is because Haemony has to do with the efficacy of truth that the Attendant

Spiritual instructions

Spirit explains, though feigning, that by the means of Haemony he himself had known what the enchanter was and was immune to his magic.

Haemony figures the word of God. Armed with the spiritual weapons and the truth of God's word, the boys need not fear the arts of Comus, based on falsehood. The word of God as ministered by the pastor[2] furnishes the education the boys most need if they are to counter the militancy of evil. In the poetic fiction, the magic power of the herb is the efficacy of that ministered word: 'divine effect' points to that spiritual instruction. With the Spirit, the children play out pretences, rehearse a doctrine for didactic purposes, on the occasion. What more idealistically Protestant gesture than to celebrate on a public, gubernatorial occasion the fundamental necessity of the ministry of the word, those 'sweet and efficacious instructions', as Milton himself was later to call them?[3]

There is a host of indications of this meaning in the language of the description. This is the Trinity text before performance:

> amongst the rest a small unsightly root
> but of divine effect he culld me out
> the leafe was darkish & had prickles on it
> but in an other countrie as he said
> bore a bright golden flowre, but not in this soile
> unknowne & like esteem'd & the dull swayne
> treads on it dayly wth his clouted shoone
> & yet more med'cinall is it then that Moly
> wch Hermes once to wise ulysses gave ...
>
>   by this meanes
> I knew the fowle enchanter though disguis'd
> enter'd the very lime twigs of his spells
> and yet came off, if you have this about you
> (as I will give you when you goe) you may
> boldly assault ye necromancers hall

The phrase 'in an other countrie' contrasted with 'this soile' introduces a Christian distinction into the figuration of the plant, the distinction between heaven and earth.[4] The flower of the plant Haemony, that is to say, its glorious result, is to be seen in heaven. And that also is expressed by the goldenness of the flower. This kind of gold is the gold of that other 'flower' amaranthus, which

Milton celebrated in *Paradise Lost*, where it is woven into the crowns of the redeemed.[5] I take it that Haemony's golden bloom, like the bloom of amaranthus, signifies the glory of eternal life, to be offered to man only in the new golden age at the end of time.

It is the first epistle of Peter, source of the religious symbolic *amarantos*, which also provides one way in which a symbolic flower can be associated with eternal life and the word of God. Peter compares the word of God to a plant:

> Being born again, not of corruptible seed, but of incorruptible, by the word of God, which liveth and abideth for ever ... The grass withereth, and the flower thereof falleth away: / But the word of the Lord endureth for ever. And this is the word which by the gospel is preached unto you.
>
> (I Peter 1.23–25)

The Spirit also describes the reception of the word, 'unknowne & like esteem'd & the dull swayne / treads on it dayly wth his clouted shoone'. Here is another distinct extension of the moly-motif. Homer says that moly is difficult for men to dig up, whereas the gods can do it. In the masque it is not a question of availability but of recognition: some men recognise the word, but commonly the swain puts his foot on it in ignorance or disdain, regularly, 'dayly', as if he trod it down in the common road.

In the parable of the sower, another kind of pastoral, where the word appears as elsewhere not as a small plant but as a smaller seed, some seed 'fell by the way side; and it was trodden down, and the fowls of the air devoured it' (Luke 8.5). Those intended are they who hear the word, but 'then cometh the devil, and taketh away the word out of their hearts'. Matthew furnishes one gloss for the 'dull swayne':

> Therefore speak I to them in parables: because they seeing see not; and hearing they hear not, neither do they understand. And in them is fulfilled the prophecy of Esaias, which saith, By hearing ye shall hear, and shall not understand; and seeing ye shall see, and shall not perceive: For this people's heart is waxed gross, and their ears are dull of hearing, and their eyes they have closed.
>
> (13.13–15)

The swain is dull, not obedient, not hearing the word truly.[6] In this and other ways the parable of the sower provides another chief way of understanding Haemony.

The 'small' and 'unsightly' appearance of Haemony is to

Spiritual instructions

'outward appearance, a very mystery of humiliation'.[7] This unprepossessing smallness is like 'the pure simplicity of doctrine, accounted the foolishness of this world, yet crossing and confounding the pride and wisdom of the flesh', as Milton himself was to put it in *The Reason of Church-Government*.[8] The shepherd lad's 'simples' are of this simplicity, and this is the humiliation the flock is taught to imitate. 'Unknowne' also conforms to this kind of Christian paradigm and suggests the scarcity of those who hear the word.[9]

The prickles on the leaf of Haemony, another obvious departure from the pattern of moly, may also be glossed from the parable of the sower. Receiving the word entails the humiliation of tribulation and persecution, which will be borne in heroic patience only by those who have 'root' in themselves:

> But he that received the seed into stony places, the same is he that heareth the word, and anon with joy receiveth it; Yet hath he not root in himself, but dureth for a while: for when tribulation or persecution ariseth because of the word, by and by he is offended. (Matt. 13.20–21)

The idea is commonplace. In a somewhat similar piece of allegorising, for example, Henry More has his spiritual pilgrim taken through 'stinging nettles' and 'prickling thistles' which 'hard'st legs would gore', in order to be led by Simon (Obedience or Good Hearing) past a barrier which is the wall of Self-conceit by means of the narrow door of Humility.[10] In Milton's more delicately restrained pastoral figure, the leaves of the plant of the word have prickles on them to signify the tribulations of obedience.

As I have already mentioned, Haemony's 'divine effect' seems to be defined in several ways that are distinctly religious. The idea of 'effect' echoes the usual Protestant description of the ministry of the word as efficacious.[11] The healing or medicinal powers of the herb in the masque probably signify the spiritual effect of the word on the flock.[12] This is what Milton himself will call the 'blest efficacy of healing our inward man'.[13] The 'gastly Furies apparition' may well suggest the fears of the mind not anchored on biblical truth.

Images of disease and healing are commonly applied in Protestant descriptions of the state of the flock. If one were to take 'mildew blast' and 'dampe' into an obviously ecclesiastical context, they would stand alongside the swellings with 'wind, and the rank mist they draw' and the 'foul contagion' spreading through the people in *Lycidas*, or the 'windes' and 'noisome vapours' which grow 'To a plague and publick wo' in Herbert's brief glimpse of the 'broken consort' of the church in 'Dooms-day'.

The 'divine effect' of the ministry of the word makes sense of the Spirit's other indication of Haemony's powers, his statement that he perceived the truth about Comus, because he had the herb about him: 'for by this meanes / I knew the fowle enchanter though disguis'd'. The earnestly admonishing poet of 'that two-handed engine' was the first to insist that one is able to know and to discern evil intent by means of the word:

For the word of God is quick, and powerful, and sharper than any two-edged sword . . . and is a discerner of the thoughts and intents of the heart . . . all things are naked and opened unto the eyes of him with whom we have to do.
(Heb. 4.12–13)

Thus the word protects the boys from 'surprisal' by the creature Comus. Not that the Lady was actually godless, when she was deceived, any more than the boys had never previously received the gift of God's word: rather that in this situation young aristocrats cannot remember the ministry of the word too often.

There is a further allusion to the parable of the sower. When 'Thyrsis' says that the shepherd lad 'bad' him 'keepe it', he is indicating that he was exhorted to 'keep' the word as a good hearer. The obedient are 'they, which in an honest and good heart, having heard the word, keep it, and bring forth fruit with patience' (Luke 8.15). Or, again, pairing 'keep' with the 'word': '. . . blessed are they that hear the word of God, and keep it' (11.28). The same idea may be in 'if you have this about you'.

Many of the religious interpretations of Haemony have been determined through etymologies of the name rather than analysis of verbal allegory. That seems to me a mistake: the primary means of understanding here, and with the shepherd lad (and with the two-handed engine), is the broad figuration of the biblical pastoral. But it is natural enough to look first to the name. When a poet offers a name in such self-conscious manner – 'He call'd it Haemony & gave it me / & bad me keepe it' – one is entitled to

Spiritual instructions

expect the name to bear some correspondence to the meaning. Spenser's method had often been to provide confirmation of significance through names.

Thyrsis, Haemony, Meliboeus: Milton is not an allegorist of hard names or a coiner of new symbolic names. A stylist, he is using a familiar poetic epithet, *haemonius*, 'Thessalian', that is to say, 'magical'.[14] It is very common in Ovid and elsewhere.[15] He called his herb 'the magic herb' to cap the idea of the word of God as efficacious. The 'divine effect' of spiritual truth is the truest magic.

What is one to say, critically, of this notorious passage of religious allegory? Its pastoral figures are expressed in concrete fashion, kept up with some lively invention, and they create a kind of understatement, a pastorly sprezzatura. The Spirit plays out dramatic pretences in a suitable poetic language, not simply issuing blatant indicators towards definition. One might look at 'leatherne scrip' as allegorical entity (a book? *The* Book?), but just as much in hand is the setting up of a pastoral device in order to introduce the herb. The 'simples' were first said in the Trinity manuscript to be 'of a thousand hews' rather than 'of a thousand names', which made the figure plainer on a literal level: these are herbs of many different colours. They have a beauty. If there is an attempt also to convey the plenteousness and manifold virtues of the word, it is oblique.[16] Yet it might also be said that in the description of the plant itself there is a visible determination to make the religious meaning clear by multiple allusions of distinctly studied, ingenious kind. The word of God is fully described, in relation to heaven and earth, to its reception, to the kind of humility, obedience and suffering it requires, and to the power which it is said to possess. Many words contribute to the pattern of intent: 'small', 'unsightly', 'prickles', 'in an other countrie', 'a bright golden flowre', 'this soile', 'unknowne & like esteem'd', 'dull swayne', 'treads', 'dayly', 'bad me keepe it', and 'by this meanes I knew', to mention more obvious examples. Milton never attempted a denser, more comprehensive verbal allegory. As I have noted elsewhere, the syntactical structure may show some signs of strain, under the pressure of cerebral definition.[17] Yet, if so, this is only a slight disruption of ease, and the whole passage is framed in dramatic context.

Milton's Aristocratic entertainments

The narrative context for Haemony is provided by the description of its giver, 'a certaine shepheard lad'. The chief difficulty with the shepherd lad is that Milton has contaminated religious symbolism with compliment to the speaker, Lawes. This contamination is perhaps the most confusing of all, in the whole crux.

The pastoral allegory is made of familiar elements. By the phrase 'shepheard lad' I take it that Milton wished to signify the type of the pastor, the good elder or minister who patterned himself on the shepherd Christ. This is the complex Milton referred to when he talked of the priesthood, in typical Protestant–biblical fashion, in *The Reason of Church-Government*: 'First, therefore, if to doe the work of the Gospel Christ took upon him the form of a servant, how can his servant in this ministery take upon him the form of a Lord?'[18] The face of the ministry must be 'pure, spirituall, simple, and lowly'.[19]

Milton's figure relies upon some of the same texts as do the treatments of pastors, good and bad, in *Lycidas* and *The Shepheardes Calender* and elsewhere in prescriptive pictures of the priesthood. It is an ideal pastor who offers the musician 'Thyrsis' the ministry of the word. He is a pastor of exemplary humility: 'Humble yourselves . . . that he may exalt you in due time' (I Pet. 5.6). His appearance – 'of small regard to see to' – belies his great skill in all spiritual virtues: he is 'yet well skill'd / in every vertuous plant, & healing herbe'. He preaches the whole treasury of the word by showing 'simples of a thousand names'. As in II Corinthians (6.10), he is humble, like a servant, yet full of rich wisdom: 'as poor, yet making many rich: as having nothing, and yet possessing all things'. As in I Peter 1.25 and elsewhere he preaches a word which is said to endure for ever. As in various descriptions of pastors, like the diatribe against bad ones in Ezekiel 34, the ministry is figured in healing. In his capacity as minister the lad laments to 'Thyrsis', like Christ to his disciples, the dullness of hearing in a people that will not recognise the word. As in the pattern of the elder given in I Peter 5, the lad gives the service of his ministry selflessly and lovingly ('he lov'd me well'), 'not by constraint but willingly; not for filthy lucre but of a ready mind', in free exchange for some heavenly singing, in fact. As a good shepherd he charges 'Thyrsis' with the challenge of the parable of

Spiritual instructions

the sower, to 'keep' the word about him and he invites the musician to join the spiritual elite, pilgrims for another country. 'Thyrsis' now says, in naive dramatic pretence, that he remembers what he was taught, and passes the word on to the boys in preparation for their dire encounter.

The chief complication is in the imagined relationship between the shepherd lad and 'Thyrsis' as musician. The lines suggest something additional to the ministry. This pastor is enamoured of music, often begs 'Thyrsis' to sing, listens in ecstasy to his song, and gives his knowledge 'in requitall'. Of course the features of herbal skill and friendship are familiar in pastoral. The poet writes a version of the literary pastoral. But, if biblical sanction is appropriate here (of which I am not entirely sure), it was David himself who loved music. It was David as king who organised music in the temple. Although he himself is familiarly the type of the divine singer, it was often said that as divine poet he addressed or gave the texts of many of his psalms to his chief musicians. This is Diodati:

> But David made a new order therin, appointing the office of holy Singers and Musicians to one part of the Levites ... To the chief of these Singers and Musicians ... David and other divine composers did give their Songs.[20]

Perhaps the preaching of a priest in church with music might be figured in David as poet giving his psalms to musicians in the temple to be sung.

By this I do not mean that the shepherd lad is, like the shepherd lad of *Paradise Regained* (2.439), David himself, historically. I am merely suggesting in the face of a considerable difficulty that Milton took an opportunity to employ an ingenious extension to the image of the pastor, so as to embrace personal reference to the speaker. This might be the means by which personal celebration and didactic allegory combine.

There can be no doubt that there is an element of personal reference in the speech, in a compliment to Lawes' singing. Many commentators have also assumed a personal reference in the shepherd lad. The only suggestion for a known contemporary that has made any sense of the reference to Lawes' singing has been that the shepherd lad is Milton himself, and that the friendship is the friendship and co-operation of Milton and Lawes.[21] The attraction of this idea is that it seems to allude to collaboration in the Ludlow masque. The difficulty is simply stated, and very real, that it is unlikely that Milton would have included such reference to himself. With such a young, relatively unknown poet, on this occasion, such self-reference would have been a breach of tact. My suggestion is that Lawes as singer is placed in relation to a Davidic order of divine music; I assume that the compliment is being made in terms of ideal biblical type.

In this regard, one might rehearse the roles of 'Thyrsis'. Lawes bears this name to indicate a relationship to the President's family, as servant: 'my father's shepherd sure'. The name also recalls singing: in Theocritus and Virgil, and thereafter, the shepherd Thyrsis sings. In the masque he is shepherd–servant to the family but of musical kind. He is also 'Attendant Spirit', an angelic guardian to the faithful. Heavenly spirits are also associated with music, and may sing. In terms of the Circe myth, he stands in the stead of Hermes, heavenly messenger to those who are 'favour'd of high Iove', that is, like Odysseus himself, *diotrephēs*, cherished of Zeus. He transmits divine instruction. Also, taking up another aspect of Hermes, as god of eloquence and courtliness, he can act as presenter of such song and dance 'as Mercury did first devise'. Apart from being musician for voices in the Private Music, he had been, as we have seen, and most significantly for Milton, a Gentleman of the Chapel Royal, the singer of psalms in a Davidic order, for it was the Davidic order on which the royal chapel was based.[22]

I would suggest that Lawes' various roles converge in this ingenious feigning speech, in such a way as to recall his royal functions also. The happy pastoral conjunction of pastor and musician in friendship suggests the Davidic order, and the allusion places Lawes as singer 'at a solemn music', royally ordained.

This is no mere adulation of courtly position. The expression is of an ideal order, by which church and court might be measured. The whole speech has shown the place of spiritual instruction. If Milton did indeed allude to the singing of the psalms at court, then he might be picturing that ministry which was concerned with the governors of the people, as Bridgewater and his family found themselves to be.

Spiritual instructions

When dense verbal allegory is contaminated with dramatic and celebratory pretence, one is tempted to the conclusion that the poet may have overtaxed sheer ingenuity in a crossing of modes. One wonders about the grasp of an audience in 1634. The point is worth pursuing, for we know so much about what Milton intended at various moments in the history of the text, about how the text was altered for performance, and about how the poet readjusted and fortified it for publication, that evidence of its fate in performance takes on considerable interest.

With the Haemony passage there is a strange omission in the performance text as represented by the Bridgewater manuscript. A whole section of the allegory was omitted. Lines 631–636 are absent, so that the audience seems to have been taken straight from the darkish, prickly leaves to the name Haemony. All reference to golden immortality had gone, together with the parable of the sower about the reception of the word. The best biblical text for word as plant had been removed, with some of the clearest evidence for the Christian application in 'unknowne' and 'dull' and 'treads'. The audience was handed quickly to the name Haemony, more decorously poetic than allegorically helpful. Allusions to the efficacy of the word remained, but I doubt whether the passage could have made much sense to any audience, however good their ears. Milton cannot have suggested the cut.

Why was it made? It may be that the contrast between 'this soile' and 'an other countrie' was omitted, because it could be construed as uncomplimentary to the people of the principality. There was an horrific danger of seeing 'this soile' as Wales. Similarly with 'dull swayne'. To patronise the locals by referring to duck and nod was one thing, to call them stupid or slothful another. The offence may not have been merely local, either. 'This soile' was a general phrase in complaint against men on earth, but the suggestion that the run of the populace does not know or esteem the word of God might seem to level a charge at the effectiveness of the ministry of the church in the whole of Britain.

If the offence was thought to be against Wales, it was accidental and illustrates again the complexities of Milton's occasional task. He had not forgotten Wales elsewhere in his text. If the offence was more generally to do with a possible failure of spiritual leadership – the ground of *Lycidas* – it was hardly accidental but rather indecorous for the occasion, even subversive. When the text was published, the religious generality was re-established, and it was joined by other material intensifying an independent-minded religious exhortation. But a censor had interfered, perhaps with good reason, with the intricacies of this notorious passage.

These difficulties, one might call them failures, can also serve to remind us of some of the things which seem notably successful, in particular the treatment of the role of Henry Lawes throughout the masque. Milton's use of Lawes strikes me as if anything more delightful, and probably more pointed, than his use of the three children.[23] It provides a delicate, shifting, even sometimes comic, pretence unsurpassed in any other masque. As with *Arcades*, the relatively small group of chief participants afforded an intimacy in pretence which could not be created in the usual court situation.

Lawes is so central to the masque, everything being presented by him to the audience, or explained by him to the children, or in general stage-managed by him, that the success of his part is crucial to the definition of tone in the whole festivity. He bears the whole otherworldly burden of instruction, an expression of vocation in the poet, as well as much of the entertainment, and, just as important, the control of courtesies.

His opening speech strikes that balance between the social comedy of pretence and a religious purpose which is the hallmark of the masque. It is a daring opening. The President, seated in state and surrounded by officials and more notable citizens, watches a 'gratulation' of some splendour. Yet the ears were first assailed with complaint, with the dimness of earth, the low-thoughtedness of men, the crown not given here below. Even from a heavenly spirit, this is uncompromising stuff. Face is saved, for all, by 'yet some there be . . .' Gentlemanly grace saves spiritual presumption. Still, the interesting thing here is that the momentary challenge is not a simple one of uncultured indecorousness in rustic comedy, as may happen at the beginning of a country-house entertainment; it is rather the contrived danger of a too strictly religious tone. Here, as perhaps he did not with the Haemony passage, Milton seems to have gauged the questions of tactful control, in the contrivance of fruitful comic risk.

Spiritual instructions

The Spirit soon takes on also the poet's role, in expressing the pleasure of fictions. Milton makes him relish playing the story-spinner: 'and listen why, for I will tell you now / what never yet was heard in tale or song . . .' The manner is infectious. And as well as the obvious delight in the inversion of 'real' roles, pretended spirit to likeness of servant, and *vice versa*, there must have been amusement in seeing the middle-aged Lawes offering to touch memories of the agile Puck or Ariel or Fletcher's Satyr, for he claims to move like them: 'swifte as the sparkle of a gleaming starre / I shoote from heaven. . .'; 'I can fly, or I can run / quickly to the green earths end . . .' Yet the comic agility of that is in part religious reminder, an invitation to think of heavenly things. Milton's humour, as always, has its point.

The fact that 'Thyrsis' invents a story of shepherd lad and Haemony as a desperate bit of fiction, pretending to explain, whilst also playing a part and elaborately defining a solemn Protestant truth, ought to do something, perhaps, to redeem that notorious description, at least from the point of view of its original dramatic interest. *Serio ludere* in this role is superb, and at this stage in the action he has not yet shown the full variety of his powers, which are to culminate in the hieratic magic of the Sabrina theophany. But if, for the sake of dramatic effect, we assume a certain edge of comic pretence in that elaborate allegory of Haemony, we are adding another dimension to a passage that could arguably do with less complexity, not more.

Once the boys have failed to complete the rescue of their sister, they neither speak nor act again, until they are conducted from the stage. The summoning of Sabrina, the request of her, the thanks to her, and the closing verses of the episode are all part of the Spirit. That at least was Milton's intention. The Spirit is still addressed as 'shepheard' by Sabrina, his role as servant to the President being still in view, but he controls with some authority, transmitter of divine wisdom, master of poetry and song and magician of the spectacle.

The Lady's silence is understandable, expressive of her helpless bondage. Someone, conscious of social decorum, was perturbed by the silence and subordination of the boys. Lawes alone addresses the Lady after she has risen from the chair: 'Come Ladie while heav'n lends us grace / let us fly this cursed place . . . I shall be yor faithfull guide.' The boys seem just to tag along. In the Bridgewater text, however, they are given some of the adjuring verses, and the President's heir, not Henry Lawes, addresses the Lady after the release: 'Come sister while heav'n lends us grace . . .' The closing couplet is also given to him. Whoever suggested the change – the party or parties I have called the 'censor' throughout the book – presumably felt that it was undignified for the President's son to remain passive for so long. Was it not their triumph too? But the poet knew what he was after and repeated his intention in *1637*.

The point is important. Milton designed this new Circean action so that the final ritual acts of winning freedom should involve some agency quite other than the family. A portion of the Odyssean power is reserved for different purposes. Though she graces the masque on behalf of the 'arriving' President and his family, it is critically unthinkable, as well as untenable from the evidence, to suggest that Sabrina might have been played by one of Lady Alice's older sisters or by anyone in the family. When the words include 'heav'n' lending 'grace', it would seem that we are discovering further aspects of special providence in some way needed to complete the celebratory statements of the masque.[24]

Other changes in the manuscript texts of this episode were made with practicalities of performance in mind but also connect with the contribution of the boys. The adjuring verses to Sabrina – 'Listen and appear to us' – were much augmented between the earliest state of the Trinity manuscript (TMS[1]) and a later stage (TMS[2a]) close to the Bridgewater text, which also shows the emendations.

In the early state, the verses 'to be said' by the Spirit were much simpler, more singly focussed on the figure of Sabrina. They may have been more expressive:

> listen and appeare to us
> in name of great Oceanus
> by Leucothea's lovely hands
> & her son that rules the strands
> by Thetis tinsel-slipper'd feet
> and the songs of Sirens sweet
> by dead Parthenope's deare tomb

Spiritual instructions

> and faire Ligéa's golden combe
> wherewth she sits on diamond rocks
> sleeking her soft alluring locks
> rise rise & heave thy rosie head

The water-gods are invoked by known properties and activities. Significantly, verse itself exercises a powerful appeal. The images seem to relate to Sabrina and to the dramatic situation concerning the Lady. After Oceanus, the list is predominantly female. Leucothea is called lovely, as in Ovid, and her hands are remembered as token of her pathetic story.[25] She has been immortalised as water goddess, rather like Sabrina, whilst her son Palaemon has become a guardian deity for seamen, just as Sabrina has taken on protective roles. Her 'tinsel-slipper'd feet' might suggest a goddess' light movement across the stage, as the Lady's too, when she is free. The sirens are remembered for the beauty of their song, also appropriate to Sabrina, who will sing. The next two couplets, treating Parthenope and Ligea, probably pick up the idea of sirens in the previous lines, but 'deare tomb' also arouses feelings associated with death, which, with the preservation of alluring beauty, suits Sabrina herself. All in all, these allusions to female water deities touch on graces of beauty, youth and singing, suiting this masque of youth and perhaps even prefiguring Sabrina's action by the mention of hands, feet and song. They create a suitable mood of sadness, for the past, tempered with the celebration of beauty and guardianship preserved for the present. The verses seem well aimed and well placed.

In the later Trinity version and in Bridgewater the list is lengthened and organised in a different way. The figures are arranged in descending order by age and authority. This is the Bridgewater text:

> listen and appe[are] to vs
> in name of greate Oceanus,
> by th'earth shakinge Neptunes mace,
> and Tethis grave maiestick pace,
> *el br*: by hoarie *Nereus* wrincled looke,
> and the Carpathian wizards hooke,
> *2 bro*: by scalie Tritons windinge shell,
> and ould sooth-sayinge Glaucus spell,
> *el bro*: by Lewcotheas lovely hands,

Milton's Aristocratic entertainments

    and her sonne that rules the strands,
2 bro: by Thetis tinsel-slipperd feete,
    and the songs of sirens sweete,
el bro: by dead Parthenopes dear tombe,
    and fayer Ligeas golden Combe,
    wherwith she sitts on diamond rocks,
    sleekinge her soft allueringe locks,
Dę: By all the Nimphes of nightly daunce,
    vpon thy streames with wilie glaunce,
    rise, rise, and heave thy rosie head, . . .

With Oceanus now come other regal figures, Neptune and queen Tethys, his mace and her majesty. Then follow two couplets of old male sea gods, each remembered by the most appropriate property, and the sequence ends with the local nymphs that dance on Severn's banks. The verse is resourceful within its formula, but the conception of the sequence has changed. Instead of something affecting and appropriate to Sabrina as feminine spirit, there is a general disposition of powers, as if in greater consciousness of hierarchies, and more like the Spirit's opening, scene-setting prologue.

    The decision to change the verses to something which is I think more typical of masques may connect with the decision to make the boys join the Spirit in summoning Sabrina. Previously, when the sole speaker had been the Spirit, Milton could simply use him as expressive mouthpiece. Now the extended adjuration, working dialogue-like by alternating couplets between the boys and designated 'to singe or not' (the organisers were flirting with the idea of the boys singing too), draws in further considerations of fitting verses to speakers, of thinking tactfully of the chief nobility. The sequence is no longer predominantly female, and a sense of grandeur has been added. As I have said, Milton knew what he wanted, with regard to the boys. In *1637* the Spirit has the whole section to himself once more. But he retained the grander, expanded verses and did not revert to TMS[1]. He seems to have been trying to balance the needs for climactic grandeur with a sense of what he wanted chiefly to signify, and the role of the boys had become involved in the practical compromises he had to make.

    In terms of spectacle and ritual, the Sabrina episode is clearly

Spiritual instructions

the climax of the action. This is a modest pastoral theophany. Sabrina seems to have risen through the stage in a chariot symbolising the waters of the river. She is accompanied by water nymphs, rising with her – the spectacle is not so very modest – but who remain inactive and mute. In her own song, which she may have sung whilst she was rising and coming across to the Spirit, the visual symbolism is continued in the imagery of the words.[26] She steps from the chariot, 'from off the waters fleet', and comes across stage, imagined as meadows.[27]

This whole section is rich in song, more, apparently, than has survived. The Spirit invokes her first in song; the following verses are marked 'to singe or not' in Bridgewater; Sabrina herself sings as she rises;[28] and after the petition to her and her saving rites, the Spirit again sings in thanks: 'Virgin daughter of Locrine'. These songs are simpler than the showpiece 'Sweet Echo', more like many other masque songs which were simple in outline and carried a narrative element indicating the action taking place. As a text, 'Sabrina faire' is beautifully decorated around the strong central verbs: 'listen ... listen ... listen and save'. The language is visual and concrete and has just a touch of authority and weight: the 'amber' may derive from Ovid, and *lacus* is from Virgil.[29] Even the straightforward spoken petition ('Goddesse deare') is well calculated in its direct simplicity. The rhyme for 'distres't' is left hanging for Sabrina herself to match in her first line, so that a formal pattern in the verse seems to resolve a crisis.

In his letter to Milton Sir Henry Wotton had the sense to realise how good the songs of *Comus* are. He commended them even above the dramatic qualities of the earlier scenes (which he calls 'the tragical part'):

> I should much commend the tragical part, if the lyrical did not ravish me with a certain Doric delicacy in your Songs and Odes, whereunto I must plainly confess to have seen yet nothing parallel in our language: *Ipsa mollities*[30]

Spectacle, song and ritualistic verse comprise the whole masque-like episode. Because it is more ritualistic than the earlier parts, it has proved particularly inaccessible to the many critics who have not approached *Comus* as a masque. Yet here the pastoralism of the masque finds its final mode, and the powers and moving allusions invested in Sabrina, which the boys like the audience stand back to watch, complete the meditation for the Welsh gubernatorial occasion. Let us take the episode element by element.

First, Sabrina's saving rites. Although she completes the rescue which the boys were attempting, she uses rites which relate back to the Lady's part of the action. That is, she undoes the 'magic' of the enchanter. Hers is the reverse of the Circean magic.

In Homer and Ovid, where Circe herself is prevailed upon to undo the imbruting spells, the victims are, in Sandys' words, 'sprinkled with better juyce, her wand reverst'.[31] When the boys contrive to fail to snatch the wand and the expected means of release cannot be used, the audience is invited to enjoy this last distinction from the terms of the framing myth:

> oh yee mistooke, yee should have snatch'd his wand
> & bound him fast; wthout his rod revers't
> and backward mutters of dissevering power
> wee cannot free the La: that heere sits
> in stonie fetters fixt & motionlesse.

In this shared game of pretences, he is not troubled long:

> yet stay, be not disturb'd, now I bethinke me
> some other meanes I have that may be us'd
> wch once of Melibaeus old I learn't

An opening has been made for the role of the Severn, but a myth must also be satisfied: as Sandys put it, 'the charms' are to be 'with charms disperst'. Sabrina's sprinklings are a 'better juyce' of purer waters.

Whilst Sabrina demonstrates that she can 'unlock the clasping charm', the 'scene' of the *kōmos* still stands behind the actors for all to see. The release picks up elements of that previous contagion, still kept in mind. The rites tackle the means to bondage stage by stage, following the sequence of the infection:

> Brightest ladie looke on me . . .

Previously the Lady had looked on a figure of falsehood and on the false images he produced; now her eyes are directed away from falsehood to remain fixed on a figure of innocent truth, embodying purity and piety. The mind has been released from the sight of the habitual pitfalls of those caught up in mundane realities of

Spiritual instructions

princely living. The world, in its normal state, is left behind.

With truthfulness before her, the Lady can be helped to confirm her purity of intent:

> thus I sprinckle on thy brest
> drops that from my fountain pure
> I have kept of precious cure . . .[32]

The breast may token the heart, which in turn indicates the will: 'Keep thy heart with all diligence; for out of it are the issues of life.'[33]

Her will strengthened, the Lady can be helped in the trial of her senses in the temptations of the lascivious feast:

> thrice upon thy fingers tip
> thrice upon thy rubied lip . . .

Trinal sprinklings are common in such fictions. Although other interpretations of fingers and lips are certainly possible – fingers may for example be hands, and hands deeds; as lips the mouth, and mouth words – it seems likely that Milton was picking up the two 'low' senses chiefly engaged in the *kōmos*, taste and touch. Sabrina has turned to the specifics of the feast–temptation in her purgations.

Finally she purges the object that symbolises the Lady's enforced acquiescence in the *kōmos*, the chair of hot luxuriousness, the habitual place of unredeemed nobility, to which she is bound:

> next this marble venom'd seate
> smear'd with gumms of glutenous heate
> I touch wth chast palmes moist & cold
> now the spell hath lost his hold.

Again, all sorts of association are suggested in the laying on of hands,[34] but it seems likely that the social festivity itself is being cleansed of residual effects of vanity and lasciviousness, by an agent of pure chastity. Marble is the stuff of pride, easy cause of luxury. After thanks have been given, the scene changes, and the image of temptation within the Ludlow feast is taken away, to be replaced by a representation of town and castle. The whole social occasion has been sanctified in image, on stage, so that the children may now move forward to the ordered expression of the dance. An earnest intelligence has reformed the image of the feast.

Milton's Aristocratic entertainments

Sabrina should be measured by Comus, by the *kōmos*; both are spirits, ideas, influences that bear upon the Lady and the occasion, images to hold in the mind. The one displaces the other, in the princely feast. Both are offered for the Lady, the President, and the whole audience to contemplate in their 'magical' effect on princely youth. We are defining influences on young aristocratic minds. The pure waters of Severn are used to counter the infections of Comus, guarding chastity, which the *kōmos* especially puts at risk: 'Shepheard tis my office best / to helpe ensnared chastitie.' Through the very arts of masquing it is being shown that the feast may be controlled by another spirit than that of the ubiquitous *kōmos*. The masque has moved into a new demonstrative phase, in which there is a vision of a people prospering by the example of piety in high places, not degrading from the centre.

To understand how Sabrina is at the centre of a people one must observe what is said about her as much as what she does. That so much is said about her is one mark of Milton's determination to use her as a major focus of contemplation. With the sense of a people and a region in mind, I wish to try to displace one simple prevalent idea about her, having repercussions for the interpretation of the whole masque, that Sabrina and Sabrina alone represents grace.

Of course concepts of special providence are relevant to the case of Sabrina. Her 'gentlenesse', her healing with 'precious viold liquors', and the festivals of the shepherds who thank her, all these things call to mind a general idea of the bounty of God acknowledged in psalms of praise. The quality of Sabrina is gentleness and goodness in general, though her 'best' office is to protect chastity. The tone had been set with the water-nymphs who took her in: they were 'piteous of her woes'. In this masque frailty in distress encounters divine mercy, in various ways. And there is the phrase 'while heav'n lends us grace'.

Yet religious interpretations have been confused by mistaken specific applications of the doctrine of grace. The account of A. S. P. Woodhouse, first printed back in 1941, was extraordinarily influential in the shaping of opinion about the religious argument of the masque.[35] According to Woodhouse, there is a typical Protestant division between the realms of Nature and

Spiritual instructions

Grace, and only Sabrina operates on the level of Grace. It is clearly wrong to say that she alone represents grace. Grace enters the action in the very first line and leaves it at the last, its channel throughout a heavenly guardian of the faithful. Haemony is as crucial a divine, saving gift as anything else. The concept of grace will not do as the unique signature of Sabrina, though ideas of providence are appropriate to her role.

The misconception of Sabrina as grace alone connects with a common misreading of the whole action, which sees a hierarchical relationship between her powers and those that have been used before against Comus, which are then assumed to have been in some way lesser or insufficient.[36] In particular, it is clear that many interpretations of Haemony have been conditioned by the idea that its powers must somehow or other be less than those of Sabrina: hence, perhaps, the many attempts to ascribe philosophy, wisdom or knowledge of some kind to the herb, hoping thereby to confine it to the human sphere and to keep the divine gift in reserve for Sabrina.

Sabrina is a 'goddesse'; masques by habit encourage one to think in hierarchies; and she does 'save' mortal frailty. But it is more helpful if the nymph of Severn is thought of as a fresh evidence of grace and as revealing providential care in another form appropriate to the occasion. From the region itself may be drawn an idea of another gift, of the possibility of another presiding spirit.[37] As I have said, the meditations of Michaelmas day, if indeed they are formative for the masque, extended to the providential care of both individuals and nations.

The auspiciousness of the occasion is felt both through arriving president and through famed locality, as the prologue makes clear. The river Severn offered itself in several ways, out of geography, history and literature, as a means by which region could be brought into the definitions of the masque as a focus of contemplation. It is the great river of the region, rising in the very heart of Wales, and in its lower reaches providing the traditional boundary between Wales and England, or the Cambria and Loëgria of ancient Britain in historical legend. Presidency and river linked Wales with England. However, Milton looked at the river chiefly through the literature of fabulous history. It was an index of mythical vision. Drayton, notably, had given the Severn some regal prominence in the picturing of Wales, in one book of *Polyolbion* using Sabrina as a judge of rival claims of England and Wales and as a mouthpiece for his Tudor/Stuart 'Cambro-British' prophecy. It is most likely that Milton looked in *Polyolbion*, when he was thinking of fitting a masque to Ludlow and Wales, although of course he would have known the Trojan/British mythology and story of Sabrina from many other sources.[38]

The immortalisation of the girl, like an Ovidian transformation, is told by the spirit at some length. Of Trojan royal pedigree, she has been given a Virgilian heroic stamp, like the Welsh people in the prologue. Yet Milton used the patriotic myth in a modified way. The story of Sabrina's drowning did not quite fit the celebratory context at Ludlow. There is no need to search for a source giving a version of the story closer to Milton's details: he deliberately changed the emphasis. He did not dwell on the immorality of Sabrina's father and he did not advertise the story as a sensational example of murder growing out of jealousy at marital infidelity. 'Stepdame' Gwendolen was somewhat played down, to become the stock figure of fable, the *noverca*, cruel stepmother. These cosmetic changes were presumably made so as not to embarrass too severely something that is partly a celebratory reference to the Trojan/British line. Yet enough was left to hint at a context of tyrannous passions in high places, in a family fallen from heroic status, and, above all, to show the victimisation of chaste innocence, echoing the action of the masque. The changes had religious point as well. Instead of being thrown into the river with her mother, Milton's Sabrina 'commended her faire innocence to the floud'. She seems pious as well as guiltless, throwing herself on divine mercy. Milton's telling of the story dwells on the guiltlessness of the girl and on a manifestation of divine mercy, providing a token of the care of providence such as may be felt to apply to the present plight of the Lady.

Thus the emphasis falls on the idea of repeated acts of providence in this place, rather than on the idea of a securely heroic nation or race. A keynote is sounded in the naming of providential 'pity' – 'piteous of her woes'. Milton's patriotic idealism tended to express itself by marking moments of providential action in history, such as might, if rightly understood and heeded, be confirmations of national greatness in a nation's

Spiritual instructions

faltering progress. This reassurance of moments of 'pity' in the masque is rather like that in the famous patriotic passage in *Animadversions*:

> Let us goe every true protested *Brittaine* throughout the 3. *Kingdoms*, and render thanks to God . . . and let us recount even here without delay the patience and long suffering that God hath us'd towards our blindness and hardnes time after time. For he being equally neere to his whole Creation of Mankind, and of free power to turne his benefick and fatherly regard to what Region and Kingdome he pleases, hath yet ever had this Iland under the special indulgent eye of his providence; and pittying us the first of all other Nations . . . (Yale 1 704)

Through Sabrina Milton could consider, poetically rather than historically, the repeated acts of providence towards a nation, in association with this place.

The 'goddess' Sabrina returns, Astraea-like, to the stage at Ludlow, returns to a princely hall such as her own, bringing with her those blessings which men themselves once drove from the place. In that sense her spectacular entry suggests the creation of a new, new–old ideal order. As in many masques, some golden age is restored. But one must immediately qualify such an idea. Milton's point is not the obvious celebratory one of simply preserving in Sabrina, for her to pass on, the supposed heroic virtue of an antique British race. Although he calls the Trojan myth to mind for the dignity of the western gubernatorial occasion, Milton does not elaborate on ideas of heroic virtue in the race. Even in fable, nothing is so unconditionally secure. Neither is there in any simple way the secure celebratory idea of Sabrina's instituting a new order, thus establishing the instauration of the new presidency as a golden era. The continuance of plenty and health is prayed for, not established. Sabrina acts for the moment, giving one of those momentary proofs of providential pity, which signal not so much the establishment of a chosen nation as a sign that God will continue to look with favour on a people seemingly chosen when it rouses itself into acts of more-than-common virtue and asks for pity. Milton's touch with Sabrina was as scrupulous, and intricate, as it was with Genius in *Arcades*, in connecting providential powers with persons and places to be celebrated.

Sabrina leads therefore towards a kind of exhortation, a shared contemplation of a truly ideal order in a nation. More than a 'state of mind' signalled by a Country ideal, the picture has a national dimension.[39] And Sabrina does not, I think, as Marcus seems to suggest, *represent* the presidency in its legal powers; rather she signals a potential which may be realised in connection with the presidency.[40] In what is said about Sabrina Milton made an affective visionary celebration of a whole land, something touching, beyond the Arcadian, the apocalyptic.

One can find an index to Milton's intentions by recognising pastoral motifs being pushed into particular directions; courtly Arcadianism is being refashioned for the Welsh occasion.[41]

The description of Sabrina's healing of the cattle with 'precious violl liquors', for example, is characteristic of Milton's intricate writing in this mode. The thought is of the evils that come by night, with the dew. The healing tokens repeated god-given aid.[42] The pastoral thanksgiving, which follows, adds a further dimension to the vision, concerning a godly community:

> for wch the shepheardes at thire festivals
> carroll her goodnesse loud in rustick layes
> and throw sweet garland wreaths into her streams
> of pancies, pinks & gaudie daffadils . . .

Thanksgiving festivals are common in pastoral, but these verses introduce the important idea of a whole people rendering thanks for divine benefits, so that when the Spirit thanks Sabrina on behalf of the president's family, he participates in the kind of pious festival, acts of charity, already practised by the pious inhabitants in this vision of the region. And they of course are the antithesis of the yokels thanking the gods amiss; or indeed of courtly Comus in his failure to render gratitude to God. The picture is of ideal pieties in an ideal pastoral land. The Arcadianism is similar to that used in *Arcades*, except that in the more public masque the poet expresses the plenty associated with a great river by a whole land and people.

The formulas of thanksgiving themselves also confirm the intention to depict a whole land. Again, a pastoral device is pushed into a particular celebratory direction:

> may thy brimmed waves for this
> thire full tribute never misse
> from a thousand petty rills
> that tumble downe the snowie hills

Spiritual instructions

> summer drouth, or singed aire
> never scorch thy tresses faire
> nor wet Octobers torrent flood
> thy molten crystall fill wth mudd

Commentators have long compared this with blessings given to rivers in *The Faithful Shepherdess* and *Britannia's Pastorals*.[43] In Fletcher and Browne the blessings have local and realistic colour. Fletcher begs protection against winds, erosion of banks by drinking animals, damming to catch fish, and spoiling of spawn by the feet of women doing the washing. Browne wishes that shepherds may present the river with lambs, that the river may predominate over other streams, that it may be protected from newts and toads, locks and weirs, keeping its fish undisturbed, and that its banks may be covered with sweet-smelling flowers and its sands be golden. Milton personifies more than Fletcher or Browne, with 'tresses' and 'lofty head'. This is for a goddess in a masque. Otherwise, he picks up the idea of finding blessings appropriate to the river, but chooses instead of rustic detail a grander, more distanced set of associations, or more generalised references to Wales. The idea of the river ruling over its tributaries is developed as much for the celebration of the snow-capped hills of mid-Wales, in which Severn rises, as it is for the dignity of the river itself. As in Drayton, it is Wales itself that is on view. And whilst there is timeliness in the mention of autumn flooding, the wish that Severn should avoid both torrid heat and 'torrent flood' recalls an antique literary context, an ideal landscape, as much as the particularities of the river itself.

The latter part of the passage develops still richer possibilities of ideal celebration, over and above the straighter 'English' pastoral. Whereas Browne wanted to keep civilisation away from his wild river, Milton pictures a landscape blessed with general prosperity including towns and estates of men. The coupling of beryl and gold, the mention of terraces and towers and of myrrh and cinnamon, seem to recall biblical visions of cities, palaces and temples.[44] This is a picture of a land such as those visionary landscapes of plenty in apocalyptic passages in the Bible. A river which brings an end to a curse for the people on its banks might be thought to remember the river of Revelation 22 and the holy water of Ezekiel 47, where ideal lands are given healing and plenty.

Milton's Aristocratic entertainments

There is a further way in which this section celebrating Sabrina's providential blessings might be measured against pastoral convention. Usually in pastoral fictions the protective deity has the identity of Pan. Pan is provider of plenty, guard against disease: '... *Pan curat ovis oviumque magistros*'.[45] Many masques ended with benedictions or prayers for prosperity in the future. Fletcher's pastoral play, ending in this way with a ritual strewing of flowers to the honour of Pan, supplies a very good analogy for Milton's floral tributes by the locals to Sabrina.[46] In the closing parts of his dramatic action Milton has taken up the protective powers and rites of thanksgiving normally due to Pan and has adapted them to fit his regal river goddess. She defends the flocks, receives floral tributes in festivals of thanksgiving, and is associated with a closing wish for continuing prosperity in the land. When the president saw Sabrina grace his feast, he was given an image to remind him of how providence would continue to bless or to pity a pious land, if piety would wish to seek such aid.

In all this, as I have said, the masque has entered a new mode of presentation. The audience is no longer shown a dark world seen with insistent moral realism. Thanks to a renewed act of mercy, ridding the hall of the customary legacy of Comus, the audience may see present place, Ludlow castle and town shown in the 'scene', in the context of the ideal. This is not Wales as it actually is, or even as it ever was; the Spirit presents a land that might be, that might promise to be. It is a *poetic* vision of a land, fixing an ideal in the minds of the beholders.

The change of mode can be felt in various ways, as for example in the treatment of the rural people. Throughout the main part of the action the audience has been issued reminders of the unregenerate state of most men, even hereabouts. In this picture of Sabrina's land all the people seem to join in godly festival. It is the mode which has changed, not the people.

These things denote something beyond compliment. The last scene presents a high-minded, idealistic meditation, in which the president and his family must share. The point is a delicate one. It engages the whole endeavour for an integrity in celebratory writing. It is true that everything in some sense pertains to the presidency, as masque faces its chief beholder; and the rule of not too much has been if not quite inaugurated then at least defined in

Spiritual instructions

the president's feast. But the care of heaven covers the whole action as much as the strength of men, and place, as much as ruling nobility, is used as a means of expressing the ideal of a people. It is as though the president, with all other beholders, is being asked to contemplate, and the idea of contemplation is implicit in the dramatic technique itself. That surely explains why Milton was determined that the boys should not participate actively in the episode but simply watch and hear and contemplate the Orphic conjuring of the Spirit, who is the poet's instructing voice.

As with the *kōmos* and chastity, there is in the use of Sabrina a serious foreshadowing of political thought such as is seen in Milton's later work. In these aspects the programme of the masque must not be underestimated. An ideal order, in which the temperate use of nature leads to prosperity for the people, and in which the piety of the people is shown, figures a paradigm which is universal, to be found in different forms throughout history. In Milton's poetry, for example, it suggests those brief moments of pastoral prosperity in the history of the race of mankind and the chosen people, as he tells it in the last books of *Paradise Lost*. There, expressing the sufficiency still in nature, Cain and Abel are shown in pastoral sacrifice, before the moment is destroyed by jealous murder. After the flood there is a spell of god-fearing pastoral prosperity, with frequent sacrifice, until Nimrod destroys the 'paternal rule'. After the captivity there is another period of prosperity, under kings, brought about by godly living and moderate life.[47] The pictures of these moments in history are in a sense admonitory, for the periods were brief, yet also bear some hope, for it is shown that God will respond, has responded, through the centuries.

The beginnning of true prosperity in godliness, for a whole people, is a common idea assumed in many places in Milton's writing, as in the opening section of the second book *Of Reformation*:

to govern well is to train up a Nation in true wisdom and vertue, and that which springs from thence magnanimity, (take heed of that) and that which is our beginning, regeneration, and happiest end, likeness to *God*, which in one word we call *godlines*, & that this is the true florishing of a Land, other things follow as the shadow does the substance.   (Yale I 571)

Through this vision of Sabrina we glimpse such a 'true florishing of a Land'. The force of this nationalistic idealism has been too little acknowledged by commentators on the masque.

Another seriousness of the masque and another foreshadowing of later writing can be felt in what might be called the suasive design, concerned with that shift of demonstrative mode. The lively treatment of evil in the earlier parts is, I take it, meant to draw the audience into proper apprehension of the pervasive nature of evil in the world, so that the final vision of the ideal may gain appeal by coming after such unflinching recognitions. The juxtaposing of the ideal and the fallen is a repeated instructional effect in his major poems. The Commonplace Book shows Milton debating the use of the arts in the late 1630s and insisting that poetry and drama could be used to move an audience to virtuous endeavour by lively pictures of the good, whatever patristic or modern puritans might say.[48] In the final synthesis of arts in the Sabrina episode the masque enacts the completion of what Milton would I think have regarded as its justification as dramatic poetry and spectacle.

If there is in this an exhortation to all concerned to fix their minds on those models of governance required by God and pitied of him at moments in the past, one can view this, in Cox's formulation, as conditional praise: Milton's compliment to the Earl of Bridgewater 'is not adulatory but conditional, for the effect of his praise depends on the earl's aspiration to the values embodied mythically in the masque' (p. 623). Yet, not quite. To focus the effect more exactly, the tone of the Sabrina episode is celebratory and not so simply hortatory as the epilogue, in which each person present is addressed in private conscience as he or she prepares for rest. One may see the method of this episode as less pointed than actually begging the question of the president's response. It offers shared meditation: the Attendant Spirit speaks, with all the magic of spectacle, speaks as a kind of angel and for poetry itself – 'wch once of Melibaeus old I learn't – to all men gathered to view that vision. If there is a submission, it is finally to the Sidneian power of poetry. Meliboeus, the supposed source of the tale, is the type of the true poet, just as the shepherd lad had been the type of the true pastor. Meliboeus is 'soothest' of shepherds who sing. Milton is making a claim for, and trying to demonstrate, the power of true poetry to move the mind to action.

Spiritual instructions

In these spiritual instructions, the voice of the true poet has joined the vocation of the true pastor. There is no more significant instance in the early Milton of the declaration of the saving power of a poetry made to raise the mind.

6 · 1634 AND 1637 – TEXTS, EPILOGUES, AUDIENCES

IN THIS CHAPTER I want to consider changes in the text of *Comus*, in manuscript and printed texts, showing what I take to be changing priorities. There is some mention of the development of parts of the text before performance, but I wish to dwell especially on those alterations made for the published version of 1637/8. As I have said, this masque presents an unrivalled history in the record of its various texts, revealing considerable complexity in Milton's address to his occasion, for performance at Ludlow and for publication.[1]

Two areas of text are under particular examination, the temptation scene and the epilogue, two crucial areas of definition in which complicated changes took place. Some changes in other parts of the text have been mentioned already. In general I have concurred with Sprott's account of the sequence of textual changes in the Trinity manuscript, discussed more fully in the Appendix. My account should be seen as complementary to his: rather than give another technical examination of the textual changes themselves, I am trying to consider Milton's intentions with regard to occasion and function as they vary in the different versions of the text up to and including *1637*.

To set these changes in context, it is worth dwelling for a moment on Milton's attitudes to national affairs about 1637, when the masque was being revised for the press. I am referring especially to the evidence of *Lycidas*, written in November of that year. The '1637' revisions in *Comus* have a good deal in common with *Lycidas*, with regard to 'public' address.

Lycidas is a poem of exceptional intricacy and demands close attention as both private and public document. In the present

1634 and 1637 – texts, epilogues, audiences

context one feature demands to be noticed and that is the surprising breadth of subject matter in Milton's poem, especially when it is placed against the bulk of the Cambridge memorial volume for Edward King. The immediate subject, the death of King, was counterpointed with another, which was national and equally the material for lament. It was only in Milton's collection of 1645 that he signalled the second subject openly, with a second prophetic part to the title: 'And by occasion foretells the ruin of our corrupted clergy then in their height'. I shall want to return to that prophetic dimension of the poem in the last chapter.

The poet's serious questionings showed a bold attempt in the twenty-nine-year-old to make the Cambridge verses responsible to an ideal of the nation. The addition to the title in *1645* showed a certain satisfaction in what he had spoken seven years before. Though its methods were more sophisticated than blatant, *Lycidas* marked the moment at which Milton first openly took on the role of writer to the nation, that is to say, in an extended English poem on a public occasion. The question I wish to address, therefore, is to assess how far that public voice of uncompromising judgement had also sounded in the revisions of the masque text for publication. The decision to publish the masque text, even anonymously, gave it a new function, for although publication was in one sense serving as memorial of the festivity of 1634, it also gave the poet a new occasion and enabled him to speak more independently of original occasion. Now, freer of various constraints, including a kind of censorship, he could address all cultured Englishmen who might read the text as poem.

In the earliest state of the text we have, that is to say, in the first version copied into and worked on in the Trinity manuscript, the temptation scene followed a simple dramatic pattern. Subsequently, even before performance, this scene underwent considerable development. The Trinity manuscript shows that Milton resorted his material so as to make the progression of the dialogue different. Then, in further revision after performance, he added two substantial passages.

In the earliest state of the text (TMS[1]) the scene was made up of two long speeches plus Comus' short final repeated offer of the cup. Comus spoke first. As in later versions, he began by explaining the binding spell ('nay, Ladie, sit . . .'), then offered youthful pleasure to placate her frowns ('why doe you frowne / heere dwell no frowns . . .'), then launched straight into the libertine argument against temperance ('O foolishness of men!'), and finished with the first invitation to drink of his cup, referring to Nepenthes and to her fatigue and thirst. During this long speech the Lady had remained silent, her action being limited to gesture: an initial attempt to rise from the chair, an expression of displeasure on her face. At the offering of the cup, she broke in with a single speech ('stand back false traitor . . .'), proclaiming the freedom of her mind, lamenting his deceptions ('was this the cottage . . .') and the ugliness she clearly saw before her ('O my simplicity what sights are these . . .'), then rejected the cup itself as the gift of an evil man. Then she apparently was meant to go straight on into her counter-arguments against luxury:

> I had not thought to have unlockt my lips
> in this unhallowd aire but that this juggler
> would think to charme my judgement as myne eyes.

This latter part could only have been acted by her turning from Comus to the audience. She begins to refer to him in the third person. Dramatically this might have been effective, suggesting a powerful compact between Lady and audience, from which the enchanter is excluded. To this statement Comus had merely replied by irritably rejecting her arguments as the 'moral stuffe' of melancholy and by offering the cup a second time. At this point the brothers were to rush in.

This was not inept as drama, and the framework of argument was all there. Nevertheless, there was something static in the two block speeches: they suggested more an exposition than a plausible exchange. By the time of performance (TMS[2]), and in the Bridgewater text, the speeches had been split up and distributed more according to the manner of a progressive conversation. Now the Lady is to break into Comus' speech after just four lines, before he has time to work on her frown. His threat of power over her through his charms is now met with fierce rebuttal in words: 'foole doe not boast / thou canst not touch the freedome of my mind'. The liveliness of this is achieved at a little loss on another count: by making her speak so resolutely so early the poet spoiled an element of surprise at the fierceness of her original delayed opening. On the other hand, the exemplary nature of her reactions is more firmly documented than before, by making her speak. We now know, from the beginning of the scene, in no uncertain way, that it will be patterned differently from the first exchange with Comus.

In TMS² also Comus was to offer the cup earlier than in the previous draft. Now, after trying to placate her frown, Comus has substantially the same lines as before about youthful pleasures, but then on 'pasted leaf (a)' he speaks his Nepenthes lines and offers the cup. So the cup has been offered before the 'philosophical' justification. The gain here would seem to be in the more progressive disposition of the elements of the dialogue, and, again, it may serve to give greater emphasis to the Lady's exemplary active virtue. A penalty in the new arrangement Milton may have realised by 1637, as we shall see: Comus no longer coaxes with so much argument before he tempts with the cup.

In these ways, then, Milton tried to make the episode more naturalistically dramatic, in TMS², whilst giving a readier sense of the active virtue of the Lady, who rebuts Comus at every stage during the encounter. Both dramatic technique and moral exemplification are in view. The Bridgewater text kept the general arrangement of TMS², differing only in that some 'tactful' excisions were made.² I am pretty sure that these excisions are not part of Milton's design and should not be counted as part of the development of the text.

Two major additions were made before the publication text of 1637. One was a new passage at the end of the Lady's didactic speech, adding a celebration of chastity to her explanation of temperance. This addition, with Comus' response to it, appeared only in the printed text, and I shall want to return to it presently. The other major addition, which appeared in the '1637' changes in the Trinity manuscript as well as in the printed text, came in 'pasted leaf (b)' and it consisted of an addition to Comus' second speech, before he first offers the cup. Following the Nepenthes section Milton now wrote:

> why should you be so cruell to yo^rself,
> and to those daintie lims wch nature lent
> for gentle usage, and soft delicacie,

> but you invert the cov'nants of her trust,
> and harshly deale like an ill borrower
> wth that wch you receav'd on other terms
> scorning the unexempt condition,
> by wch all mortall frailtie must subsist
> refreshment after toile, ease after paine,
> that have bin tir'd all day

This is now a persuasive generalisation of the case, addressed to the Lady as mortal needing refreshment and rest. Its function is to reinforce the moral challenge; its cunning related to the author's wish to examine social attitudes more trenchantly. Comus' appeal to the 'unexempt condition' of 'mortall frailtie' is in fact a nice perversion of the dominant religious sense of man's fallibility. That which had always supported the masque is through insidious perversion being brought further into view in *1637*.

The language of covenants and borrowing also prefigures Comus' speech against temperance later in the episode. One might say that a redundancy had been introduced. However, Milton evidently wanted the suggestive power of the new insidiously generalising moral formulation more than he cared about the slight redundancy, and in one way the new passage can also be justified on dramatic grounds. When the scene had been reordered in TMS[2] and the offering of the cup had been transferred to a position before Comus' speech of libertine philosophy, the persuasive effects of these arguments had not been tried before the first act of temptation itself. The 1637 addition suggests that Milton wished to restore something of the persuasiveness of Comus' verbal display. Again, a powerful moral realism is being sought, above other considerations, in the development of a publication text.

One might express gain and loss in dramatic effectiveness in another way. Previously Comus had touched on the Lady's *personal* fatigue and thirst, before offering the cup:

> poore ladie thou hast need of some refreshing
> that hast bin tir'd all day wthout repast
> & timely rest hast wanted heere sweet Ladie
> this will restore all soone

On pasted leaf (b) the reminder of her need for rest and refreshment comes first, rather powerfully, in *general* terms:

1634 and 1637 – texts, epilogues, audiences

'refreshment after toile, ease after paine, / that have bin tir'd all day . . .' The new generality is encouraged by the sense of shared experience. On the other hand, there is now a slight awkwardness in syntax. The new passage seems not perfectly assimilated. The second-person subject of 'that have bin tir'd all day' (replacing the earlier familiar form 'hast') does not seem to follow naturally from the third-person generalities of the new lines before. One has to go back four lines, in fact, to 'you receav'd', to pick up the continuity of second-person subject. This is measuring small things, but a general moral forcefulness has been gained at the cost of a slight embarrassment to the plausibility of the dialogue as speech.

In these changes something may be typified about shifts of authorial attitude with regard to occasions and audiences. The gains in this new passage will be seen elsewhere in *1637*. The recognisably 'cavalier' note of the cynical 'daintie lims' argument and the cunning perversion of religious language help to place the published version as an even more independently outspoken authorial comment on the moral state of the real world about him. Whereas in developing the text of the episode from the earliest Trinity draft up to the time of performance Milton had tried to foster dramatic realism and didactic exactitude at the same time, within the constraints of using his noble actors, in the changes after performance he was willing to compromise those dramatic concerns, a little at least, in the interests of a more comprehensive view of the insidious mores of courts seen through the spirit of their festivities. There is a perceptible shift in sense of audience and mode of address.

One can look in a similar way at the other major addition to the temptation scene in *1637*, the substantial new passage added at the end of the debate. This new conclusion is a sustained and in some ways a self-contained exchange. I quote it therefore in full:

> Shall I goe on?
> Or have I said enough? to him that dares
> Arme his profane tongue with reproachfull words
> Against the Sun-clad power of Chastitie
> Faine would I something say, yet to what end?
> Thou has nor Eare, nor Soule to apprehend
> The sublime notion, and high mysterie
> That must be utter'd to unfold the sage
> And serious doctrine of Virginitie,

> And thou art worthy that thou shouldst not know
> More hapinesse then this thy praesent lot.
> Enjoy your deere Wit, and gay Rhetoricke
> That hath so well been taught her dazling fence,
> Thou art not fit to heare thy selfe convinc't;
> Yet should I trie, the uncontrouled worth
> Of this pure cause would kindle my rap't spirits
> To such a flame of sacred vehemence,
> That dumb things would be mov'd to sympathize,
> And the brute Earth would lend her nerves, and shake,
> Till all thy magick structures rear'd so high
> Were shatter'd into heaps ore thy false head.
> *Co.* She fables not, I feele that I doe feare
> Her words set off by some superior power;
> And though not mortall, yet a cold shuddring dew
> Dips me all o're, as when the wrath of *Iove*
> Speaks thunder, and the chaines of *Erebus*
> To some of *Saturns* crew. I must dissemble,
> And try her yet more strongly. Come; no more,
> This is meere morall babble

The sequence looks the same as in 1634; on the face of it, we have merely greater force in the Lady's words and a new acknowledgement of that force by Comus. New details fit the context: the presiding spirit of the *kōmos* arms his profane tongue against chastity, as he should; his 'deere Wit' and 'gay Rhetoricke' are exposed as fashionable false learning; the Lady is a virgin, seeing her own virginity in the light of religion; and Comus may sound a little like Caliban ruing Prospero's power, but his reference to Erebus and 'Saturn's crew' confirm a hellish pedigree. And the new words do not lack actable power.

Nevertheless, a more insistently didactic note has been struck. Here, as in the *1637* epilogue additions, there is that haughty distinction of ears. What Comus cannot understand is the mystery of godliness in the word of God. The problematical 'Sun-clad power of Chastitie' might be seen in this context. Commentators have assumed that the phrase carried religious significance, and 'Sun-clad' has often been related to a canzone of Petrarch (viii 1) addressed to the Virgin Mary (Vergine bella, che di sol vestita), whilst registering that the origin of the image may be found in the 'woman clothed with the sun' of Revelation 12.1.[3] One cannot deny the suggestive power of glorious woman clothed with the sun.

1634 and 1637 – texts, epilogues, audiences

Still, it may be easy to give 'Sun-clad' the wrong specificity. For one thing, the woman in Revelation was usually taken to stand historically for the Jewish nation or the Christian church.[4] Milton's reference may not be to her, primarily. What may be more important is the metaphor itself, the clothing with the sun, which has a wider biblical currency. It would seem to denote more generally some state associated with the presence of God. Commentators recorded a cluster of related images.[5] One appropriate text might be Matthew 13.43, where there is also that distinction of ears: 'Then shall the righteous shine forth as the sun in the kingdom of their Father. Who hath ears to hear, let him hear.' That is to say, the sun image may simply express a state of righteousness.

This part of the debate, the 1637 additions to the epilogue, and the Haemony allegory all share a similar biblical context. All three make distinctions between those who have ears for God's word and those who have not. All three, like the allegory of the 'two-handed engine' in *Lycidas*, are concerned with an advertisement of the word of God and some celebration of its power. Chastity is called 'Sun-clad' not because it contains magical power in any literal sense, but because it is ordained as righteous and therefore shares in the ultimate immunity of all Truth from the clever imputations of profane tongues. Similarly, virginity is celebrated because it points, in biblical metaphor, to the greater mystery of the heavenly state. 'The sage / And serious doctrine' of virginity is a kind of metaphor for the teaching of the New Testament about the kingdom of heaven. The Lady's virginity has to be thought of as literal and figurative at the same time.

The new section of the debate comprises one extended figure demonstrating the power of the word and the inevitable triumph of truth over falsehood. Because it demonstrates the triumph of truth, it gives sharper, or more obvious, irony to Comus' final resolve: 'I must dissemble . . .' The time for that is past. The 'superior power' that he acknowledges in the Lady's speech is the word itself in her speech. The earnest Protestant poet is using her as mouthpiece. Comus' 'magick structures' are revealed as his perversion of the truth. This power of the Lady over falsity is similar to that Milton had given to Haemony 'gainst all enchauntments'. It is also the same prophetic triumph of truth as that which he put into the mouth of Peter in *Lycidas*, also in 1637. All these passages are public statements, or exhortations, fired by reformation idealism.

The new passage is bound together by a trick of allusion. Warton, followed by Hughes and Bush, noted that 'brute Earth' is Horace's *bruta tellus* from the thirty-fourth ode in the first book (lines 9–12).[6] The allusion is worth pursuing, for it makes a wry device. In this poem Horace had wondered whether the unusual phenomenon of thunder coming out of a clear sky should be interpreted as an indication of Jove's wrath at his impiety. Ought he to repent, and worship the gods with regularity? Pious scholarship of Milton's time, rather blurring the sophisticated tone of the original, saw the ode as a repudiation of the 'foolish wisdom' of Epicurean or Cynic atheism, Comus' brand of philosophy. '. . . having followed the Epicureans, he had been little studious in worshipping the Gods', says the headnote in Fanshawe's translation, echoing the usual view of the poem as a figurative demonstration of the power of the truly divine.[7] Milton's line – 'And the brute Earth would lend her nerves, and shake' – might betray the memory of Horace's verb, *concutitur* (is shaken), as well as of *bruta tellus*.[8]

But Horace was still in the poet's mind as he was framing Comus' response. The enchanter acknowledges the power of her words 'as when the wrath of *Iove* / Speaks thunder'. Though he has elaborated the idea, Milton has made Jove's power be felt, as in Horace, even in the regions of the underworld: 'and the chains of *Erebus* / To some of *Saturns* crew'. Bearing the whole Horatian poem in mind, one can see that Comus' reply completes the allusion and rounds off a figure which has given shape to the whole new inserted passage: the Lady claims the power of heaven in her arguments against epicureanism; Comus, a creature known to hell, acknowledges the fear of God induced by thunder. The might of Jove is in the word of God uttered by the Lady. The addition has the incisive wit of mature Miltonic allusion, but it is also, at base, idealistically religious in assumption and didactic in attitude.

This addition might well have run into censorship, had it been included before performance.[9] I think also that this new passage, finely tuned though it is, would have been somewhat disruptive to performance, just as it has been to subsequent critical readings.

1634 and 1637 – texts, epilogues, audiences

Some subtle confusion is caused. We have now *two* celebrations of chastity or virginity spoken by the young aristocrats. The speech of the Elder Brother already asked for delicate understanding, with regard to tone. The introduction of a second passage for the Lady herself in such a way as to describe chastity and virginity as religious virtues, even as symbols of religious mysteries, creates a problem of accommodation with the earlier speech. There is no hint of exposure of immaturity in this speech of the Lady, though it might be thought youthful in its idealism. From the history of criticism of the masque, it seems to me pretty plain that many modern readers who have studied the masque in its published form have allowed the tone of the second new passage to affect their assessment of the tone of the first. From that point of view, considering certain nuances of the dramatic exploitation of occasion in 1634, it was not a good idea to add the new fiercely doctrinal passage to the debate.

Again, a general conclusion begs to be drawn. In *1637* the mind of the poet was not quite so scrupulous of the delights of occasion. In fact it must have been an act of imaginative reconstruction for him to recapture all the old priorities. The new decorum concerned what was right and fitting to say in exhortation to a more general readership of that particular time. When, in adding to the debate, Milton took the opportunity to make a demonstration of prophetic kind about the ultimate power of truth, the context of *Lycidas*, the context of the struggles of the true church in history, was not far out of view. The sense of the contemporary is more present than ever: 'deere Wit', 'gay Rhetoricke' and dubious sexual mores are understood to be presently at work in the world. These new passages in the temptation scene – and in this one may look forward to the enlarged epilogue for the printed text – seem to want to tell readers that the poet had seen god Comus and his associates well settled in the Britain of 1637.

The most comprehensive evidence of Milton's changed priorities, or changed opportunities, in *1637* comes from the alterations he made to the epilogue. The epilogue, however, is not easy to assess, especially in the enlarged version of the printed text. Again, the alterations of *1637* can be judged against a sense of the functions of the epilogue in TMS[2]. (Strictly, a passage of related imagery in an early version of the prologue in the Trinity manuscript might also come into question.)[10] I would like to begin to take the measure of the epilogue by noting ways in which Milton adapts the conventional endings of other masques.

At court, masque nights were long. They began after supper and went into the small hours. After the revels, the social dancing, a song often marked the end with some reference to time. 'Then yield to Time, and so must all', sang the chorus at the end of Jonson's *The Vision of Delight* in 1617.[11] Sharing this conventional reference to time, Milton's ending alluded to Hesperus, the star that is visible after the setting of the sun.

The ending of *The Vision of Delight* looked back in time, with a reference to mundane mortality. A masque poet might also look forward, to greet the morning, and thence the future. In *The Masque of Oberon* (1611), Phosphorus, herald of the day, commanded the dancing fairies to disappear with himself: 'Then, doe I give way, / As night hath done and so must you, to day.' *The Haddington Masque*, presented at a wedding in 1608, also ended with the imminence of dawn. Its final epithalamium had the refrain 'Shine, Hesperus, shine forth, thou wished starre'. During the night, evening star had given way to morning star, one Hesperus to another. *The Triumph of Peace*, of 1633, a recent example for Milton, also ended by figuring the approach of morning. So did many other masques.

Then again, performers and beholders were sometimes invited to take their rest, after a long night out. In *Albions Triumph* (1631), where the valediction was addressed chiefly to the king and queen, Townshend wrote 'angels sing them to their rest'.[12] At Ludlow, of course, an angel does sing the masquers to their rest.

These valedictions or epilogues looked back and forward in time, then, lamenting the transience of the splendours of the masque but also registering the length of those splendours through the night. Poets could compensate for the work of time in various explicit ways, as through the idea of lasting fame, as Jonson did in several masques including the two for the Caroline court, *Love's Triumph* and *Chloridia*. Optimism for the future was a marked feature of the art and political celebration of the court of Charles; for the first time that anyone at court could personally remember there was a relatively youthful pair on the throne. When the

1634 and 1637 – texts, epilogues, audiences

ending of masque nights was made more in the gesture of a wish for future blessings, it provided a means of suggesting that the evident bounties of the present might indeed extend into the future, in the life of the court and nation generally. *Pan's Anniversary* (1620), *Neptune's Triumph for the Return of Albion* (1624), *Albions Triumph* (1631), *The Triumph of Peace* (1633) and *Coelum Britannicum* (1634) all end with this idea of continuing blessings for court or nation. Or, more dramatically, time may simply be outfaced in bold assertion at the end of the night, as when Astraea said she wished to stay on earth instead of returning to heaven, at the end of Jonson's *The Golden Age Restored* (1615), or when, in *Coelum Britannicum*, Time himself is asked to stand still.

Turning from these conventions at court to Milton's epilogue for Ludlow, we can quickly see an affinity in motifs – Milton had of course studied some models – but also a different religious emphasis, even in the shorter Trinity version of 1634. This is the epilogue as it seems to have stood in the Trinity manuscript soon before performance:

> To the Ocean now I fly
> and those happie climes that lie
> where day never shuts his eye
> up in the broad feilds of the skie
> ther I suck the liquid aire
> all amidst the gardens faire
> of Hesperus & his daughters three
> that sing about the golden tree
> there aeternall summer dwells
> and west winds wth musky wing
> about the cedar'ne alleys fling
> nard, & casia's balmy smells
> Iris there wth humid bow
> waters the odorous banks y^t blow
> flowers of more mingled hew
> then her purfl'd scarfe can shew
> yellow, watchet, greene, & blew
> and drenches oft wth manna dew
> beds of Hyacinth, & roses
> where many a cherub soft reposes
> now my taske is smoothly don
> I can fly, or I can run
> quickly to the earths greene end

Milton's Aristocratic entertainments

>where the bow'd welkin slow doth bend
>and from thence can soare as soone
>to the corners of ye moone
>mortalls that would follow me
>love vertue she alone is free
>she can teach yee how to clime
>higher then the sphaerie chime
>or if vertue feeble were
>heaven it selfe would stoope to her.

Like other masque poets Milton turns his valediction about considerations of time. The epilogue is designed for the close of day not the anticipation of the dawn, but as he describes his abode in the Elysian skies, where there is constant light, the Spirit is making a version of the lament for the end of festivity and its bright delights, and is seeking a mode of compensation.

However, the pious differences are obvious. The Spirit does not seek to dwell on present or passing splendours. He issues an invitation to move in thought to a new place, to the heavens. Masques often claimed that heaven had come to earth; the Spirit asks earthbound men to think of somewhere altogether better. The 'broad feilds of the skie' are not heaven itself, they are the heavens, the 'sphaerie chime', 'before the starrie threshold of Joves court', as it is put in the opening speech of the masque. But the Spirit lives in a place which is on the way to the court of heaven.

The conflation of various ideal abodes from ancient poetry, abodes associated with happy spirits though also with death, to produce a figure for the bright heavens, is something that is repeated in Book Three of *Paradise Lost* (563–571), where Satan enters the outer confines of the new world, and the heavenly bodies are like bright islands in the sea. Hence the association there and in the epilogue with various mythical islands and lands far off in or by Ocean: the gardens of the Hesperides, Isles of the Blessed, or Elysion at the world's end.

In the Ludlow epilogue actual nightfall is suggested in the dew. The dew drenches not Welsh but Elysian flowers. The flowers allow play on the word 'beds' – why do commentators so often fail to note it? – for to the flowers Milton attaches his final reference to rest or sleep: 'and drenches oft wth manna dew / beds of Hyacinth, & roses / where many a cherub soft reposes'. Cherubs are angels;

1634 and 1637 – texts, epilogues, audiences

they are given manna, 'angels' food'. Angelic spirits provide the pattern of repose for men on earth to contemplate.

This is of course a version of ease and refreshment offered to the souls of men in the Elysian fields, as in the fourth book of the *Odyssey* (4. 561–568) and in many other related passages of poetry.[13] It is hard to know just how loudly Milton wished to sound the note of death in this repose (an issue relevant to the extended epilogue of *1637*), but the flowers hyacinth and rose, as well as bearing fragrance and the freshness of spring and summer, carry with them the memory of decay and death. Repose is sleep or mortality and also Elysian joy. There is a double effect: something dying, something better going on.[14]

Just as with the vision associated with Sabrina, this picture of the happy place is meant to move minds. Sabrina's land completed the suasive design for the public masque, concerning a people; the imagery of the epilogue for the individual, as he turned to pious rest, withdrawing from the social occasion.

In fact Milton exploited the eclectic *topos* of the Hesperian or Elysian place many times in his poetry. The aromatic herbs of the epilogue are like those he used, for example, in the fifth book of *Paradise Lost* (291–294), at the entry of Raphael into the earthly paradise. There they impress the sense and whet the appetite for the meal. In these passages Ovid's description of the preparations for the immolation of the phoenix (*Met.* 15.393ff) may be remembered, at least for the nard and cassia, whilst odour-bearing winds might recall Claudian's lush description of the garden of Henna.[15] In this rich, if commonplace, allusion, there may be marks of Christian language too.[16] The Psalms may have contributed.[17] Refreshing dews and waters and the mention of manna and the rainbow all invite religious associations.[18] These gardens display the profusion of heavenly grace nearby.

As the Spirit signals his departure, the movement of the quick heptasyllabic lines and the half-comic use of 'mortalls' show also the influence of Shakespeare's spirits of comedy, Puck, the fairies and Ariel. There is no seriousness lacking in the exhortation, though. Man's virtue can help him higher than the fields of aerial spirits. Heaven itself is reached in allusion in the very last lines of the epilogue, which also give the statement of grace.

We have travelled a long way from the simplicity of

Townshend's 'angels sing them to their rest' or the mundane observation of Jonson's 'Then yield to Time, and so must all'. The epilogue of TMS[2] gave religious placement to the pleasures of the masque just seen, leading the mind heavenwards at bedtime, and completed the offering of a rather determined young poet, whose pastor-like piety would not finally bow to earthly grandeurs.

I want to say little about the truncated Bridgewater manuscript version of the epilogue, which shows considerable interference with Milton's intentions. Someone decided to move the first, 'Hesperian' part of the epilogue to the beginning, as a sung prologue. There was a wish to exploit a strength in resources, the singing of Henry Lawes. The action was now framed by his songs, in prologue and epilogue. The short remaining section of the epilogue was also sung.

The truncated Bridgewater epilogue still allowed the Spirit his heavenward flight, and the poet his pious exhortation, but the prior persuasions of poetry are largely taken away. The effect of the cut on the dynamics of the poetry is much as with that in the Lady's soliloquy, where the Bridgewater manuscript left her to sing without showing how she had revived her spirits to do so. With the epilogue, as elsewhere, Milton stuck to his intentions in print.

In the changes in the epilogue in 1637 there was no complete transformation of function, and Milton did not lose all sight of the original occasion. All the elements relate in some way to festivity and to a sense of an ending. Nevertheless, he reinforced the moral and religious generality of the passage, as we have seen elsewhere, and tended to blur some of the more specific applications to occasion. There was a greater distance from actual masquing.

Near the beginning of the description of the gardens of Hesperus Milton began a major change, then thought better of it. The first bit was as before: 'all amidst the gardens faire / of Hesperus & his daughters three'. Then instead of the original 'that sing about the golden tree' (a line which reflected song in masque) he tried a new extension to the image. The extension would I think have turned it into an allegory. The manuscript is difficult to decipher, but Milton seems to have written

> where grows the right-borne gold

1634 and 1637 – texts, epilogues, audiences

This must be an incomplete line. It seems to introduce the idea of the golden fruit of the Hesperides as the gift of eternity and reward for heroic virtue in man, as in the cancelled passage of the prologue in 1634. The right-born (or is it right-borne?) gold is presumably immortal life, transferred from paradise to heaven, to be recovered again by man.

Dissatisfied with this, Milton crossed through 'grows the right-borne gold' and completed the line instead as 'where upon his native tree'. The intention was still, I take it, to lead into the moral allegory of Hercules and the golden apples. Then he gave up the idea of allegorising this section of the epilogue and substituted the original reading, 'that sing about the golden tree'.

Had the allegory been developed, it would have reflected the action of the masque on a moral rather than occasional plane. Like the cancelled passage of the 1634 prologue it would have expressed the triumph of virtue, the transience of earthly pleasures being confronted by golden eternity won with heroism by man. But such an allegory, coming at this point, would inevitably have caused other changes in the verse, because it would have equated the Hesperian gardens with the heavenly state of eternal joy for man. The distinction between the heavens and heaven would have been closed long before the end of the speech by some perhaps elaborate new attempt at underlining the moral meaning.

The next major change in 1637 was the insertion of four lines between the singing of the three Hesperides and the eternal summer:

>   along the crisped shades and bowrs
>   revells the spruce and jocond Spring
>   the Graces and the rosie-bosom'd Howrs
>   thither all thire bounties bring

Spring revelling furnished a new correspondence with masquing, strengthened by the word 'jocond', suiting festive mirth. At the same time, the freer expansion of the whole *topos* made it more like its equivalent in the description of the earthly paradise in Book Four of *Paradise Lost*: '... while universal Pan / Knit with the Graces and the Hours in dance / Led on the eternal spring' (266–268). There is a cluster of images. Both passages link Graces and Hours with dance and spring. In the epilogue, where they bring bounties which may also have been intended as correspondents to the splendours of masque, Milton seems to have thought these gifts would explain more fully what it means to have eternal summer: he inserted the word 'that' in the next line – 'that there eternal Summer dwells' – presumably to mean 'with the result that' or 'in order that'.

The preoccupation is with time and the seasons still. The Hours traditionally bring the blessings of all the seasons. The Graces, expressing gracefulness and beauty and festive joy, are sometimes also, like the Hours, depicted bringing fruits and flowers of spring and summer. Hours and Graces had often been associated before.[19] There may be a greater placement of youth and youthful joy generally in the 1637 epilogue.

These additions gave fuller expression to the *topos*, yet the elaboration also somewhat obscured the precise applicability of the original: the explicit mention of the traditional spring does not so neatly meet the Ludlow occasion, set at the end of summer. But the picture has been augmented to make it more moving, and that was an important motivation.

The other changes in 1637 concern the addition of a new allegory at the end of the description of place. First, connective adjustments were made. The original closing repose of aerial spirits – 'where many a cherub soft reposes' – was changed into the cyclical generation of Adonis. The line became 'where young Adonis oft reposes'. Having taken out the angels, Milton had also to take out the 'manna', angels' food, as qualification of the dew. This he replaced first with 'Sabean', conveying eastern fragrance, but then erased that and tried 'Elysian', more openly suggesting a blessed state in connection with death.

Another addition was made to introduce the new allegory: 'list mortals if yor eares be true'. This turned a quadruple rhyme into a quintuple, so 'yellow, watchet, greene, & blew' was deleted, incidentally removing one of the more festive features of Iris. The new line is a clear indication that a religious allegory is to follow. As I have noted before, it is a version of the much-repeated admonition in the gospels and the Book of Revelation to attend to the word of God: 'He that hath ears, let him hear.'[20] It strikes that hortatory note that is sounding more insistently in *1637*.

1634 and 1637 – texts, epilogues, audiences

The transition to the Adonis myth was now made as follows:

> flowers of more mingled hew
> then her purfl'd scarfe can shew
> & drenches wth Elysian dew
> (list mortals if yor eares be true)
> beds of hyacinth & roses
> where young Adonis oft reposes
> waxing well of his deepe wound
> in slumber soft, & on the ground
> sadly sits th'Assyrian Queene

The Adonis myth offers a number of possible connections with the preceding material. As a lamentation for mortality, it meets the idea of the passing of youthful beauties, suiting the end of a masque. It carries with it the tradition of a summer festival, the Adonia. Adonis, like Hesperus, could be linked with the sun. There were also associations of Adonis with gardens, through the miniature 'gardens of Adonis' and of course also in the sixth canto of the third book of *The Faerie Queene*. And on a moral plane, it introduced the idea of lust or at least of the deluded love of mere earthly beauty.

A problem is to see which possibilities Milton wanted. The inclusion of hyacinth and roses *within* the new allegory immediately suggests that transience and mortality are still in view.[21] The Adonis myth was based on the death, apparent death, or disappearance of the youth. That Milton also wished his readers to remember the rites of the Adonia as practised in Old Testament times is proved by his use of 'sits' for the figure of Venus/Astarte, the Assyrian queen. The text to which commentators infallibly turned was Ezekiel 8.14: 'Then he brought me to the door of the gate of the Lord's house which was towards the north; and behold, there sat women weeping for Tammuz.' Tammuz was taken for Adonis, and commentators found means of linking mourning figures of Venus herself with the sitting posture of these idolatrous women.[22] It is evident, then, that the lament for the close of masque has been deepened and extended into a more general figure of lamenting mortal things and earthly love, and the lamentation has been tied in a new way to youth and seasonal festival. The idea of seasonal decay is also given in the word 'oft' and by the habitual recovery through a kind of sleep. These correspondences make it certain that Milton here associated Adonis with the sun, as was virtually standard in the interpretations of the myth in his time.

Thus far I think no completely new ideas have come in through the Adonis myth, but the direction of attention has changed. The idea of response was there before, and so was the sunset or westerly place. However, by introducing Adonis' cyclical recovery Milton was now talking more obviously in a general way about the whole frame of nature and the whole rhythm of the world in time. And it would seem that greater emphasis upon transience was being developed for a moral purpose: the invitation to the ears of the faithful to be aware of some religious truth seems to suggest that Venus, sitting mourning 'on the ground', is open to moral judgement. Her Old Testament record would indicate the same.

That phrase 'on the ground' is not so much indication of location (where *is* she, on that 'ground'?) as morally suggestive, an image. This Venus is limited to a love of earthly, mortal things, even perhaps to a lust for youthful beauties. The Spirit catches the habits of men: those who mourn like Venus about the passing of youthful beauties are caught in inevitable lament. The transience of the masque of youth has been transmuted into a general moral lesson.

The glance at the lamentations of the earthly Venus provides the transition to the next new section of epilogue, the allegory of Cupid and Psyche. With Cupid and Psyche we have almost moved out of the fallen world. Cupid is Love; he is called celestial Cupid, 'farre above in spangeld sheene', because he is not the earthly love which has just been on view. The spotlessness of Psyche is like the 'righteousness of saints' (Rev. 19.8). Psyche is the beloved of Christ but not yet married to the Lamb, until God wills the final events told in Revelation – 'till free consent the gods among'. When that marriage takes place, God has promised, Jove hath sworn, that he 'shall wipe away all tears from their eyes' and there shall be 'no more . . . sorrow, nor crying' (Rev. 21.4). Laments for transience are then ended. Hence the birth of Joy. Because 'there shall be no more death', the twin to Joy is Youth, a new eternal youth – 'I will make all things new' (v.5). There is no need to contaminate the allegory with overmuch Platonism or to think, as some have done, of Adonis as the soul of man in one state and

1634 and 1637 – texts, epilogues, audiences

Psyche as the soul in another.[23] This is myth brought to the service of the Bible.

Cupid and Psyche, like Venus and Adonis, still meditate an ending (though now to the fuller extent of history), and give new connections with youth and joy, such as suit the masque. But the poet is now more firmly asking the reader to remember that there is a love of things other than these earthly pleasures. And whereas the love of earthly beauty leads into a festival of mourning, the Adonia, the love of heavenly beauty, the struggle of the saints, beginning in long labour such as Psyche's, ends in a festival which is eternal in its youthfulness and joy. Just as he noted in disagreement with Tertullian,[24] so here Milton is practising in his poetry the drawing of the mind to eternal festivals. In the afterword to *1637* Milton made poetry justify itself yet more.

One could say that on a masque night a poet should draw all present together in an ideal celebration, in the happiness of the event. Even poets of independent voice, like Jonson, did not usually seek to divide their audiences in the closing gestures of a masque. The Attendant Spirit had made other superior, scathing remarks about men, in the body of the masque, but in the epilogue the line 'mortalls that would follow me' was always somewhat worrying, because it implied that some even amongst those present would not wish to. On the other hand this might be accommodated as a risk made to provoke momentary tension to be smoothed in the security of a smile: most men, and those present, *would* wish to follow. In 1637, however, the new line 'list mortalls if yoʳ eares be true' put in more open doubt the piety of men, readers included.

In this general shift of tone in the published text, towards sharper and more independent discrimination, there is the suggestion that the aristocratic and courtly world of the 1630s, its mores often exposed through its tell-tale festivities, is being more firmly placed. This need not be the hardening of the Miltonic puritan arteries. It may or may not mark a failing of the nerve about associating the causes of his own career with that of the present aristocracy. Certainly it derives from a changed sense of function. The poet of the published poem, more conscious of his role as shepherd to the nation, could play more archly in his own voice and begin to make dissociations of self from participation in

Milton's Aristocratic entertainments

the rites of a social milieu about which more and more questions arose. The leadership of the Protestant nation seemed to Milton to go more and more awry. The events of the intervening years would have contributed. Whatever the changes of attitude, the opportunities for their expression have always been there in a masque on these themes, for the *kōmos* was expressive of the quality of the leadership of nations. Did that lamentation of Venus, in *1637*, reflect back on masques and courts at large, as a kind of judgement on an effeminate people beguiling young nobility with merely earthly pleasures?

7 · THE SENSE OF VOCATION IN THE 1630s

REMARKABLE THOUGH IT IS, Milton's Ludlow masque resists simple judgement. If one takes the development of all the various versions into account, there are shifting patterns of intent, competing functions, and many local gains and losses in the text to consider. But there can be little doubt that the conviction of the young poet, his fundamental seriousness of intent on a public occasion, was one of the underlying factors to make it so remarkable, as also problematical for those organising the masque. The achievement and promise of the poetry have always been plain to see, the innovation in the masque form, and the grace of some of the social gesture; I am not sure that Milton's writing for the aristocracy has always been given its due importance for the seriousness of its reformist thought, partly because of interpretative difficulties with key parts of the text.

One way of placing its significance in his career is to realise the sense of vocation expressed in the two entertainments. Indeed, the sense of vocation is crucial to document for the whole formative period of the 1630s, through the major occasional poems, *Arcades*, *Comus* and *Lycidas*. *Lycidas* is obviously an impassioned statement about vocational ideals; vocation is more firmly announced in the aristocratic entertainments than is usually realised.

To think of aristocratic entertainments having genuinely reformist programmes is intriguing in itself. At first view there is a clash of values between the earnest young poet and his aristocratic audiences, if we take the familiar stereotypes of broad differences in attitude between landed nobility and the rising 'puritan' groups, to which Milton might be thought to belong. For example,

Milton's Aristocratic entertainments

this is an opening working definition of those differences in Lawrence Stone's *The Crisis of the Aristocracy*:

> The life of a nobleman was one of comfort and leisure, based on a country house, financed mainly from agricultural profits, and supported by a huge train of servants. The code by which these men lived differed radically from that which rose up to challenge and temporarily to overthrow it in the middle of the seventeenth century. The capitalist/Protestant ethic is one of self-improvement, independence, thrift, hard work, chastity and sobriety, competition, equality of opportunity, and the association of poverty with moral weakness: the aristocratic ethic is one of voluntary service to the State, generous hospitality, clear class distinctions, social stability, tolerant indifference to the sins of the flesh, inequality of opportunity based on accidence of inheritance, arrogant self-confidence, a paternalist and patronizing attitude towards economic dependants and inferiors, and an acceptance of the grinding poverty of the lower classes as part of the natural order of things. If in this age of confusion and turmoil many men – even Cromwell himself – seem to straddle the two ideals, this does nothing to minimize the essential contradiction between them.[1]

There would be some justice in saying that the scrivener's son was trying to cast this aristocratic family, and thence others, in a mould more reformed than that which already shaped them. Not that Bridgewater and his family had not demonstrated kinds of reformed purpose, more than most leading families in the nation. To ally with them, for Milton, may have felt to be seconding Spenser's partisan praise. What is more, the Countess of Derby had not a little of the active independence of the 'capitalist/Protestant ethic' mixed with her concern for station, and Bridgewater was a sober-minded, hard-working man, not at all one of 'arrogant self-confidence': though a staunch royalist, he was no showy cavalier and not at all tainted with tendencies of false religion. His family showed an interest in supporting idealistic Protestant divines and was prepared to hire a Huguenot governess, and the earl himself evidently took an active interest in the religious education of his children, even to the extent of warning against Arminian doctrines, if we are to believe the testimony of John Collinges.[2] To a large extent Milton found an apt audience in this aristocratic family. Yet, as the history of textual changes shows, only so much preaching, ultimately, could be compassed in the social ritual.

Any poet writing for patronage or occasional celebration who

The sense of vocation in the 1630s

was worth his salt – and most were not, in Milton's eyes, when they produced the 'trencher fury of a riming parasite'[3] – understood that the decorousness of the social gesture and the self-evident integrity of the poet were considerations which went hand in hand. Servility in compliment failed to protect the dignity both of patron and writer. By presenting *exempla* against which the honoured parties could view themselves, or the occasion, or place, or whatever, the poet could invite his audience to share with him in the contemplation of those images and to join him in the pleasures of an invention which had found some new but evidently apt way of associating exemplary fictions with the real situation. The target was shared contemplation. In the act of shared contemplation, when it was managed properly, everyone was to become an understander, within the terms of his social role. *Arcades* paid the best compliment by courteously assuming the countess' ability to feel the wit, grace and seriousness of the gesture offered to her.

Better poets had various ways of contriving shared understanding, from Sidney's confident challenging of his queen, at Wanstead, to Marvell's dexterous teasing of the Fairfax family. Ben Jonson was of course the most imitated practitioner for such occasions in the first half of the seventeenth century. Milton would have been aware of his example. As well as in the masques and entertainments themselves, we can see in *The Forest* Jonson's copybook of how to address the nobility in celebration whilst protecting and defining the integrity of the poet. Jonson was also notable for his many complaints about the lack of understanding in his audiences, a problem which other writers would have appreciated but which he may often have helped to bring on himself. In fact, Jonson's was a particularly complicated case. Defining his own role in relation to his elite audiences, he was often secure, in exemplary fashion, in the aristocratic code, but sometimes also precarious, sometimes as obtrusive as hidden in the gesture. There was, in fact, always risk in such celebratory poetry, risk to be lamented or enjoyed.

Servility and lack of intellectual centre were the least of Milton's dangers. Young as he was, when he wrote his aristocratic entertainments, he had a more thoroughgoing idealism than Jonson. His danger was that he would test too much, and serve too

Milton's Aristocratic entertainments

little. It was not for lack of attention to grace. He showed the same determination to refine the medium as he did, in various ways, in all the major poems. The masque ritual itself came under comprehensive review. The nobility of poetry itself was at stake, as well as that of the social elite. It was a question of the sense of vocation, in all concerned. Most crucially of all, Milton's prescriptions for the nobility drew as Jonson's could not on the dynamics of the politics of reformation. In Stone's terms, the two poets tended to celebrate the opposing ethics. Milton's entertainments must be placed in the context of reformation idealism.

Milton's solutions to the problems of address suggest that he had considered them carefully and that he was then sympathetic to the whole endeavour for a truly aristocratic art. That is to say, he wished to explore a poetry which used its occasions to display the moral and literary refinements of an ideal leading class. Many of the preoccupations of the entertainments, like godliness and chastity, which have sometimes been seen to express merely personal characteristics of the poet, are as much the personal emphases of his more public thought, nurturing a set of ideals against which the honoured nobility should also measure itself. The models of behaviour were openly presented; appropriate evil was equally on view. Sobriety and intellectuality were added to the fictions of masquing. Milton took risks, as occasional poets had to, on pain of dullness, and he touched a hint of teasing in his angelic spirit, but his were not the risks of frivolity.

Because of its greater range of concerns on its more public occasion, *Comus* took many more risks than *Arcades*. That a censor, rightly or wrongly, thought the decorum defective in parts, that Milton himself may have wished himself freer of the constraints of actual occasion, when he came to revise for *1637*, that he seems to have experienced difficulty in controlling the compromising functions of some sections of his text, all these things should not obscure the remarkable attempt to unify means and functions in the masque as a whole. As I have said, the braveness of this reformed and reforming masque helped to make it so special. With that in mind, therefore, I wish to sketch reformist programmes in the major occasional writing of the 1630s. There are patterns of responsibility to be traced, above all in the poet's sense of his own role, in *Arcades*, *Comus* and *Lycidas*.

The sense of vocation in the 1630s

These three occasional pieces can be seen to have public perspectives, though the perspectives were somewhat different in the different textual versions. Before he took to exhorting the nation in prose, in the 1640s, Milton's most publicly responsible texts were those for specific occasions for particular elite audiences, aristocratic and educational. These three pieces, printed with individual headings at the end of the 1645 collection, can be seen there especially as having national as well as local concerns in mind. One might define their national dimension in two ways.

First, the fact of publication made the poems responsible to a wider audience, in 1645. With *Lycidas*, designed for publication from the start, Milton patently spoke not only to the Cambridge community organising the memorial volume but also through that community to the country at large. When *Lycidas* was published for the second time, in *1645*, times had changed, address to the nation was now direct, and Milton adjusted the headnote of his text according to his sense of the new occasion. Both *Comus* and *Arcades*, as we have seen, underwent instructive adjustment in preparation for publication.

But secondly a national responsibility may be defined by the very nature of the elite groups originally addressed. In the entertainments and the Cambridge elegy he was identifying with key groups in the leadership of the country, and considering the responsibilities of the serious poet to these different groups to which he was allied. In *Lycidas* he reminded his audience of the best role of a godly educational community, training shepherds for Britain; in *Comus* good education and good governance in the nobility were his themes from the start. The poet's responsibility is to remind these groups of their responsibilities. To some extent the same was even true of *Arcades*, with its seeking out of a pious pattern of nobility and its definition of true Arcadianism, signalled in its title in *1645*. The vocation of the poet in these situations is to be the true shepherd, in whom the sense of personal mission and the sense of national destiny are inextricably combined.

Religious instruction stands at the back of all these pieces, as the first assumption of their programmes. In the masque the education of the nobility is shown to include, beyond all else, the foundation of religious doctrine. The primacy of religious truth, as given in the word of God, is advertised by the Spirit at the beginning, where he speaks of 'that golden key'. The picture of the prosperous nation is based on godliness. In *Lycidas* the analysis of the moral state of the nation has been taken one stage back. Whereas the occasion of *Comus* invited the exemplification of aristocratic mores, in which the prior necessity of an effective ministry was also prescribed, in *Lycidas* what is under examination is the quality of that spiritual leadership itself. In its public aspects, the poem centres on the educative role of ministers in a reforming state. Thus the two poems prepared for publication in 1637/8, at the time of rising puritan fury at the repressive punishments of Bastwick, Burton and Prynne, offered comment on the examples of leaders in both civil and ecclesiastical spheres.

Hardly surprisingly, images for the word of God are found at the heart of both poems. 'Truth' is to be 'bred up . . . between two grave & holy nurses the Doctrine, and Discipline of the Gospel'.[4] Doctrine and discipline in *Lycidas* turn on the speech of St Peter, in which the witty unity of the passage depends upon words and images associated with the word of God. One might dwell on different facets of this poem, replete with too much meaning perhaps, but as a polemically intended reformist poem it has the speech of Peter at its prophetic core.

Edward King was the son of a bishop, a favoured young man. In the monody Milton depicts him as a model pastor in the making, one of the rare examples to other ministers and to the flock. Cambridge is treated as a model educational institution. The loss of a good pastor becomes a national theme. Hence the questioning, as of tragic lamentation, of the workings of providence. How can it be that Britain, a nation of Protestant championship pitied of God in the past, a covenanted nation perhaps, should be less and less served by its priests? The anguished gesture of the poem is of course seen in the context of Milton's own sense of vocation, deepening his dismay at the proliferating errors of the Laudian church, misled by its leaders, betrayers of the cause of the reformation itself.

As he was to express it later, in *Of Reformation*, what had failed, or what was now failing in the 1630s, was not so much the doctrine as the discipline:

The sense of vocation in the 1630s

The pleasing pursuits of these thoughts [of reformation] hath oft-times led mee into a serious question and debatement with myselfe, how it should come to passe that *England* (having had this *grace* and *honour* from GOD to bee the first that should set up a Standard for the recovery of *lost Truth*, and blow the first *Evangelick Trumpet* to the *Nations*, holding up, as from a Hill, the new Lampe of *saving light* to all Christendome) should now be last, the most unsettl'd in the enjoyment of that *Peace*, whereof she taught the way to others; and although indeed our *Wicklefs* preaching, at which all the succeding *Reformers* more effectually lighted their *Tapers*, was to his Countrey men but a short blaze soon dampt and stifl'd by the *Pope*, and *Prelates* for sixe or seven Kings Reignes; yet me thinkes the *Precedencie* which GOD gave this *Iland*, to be the first *Restorer* of *buried Truth*, should have beene followed with more happy successe, and sooner attain'd Perfection; in which, as yet we are amoungst the last: for albeit in *purity* of *Doctrine* we agree with our Bretheren; yet in Discipline, which is the *execution* and *applying* of *Doctrine* home, and laying the *salve* to the very *Orifice* of the *wound*; yea tenting and searching to the *Core*, without which *Pulpit Preaching* is but shooting at Rovers; in this we are no better then a *Schisme*, from all the *Reformation*, and a sore scandall to them.

(Yale 1 525–526)

Political conflict had spread by the 1640s, but the blaming of prelacy, the preoccupation of the first prose tracts, is already on view in *Lycidas*. In the tracts Milton was to claim that the bishops had degenerated in the same way as they had with increasing riches in the reign of Constantine, and at other times, giving up the exemplary 'mean and plebian life' as of the shepherd lad of the masque to be 'lords of stately palaces' eating 'delicious fare'.[5] Corrupted prelates failed to teach by example, encouraged the hireling curates, collected benefices, and discouraged 'faithful shepherds of the flock', thus further ensuring the dearth of spiritual food for the people. In *Lycidas* this is scrambling at the shearer's feast and shoving away the worthy bidden guest.

Of all the biblical language muscularly compressed into the pastoral of Peter's speech – a passage, pivoting on the withering oxymoron 'blind mouthes', far overpowering Spenser's equivalent expressions in *The Shepheardes Calendar* – one influential source besides Ezekiel 34 is this passage from Isaiah, as it was to be again in a parallel passage in *An Apology*:

His watchmen are blind: they are all ignorant, they are all dumb dogs, they cannot bark; sleeping, lying down, loving to slumber. Yea, they are greedy dogs which can never have enough, and they are shepherds that cannot understand: they all look to their own way, every one for his gain, from his quarter.

Come ye, they say, I will fetch wine, and we will fill ourselves with strong drink; and tomorrow shall be as this day, and much more abundant.

The righteous man perisheth and no one layeth it to heart: and merciful men are taken away, none considering that the righteous is taken away from evil to come.   (56.10–57.1)

Something like *kōmos* infects the lords of the church, and the health of the nation is measured by the way it feels the death of the righteous man. Commentators saw this passage in Isaiah as having an occasion very like Milton's in *Lycidas*. Here is Diodati, expanding on the sense of impending evil and including both civil and ecclesiastical leaders:

Another prophetick speech, by which *Isaiah* declares, that the chief cause of the dispersion and destruction of the Lords flock by their enemies, was the disloyaltie and negligence of the shepherds, as well Ecclesiasticall as politick. . . . It is likely that in the time of these Prophecies God did take out of the world divers persons noted for piety and virtue, which was a presage of great approaching evils, from which God would exempt those his faithful servants.

Milton knew the uses of Isaiah. In this way he employed the occasion of the death of the good shepherd King, one of the righteous the poet himself would lay to heart, as he feared the evil to come.[6] Elegy shaded into lamentation and prophetic warning, each a kind of laying to heart.

In this astonishing, many-sided poem, a virtuoso performance, one of the most surprising features is the way in which it is touched by something like a populist rhetoric in public address. The new headnote 'And by occasion foretells the ruin of our corrupted Clergy then in their height' seems to have offered to say, in 1645, as some George Wither might have said, see what a true prophet I was: history has fulfilled the omen of the death. The prophetic element in *Lycidas* is expressed in various ways, as in the portentous opening, 'Yet once more', and in the historical perspective of the St Michael passage, seeing present corruption from within as equivalent to Catholic invasion from without in 1588.[7] Yet it seems to me that the central prophetic gesture, which has I think not been recognised, is embodied in the way the occasion of elegy has been made to conform with the omen of the

The sense of vocation in the 1630s

death of the righteous man. At least, that is what Milton himself chose to advertise, in retrospect.

Such an omen was read in the same period in the deaths of other noted pious men in times of impending trouble. In this way for example, Archbishop Ussher had offered to signify his own death, according to his first biographer, Nicholas Barnard. After giving dire warnings of the fatal effects of catholic infiltration, the work of Milton's grim wolves, Ussher had reputedly added

> therewith, how willing he was, if God so pleased, *to be taken away before that evill to come*, which he was confident of, unlesse there were some speedy Reformation[8]

Ussher's prophecies carried great weight with ardent reformers, right into the beginning of the eighteenth century.

The same formula was applied to the death of that exemplary righteous man, George Herbert. This is Herbert's first biographer, Barnaby Oley, in 1652, offering to mythologise Herbert's death (1633) with that of Nicolas Ferrar (1637) and Thomas Jackson (1640), in this case from a royalist point of view:

> I shall be bold to *instance* in *Three*, who died in peace; few considering (some did) that they were taken away from the evil to come, lest their eyes should see (what their spirits foresaw) what is come on us, on whom the days not of visitation only, but of vengeance, even the ends of the world are come.[9]

In *Lycidas* the warning is specifically about the quality of most of the shepherds. As well as the blindness, slothfulness, open-mouthed appetite, lack of understanding, and dumbness of corrupted shepherds, Peter points to the failure to minister the word to the flock and to the 'wind' of insubstantial instruction and mere ceremonies in the Laudian church.[10] In *Comus* the complaints, reinforced in *1637*, had been at the general unregeneracy of the people, figured in the ears that would not hear the word; in *Lycidas*, as in the episcopal tracts, Milton offers to show the cause of the lack of good ears.

The rising emotion of the 'blind mouths' passage depends upon the gradual revelation of the greatest betrayal of reformation, that is, the reversion into superstition.[11] The 'rank mists' of unsound teaching obscure with the darkness of superstitious ignorance. The effect of ritualism without sound instruction is to foster a contagion that will spread. Then the final lines express the actual incursion of Catholicism into the weakened nation: 'Besides what the grimme wolf with privy paw / Daily devoures apace, and little said'. As editors have noted, Milton mollified the contemptuous, accusatory 'nothing sed' in the manuscript to 'little said' for the Cambridge volume, but reverted to the sterner reading in *1645*. One thinks not only of the old bugbear of Jesuit infiltration but also of a new fashionability and freedom of Catholicism at court, connected with the queen and her new chapel, begun in the late 1620s and finished in 1635. Prominent families were showing their Catholic affiliations again.

The point about lack of discipline in Britain's reformed church is driven home by that prophetic denunciation 'nothing sed'. The twin 'nurses' of Truth, doctrine and discipline, support the whole of Peter's speech. It is true that many of the abuses of corrupted discipline which Milton was to expose in the tracts do not appear specifically in the poem: extortionate law-suits; the tyranny over consciences; the rash of excommunications; the use of power for the protection of self-interest. In *Lycidas* the sense of abuse is more generalised and the concern is more about the quality of the ministry itself, in tune with the subject of the poem. But in those two notorious images which frame the passage, the keys and the two-handed engine, Milton shows the discipline given to ministers and the power of the word of God, on which the discipline depends.

There is a witty continuity of reference through the passage. The image of the two-handed engine completes a sequence begun with the keys and continued throughout in the metaphor of the church as the fold of the flock. Peter, as founder of the church, as questioner about wise steward, and as writer about pastors – a 'pilot' to those who follow – is given a grim prophetic wit. The sequence elaborates the contrasting yet complementary offices of the keys. The one key is golden and is used for opening. This is the key which the Attendant Spirit in the masque says few try to possess. To hold this key as a pastor is to bear the responsibility of preaching the word 'that ope's the palace of aeternity'.[12] This is the glorious spiritual office for which King was trained and in which so many prelates and hirelings fail.

The other key is of iron and shuts off access to God's house, or to eternal life, because it denotes the controlling discipline of

The sense of vocation in the 1630s

ministers of the church as stewards of that house. The 'power of the keys' in this sense is an administration of discipline, 'a power not committed to Peter and his successors exclusively, or to any individual pastor specifically, but to the whole church collectively'. So Milton was to rationalise it in his *Christian Doctrine*.[13] We do not know his position on this difficult ecclesiastical question in 1637. His general sympathies we may guess at. This kind of discipline reformist observers saw increasingly corrupted in the Laudian church of the mid 1630s. There was popular outcry against 'halings and amercements in the use of her powerfull Keies', to use Milton's phrase from *The Reason of Church-Government*,[14] that is, in particular, the arbitrary and extortionate use of the ecclesiastical courts.

The keys which Peter carries in *Lycidas* therefore figure the whole responsibility of the pastors, the whole 'execution and applying of Doctrine home'. But because all such discipline is founded upon doctrine and derived, according to the Protestant ideal, from the word of God, the betrayal *can be thought of as of the word of God itself*. It is with nicely wrought justice that Peter warns the false pastors of the powers against hypocrites that are in the word of God itself, symbolised in that aspect in the two-edged sword waiting at the very door of the heavenly house so ill-stewarded: 'But that two-handed engine at the doore, / Stands ready to smite once, and smite no more.'

A chief text behind this is one I have already quoted in connection with Haemony, Hebrews 4.12–13. His word is, as it were, God's instrument in this case. Diodati, again, on this passage:

he attributes that to Gods word which belongeth to God himselfe, or to Christ working by it, and mortally wounding the unbeleevers and rebellious mans soul by a lively feeling of Gods curse, and against which there is no defence or remedy, seeing that it doth penetrate into all parts of man.

This is, in Milton's own phrase in *The Reason of Church-Government*, 'the quick and pearcing word' which enters to the dividing of the soul. As the shepherd of God's people, and on Milton's behalf, Peter warns the false pastors that they will feel soon 'the most effectual and penetrant power of Gods Word'.[15] He speaks sternly and shakes his 'mitred locks' at the leaders of the Church, just as

John had written to the 'angels' (pastors or bishops) of the seven churches in Revelation. Both warn of the power of the word, at the door.[16] That which the betrayers of reformation have abused will prove the 'engine' by which their falseness is exposed and punished.

The hardly radical change from 'nothing sed' to 'little said' may indicate censorship by the university, or the poet's tact in anticipation of censorship. If on the other hand it represents actual indecision in Milton's mind in November 1637, it could indicate that he saw the prelacy as on the very edge of perdition, as almost but not quite over the edge. Or at least he was willing to make that hortatory gesture. By 1645, when prophetic denunciation had become retrospective judgement, the sterner reading was quite clear: corruption in the clergy *was* then, in 1637, in its height.

The condemnation is the climax of the series of lamentations of the mourners, in which explanations for the death have been sought and blame apportioned. The effect of addressing all this to the dead Lycidas is curious: it seems to ask the reader to become partisan, to share in the fellowship of the dead righteous man. Provocatively, the poem assumes that the collegiate body of Cambridge will identify with the poet's reformist programme. As a political poem, *Lycidas* sought to galvanise its own audience. It challenged an Erasmian, reformist society in Cambridge and thence in the nation at large, for whose pleasure and respect a monody was written such as had never been written before in English, but an elite which was also to be disciplined to make better examples to ministers and people than the run of the prelates. And discipline could only be founded on doctrine, on the word.

The sense of vocation so feelingly evident in *Lycidas* may also be seen throughout the period of the 1630s covered by this book. I would argue this for the sake of the seriousness of the programmes of the entertainments. For convenience and for the sake of definition, my points are ranged against those of John Spencer Hill in *John Milton: poet, priest and prophet*.[17]

With regard to the offices of priesthood and poetry, it has often been assumed that the second was confirmed when the first was relinquished. The date of Milton's being 'church-outed' by the

The sense of vocation in the 1630s

prelates has often though not uniformly been put back to around the early 1630s. Hill's arguments against this traditional view seem to me well taken: it was not simply a question of being either priest or poet, rather that both possibilities were constantly in his mind, in the 1630s, and that these twin vocations could co-exist, though perhaps with more difficulties about priority than Hill is willing to allow. At any rate, hard evidence is lacking for an intention to abandon the priesthood before 1637. Nevertheless, one must have reservations about Hill's argument for assuming a continuing determination to enter the ministry beyond that year.

For the early and mid 1630s there seems less difficulty in thinking in terms of the two possible vocations, though even then the question of priorities arose. The intention to become a poet, that is, a poet in English for the nation in the line of Spenser, was announced with something of a youthful fanfare in *At A Vacation Exercise*, back in 1628. It was repeated thereafter. In Milton's famous later declaration, poetry was 'of power beside the office of a pulpit, to imbreed and cherish in a great people the seeds of vertue, and publick civility'.[18] The intention to become a priest had been assumed at least since entry into Cambridge in 1625. The vast majority of Milton's contemporaries at Cambridge took orders. As Hill and others have pointed out, under the terms of Article 34 Milton became of eligible age for ordination on 9 December 1632, his twenty-fourth birthday. It would seem that there was a neatness to the original plan. The MA graduation in the summer of 1632 came shortly, that is, some five months, before the statutory eligibility for orders. Hill and Parker are probably right in arguing that the 'Letter to a Friend' and its enclosed sonnet 'How soone hath Time' refer to his eligibility for the priesthood. In this letter Milton is explaining not his abandonment of the priestly calling but rather what seemed, to an earnest adviser, perhaps in 1633, like an alarming sign of procrastination after his twenty-fourth birthday. At the time of writing *Arcades* he was presumably still thought to be destined for orders which he would take when he felt ready.

Milton's statement that he was 'church-outed by the Prelats' because of their tyranny over consciences, later rationalisation though it is, must indicate that developments in church administration under Laud had a lot to do with his decision to abandon the priesthood. When it came, the abandonment was a step taken with the greatest bitterness. Already, back in 1632, in 'How soone hath Time', Milton had shown ambivalent feelings towards those readier spirits, his contemporaries, who had already found benefices and arranged to take orders. Although his influence was felt earlier (for Milton's friend Gil, back in 1630), Laud's reign at Canterbury began in 1633. Puritan opposition to his measures of conformity grew steadily year by year. By 1637 outcry was very loud. By 1639 the nation had been drawn into war with Scots Presbyterians. It was cruelly ironic that Milton's further, scrupulous period of self-cultivation after he had finished at Cambridge in 1632 took him into an agonising period of alarm for those, like him, attuned to reformation idealism of the old kind.

Crisis of conscience gives a special edge to *Lycidas* in 1637. The situation to be inferred from that poem has its own ironies about the sense of vocation. In the Trinity manuscript the text of *Lycidas* follows directly upon the Ludlow masque.

The masque was written in 1634; and during 1635, 1636, and the first ten months of 1637 Milton *wrote no more poetry*.

Parker, whose words these are (p. 126), links the apparent cessation in composition to a continuing tension between Milton and his father. Milton senior, like the Friend to whom Milton replied in the letter, may have expected his son's preparations to be more visibly leading towards ordination. That is to say, though poetry and priesthood might co-exist, there was a danger that poetry might interfere with the priority of the priestly calling. Some such debate may be behind Milton's cleverly persuasive *Ad Patrem*. We shall probably never know the precise nature of the debate between Milton and his father about his vocation, but if Parker is right to suggest that an apparent cessation in major composition between 1634 and 1637 has something to do with renewed determination to be seen to be moving towards a career in the church, then what a paradox there was at the heart of the heart-felt *Lycidas*: Milton spoke out publicly at last about the state of the priesthood for which he had been so long designed, but only by writing a substantial poem did he do so.

If *Lycidas* actually defines the two vocations of poet and priest,

The sense of vocation in the 1630s

the idea of the shepherd spanning both, as it spanned also his career and that of King, then the two aristocratic entertainments surely advertise those two vocations also. And the vocations are advertised with conviction, on the assumption that they should be. Milton was not one to hide his callings.

The vocational signature is clear in the invention of the roles of the two daemonic presenters. Genius linked song with nightly pieties. Like the Attendant Spirit, he is servant to place and servant to God. The Ludlow masque encompasses both vocations in the most determined way. At two crucial moments in the action 'Thyrsis' calls upon the authority of Milton's two offices for the truth. First, he recalls the office of a true pastor who preaches the word home: the complex of associations around the shepherd lad unites poetry and song with the ministry, seeming to assume the prospect of their happy co-existence. Then he calls upon the true poet, Meliboeus old, the source of the story of Sabrina and the means of furnishing a persuasive vision of an ideally governed land. The masque thus gives what one can only call programmatic expression to the ideals of these vocations. (One might note, also, that had the vocational expression of the masque been looked for, two notoriously difficult sections of Milton's text, around Haemony and Sabrina, would have been a good deal easier to understand.) Milton's text for Ludlow displayed the possibility of a society in which these vocational responsibilities could function to glorious effect. There is plenty of realism about pinfold earth in Milton's masque, but the display of these vocations embodies a kind of heroic hope. In retrospect the heroic Protestant visions seem a poignant thing: when again, in the poetry at least, would that hope of the reformed nation be possible?

Hill notes in general of the earlier verse that

> a longing for the 'prophetic strain' . . . and the carefully nurtured belief in the immortality of fame to be achieved through his poetic priesthood are the convictions of a largely unfocussed idealism. (p. 63)

One cannot call Milton's sense of vocation through the middle 1630s and in *Comus* as unfocussed as that. A very considerable prejudice is working at the expense of the seriousness of the entertainments. To invoke the longing for the prophetic strain is of course to recollect *Il Penseroso* rather than the more public occasional poems. An instructor to the nation can only instruct in his more public works.

Hill also underplays the anguish of *Lycidas*. The evidence of this poem suggests that 1637 was a crucially difficult year for Milton with regard to the ministry, yet Hill is keen to keep open the possibility of a church career even after the return from Italy in 1639, when the Bishops' Wars were disturbing the nation, until the Laudian canons of 1640 finally closed the door to liberty of conscience in the priesthood. In fact, he is determined not to put the abandonment of the priesthood too early, as had often been done before. The Laudian canons may well have put the seal on Milton's decision, but one can also speculate about the meaning of earlier decisions, as for example to go on an Italian tour. That was not an obvious preparation for orders. The decision to go to Italy was probably taken in late 1637 or early 1638, during the period I have dwelt on in the last chapter.

Perhaps one may give further focus to the writings and publications of 1637 and 1638 by taking Hill's third 'vocation', that of the authorial office of prophet to the nation, the role which Milton developed in the years of writing polemical prose. Here again there is danger of underestimating the import of the writing of the 1630s. Hill has argued that Milton's sense of himself as prophet to the nation did not come all at once but 'evolved gradually over a considerable period of time' (p. 77). There is obvious sense to this thesis, which serves to highlight Milton's finally isolated position at the Restoration. In fact, Hill wishes to point chiefly to two periods, both after the early years.[19] Yet it might also be said that the evolution had begun much earlier, that Milton showed signs of speaking prophetically as soon as he wrote publicly for the nation or served important groups in the nation, in the 1630s. It is no accident that the masque uses figures of hearing, like Jeremiah, to point to the general deafness of the people and to plead for the special hearing of a spiritual elite. The use of the prophetic voice in *Lycidas* was explicit, politically clear, exploiting the reformers' mythology.

The scope for such prophetic utterance was to do with the developing public functions of the substantial works of the 1630s. The more publicly Milton could conceive of the function of a text,

The sense of vocation in the 1630s

the more stringent the instructing voice seemed to be, and the more likely it was, as these years went by, to touch moments of something like prophetic exhortation. As we have seen, when he broke his silence in 1637 and decided not only to write *Lycidas* for Cambridge but also to publish the masque text, as poem to the nation, he not only restored a passage in the Haemony allegory which sounded an ardent reformist note about the clergy but also added other passages which came close to the prophetic in tone. The Lady was now cast as lecturer to the nation, as she pressed the necessity of chastity against assumptions of 'cavalier' indifference. The Spirit, more hieratic than ever, challenged his affluent audience in the new epilogue to separate itself from all worldliness. What we have, within the timespan of the history of the *Comus* text up to *1637*, is the story of the attempt to establish an independent, instructing voice, out of concern for the nation, and the final approaching in *1637* of something like the prophetic mode.[20]

Doctrine and discipline had been everything to Milton in the long preparations for his life tasks, until providence, or history, began to dictate to him and to limit and modify his options. The process of adjustment was to be repeated many times through his life. It may be as important to see the writing of the aristocratic entertainments as embodying Milton's vocations and political idealism, as it is to see the publications of 1637/8 as marking the beginning of some narrowing or changing of vocations and some isolation from the establishment. One must acknowledge the synthesis he tried to achieve in these entertainments when he first wrote them. He was seeking to define the role of the ruling class within the reformed state. Always he thought in terms of the influence of the elite, with the magistrates, with the pastors, with the scholarly community, with the educated young of the governing class, and so on. At Harefield the young poet presented himself to the family as one who would instruct in verse as if he held the office of the golden keys. I can only assume that when he chose the *kōmos* as the test to young nobility at Ludlow, gave full play to the evil of 'cavalier' evasions and temptations, showed the primacy of religion, glimpsed the happiness of the pious nation, and pleaded for the understanding of a spiritual elite, he was writing in hope for the cause of reformation in Britain, not underestimating the difficulties of establishing a true elite amongst nobility and gentry, but imagining that such an elite might exist. He was following his calling by fighting the battle where he thought it might be fought, amongst the leaders of the people.

Providence, with its unsearchable dispose, was to open a much wider gulf between the poet and his aristocratic audience than even he in his most pessimistic moments might have thought possible in the 1630s. Some fifteen years after the performance, the Elder Brother, himself embittered by political developments and crippling burdens of insolvency, endorsed one of Milton's books which came into the Bridgewater library, the *Defensio: Liber igni, Author furcâ, dignissimi* – 'the book deserves the flames, the author the gallows'.[21] We tend to think of Milton's relationship with aristocracy through hindsight, knowing the struggles of Civil War. There is the later castigation of 'wanton mask', badge of degenerate courts in *Paradise Lost*, a pernicious ritual rejected as sharply as false priests or false poets. Hindsight should not blur the relationship in the mid 1630s. It was not simply that the naively idealistic scrivener's son had flirted with nobility, sought their company, then found them wanting. The moral and political stringencies in Milton's attitudes are consistent throughout his life. He had not played with the nobility. He had asked them to share in the contemplation of their own roles, defined in his zealous way. Out of a sense of his vocations, in service to his Protestant country, he had held up the mirror to true nobility and responsibility in the governors of the people. In that sense, as I have said, for them and for the nation, he wrote truly aristocratic entertainments.

APPENDIX

THE AUTHENTICITY OF THE BRIDGEWATER MANUSCRIPT AND THE IDEA OF THE CENSOR

THE BRIDGEWATER MANUSCRIPT is a presentation copy of the masque, written out in an unknown copyist's hand for the earl and his family to keep as a memento of the occasion. In all probability it records what was actually performed on 29 September 1634. Similar presentation copies exist of other masques and entertainments.

The Trinity manuscript and the printed text of 1637, both carefully revised by Milton himself, give us very extensive evidence of his intentions, probably an unrivalled amount of evidence, for any masque. Judged against these, how authentic is the Bridgewater text? By the term authentic I mean of course to ask whether Milton himself initiated or had anything much to do with cuts and transpositions of material in the Bridgewater text. I have taken a line all through this book, that he had little or no part in these alterations. However, the matter has been the subject of some debate, and I need to make my position clear, especially in relation to what Diekhoff and Sprott have written in their careful consideration of the *Comus* texts.[1]

Let me focus on the relationship between the Bridgewater text and Milton's revisions for *1637*, seeing in the one case what changes those organising the actual performance made to Milton's intended text (judging against the state of Trinity in 1634) and in the other how the poet himself affirmed or reaffirmed his intentions, as he prepared for print. The general position has been set out by Sprott in his invaluable study of the texts. With these general conclusions concerning the sequence of versions I have no quarrel:

Appendix

In 1637 the passages that had been shifted or suppressed for BMS have been restored. The material of the prologue of BMS has been returned to the epilogue, the speeches that had been redistributed among the brothers are given back to the Spirit, and the cut passages have reappeared; the whole text has undergone light revision, a few lines have been omitted, and new passages have been interpolated. Obviously the compositor could not have worked from BMS, even if such a presentation manuscript had been made available to a printer, but has set type from a copy that was a revision of TMS.

(p. 26)

But there is something like a hidden assumption here. Because the sequence of events regarding the extant copies is in general clear – the revisions for *1637* come after the creation of the Bridgewater manuscript text, which in turn comes after the early states of the Trinity manuscript – it is tempting (and one does it constantly) to think of Milton working according to this temporal sequence, always having the 'latest' state of the text before him as he revised. That is to say, the idea of *restoring* and *returning* things, in the sentences above, has tacitly assumed or implied that Milton himself was working from the 'latest' version of the text. The admitted doubt about whether the compositor would have had such a presentation copy in his possession does not quite cover the issue. The more important question is whether Milton would ever have wanted to put something like the Bridgewater text into the hands of the printer. Would he have regarded such a text as authentic, as satisfying his intentions, three years after the event? Would he ever have wished to consult the Bridgewater text (or the like) for his revisions in 1637?

It would be absurd to be categorical about an issue that is bound to remain conjectural, but it seems to me more plausible to assume that Milton initiated none of the changes recorded in the Bridgewater text than it is to assume that he worked in consort with Lawes or some others to produce those changes. I reach my conclusion from what seem to me weighty considerations of Milton's design and intention, and of the meaning of certain passages, set against the equivocal and inconclusive evidence of textual criticism alone. Of course I am not saying that the poet did not know of what happened at Ludlow – in the lack of firm information, I assume that he did, presumably after the event –

Authenticity of the Bridgewater manuscript

but I would suggest that it is safer to say that he chose not to recognise that version of the text.

My evidence here concerns only major cuts and changes in the Bridgewater text, most of which I have mentioned already in the course of the book.

1. Much of the Lady's opening soliloquy. These lines, written in rather Shakespearian dramatic style, display the Lady's virtuous mind, but include much that is explicitly religious and make her name chastity and document her fears at the outset. It is sometimes argued that this very substantial cut was made in the interests of shortening Lady Alice's considerable part. That may be. However, such a suggestion does not explain why one passage rather than another was chosen to be cut, and if we view this cut in the light of others made in Bridgewater, not all in the Lady's part, we might conclude that the 'censor' was encouraged to leave out something that was on the one hand psychologically realistic, the Lady's fears, which could seem to detract from her role as moral exemplar; and on the other to steer clear of passages that were too explicit about the moral and religious case. I have already argued that Milton designed an exemplary psychological progression in this speech, showing how the Lady's spirits were enlivened so as to be able to sing her plaintive song, and this psychological progression was ruined by the Bridgewater cuts. The 'censor' damaged the precious realism of the part, which the poet has so carefully forged in order to combine an exemplary role with a sense of religious truth.

2. The excised lines about the ignorant swain in the allegory of Haemony as word of God. I have already suggested that this cut ruined the religious allegory for the sake of eliminating possible offence to the Welsh region or to the whole church in Britain, failing to form the nation with its ministry.

3. A passage of four lines[2] in which the Lady talks to Comus of his trying to ensnare her 'credulous innocence' with 'likerish baits fit to ensnare a brute', that is, his inebriating cup. Probably this was too stark in its moral realism for the 'censor': it admitted that the Lady was vulnerable and credulous to begin with, and it brought the luxury of the feast-temptation into focus. But the speech has a considerable importance in Milton's presentation of

Appendix

the role of the Lady, whose first encounter with Comus was marked by her helplessness in the face of devilish disguise, and whose second conversation with him is to be marked by her determination not to be deceived again by false appearances. To take the passage away is to remove one of the clearest pieces of evidence about the difference in her state of mind in the two scenes with the enchanter.

4. Comus' summary argument against virginity, which makes explicit the connections between such a line of thought and the habits of courtly 'feasts, and high solemnities'. Presumably the passage was thought too disturbing, too exposing in its moral implications, for the festive moment, but it was of course absolutely central to the expositions in the masque of the *kōmos*.

5. A line about Sabrina's healing of the local herds with her 'precious viold liquors'. This was omitted in Bridgewater together with the previous line, which is about diseases in the cattle, their 'strange pinches'. I take it that the scrupulous censoring hand, primed perhaps by the previous incidence of a case of discourtesy to Wales, feared the implication that the cattle around Ludlow parts were in constant need of veterinary care. But the idea of healing with the precious dew was important in the presentation of Sabrina as agent of God's providence.

6. The passive silence of all the children during the Sabrina section. Milton gave the children no part in the summoning of Sabrina, in the petition to her, or in thanking her; and all the closing verses were for Henry Lawes. Of course they danced, in triumph, but dramatically this section is for the showing of Jove's guardian spirit and for revelations about the region, with its own kind of providential history and blessings. In the Bridgewater text the boys were given some of the adjuring verses, and Lord Brackley, not Henry Lawes, invited his sister to rise from the chair. The conflict is between a passivity symbolically appropriate and the possible indignity of having the President's sons mere spectators. Milton printed his original intentions in 1637.

These examples are selective; I do not wish to make a detailed examination of other changes or to try another examination of the evidence of textual transmission, ably described by Sprott. I think that these are enough pieces of evidence to indicate some general

Authenticity of the Bridgewater manuscript

conclusions about the authenticity of the Bridgewater text. Diekhoff's comment, that in Bridgewater 'no compliment disappeared',[3] is accurate enough, but leaves the other half of the story untold: what disappeared in Bridgewater were passages construed by some careful censor as *uncomplimentary* or indecorous. The criteria would seem to be a precise sense of tact with regard to occasion, especially concerning the President's family, and the conventional restraints upon religious language in such theatricals. The Bridgewater manuscript is a fascinating document, from a social point of view. It shows us how the poet's festive yet high-minded design, already carefully balanced between proper moral definition and the needs of occasion, came up against the further compromises of the actual social function, as judged, surely, by eyes other than his own. Most commentators have speculated that Lawes and Milton collaborated in the preparation of the masque, and there may well be much truth in that. Consultations of some kind must have gone back through various stages of the text prior to performance to the original briefing that preceded the putting of pen to paper. That is reasonable speculation. I am much less convinced that Milton himself played much part, if any at all, in the alterations embodied specifically in the Bridgewater text. I would conjecture, as I have said, that this text was developed after the masque had left Milton's hands and gone to Wales. In each case listed above manifest damage was done to the design. Seeing the problem of authenticity from the point of view of an interpretative rather than a textual critic, I would want to reverse the resolution of these doubts in Sprott's account. After weighing the evidence finely, he concludes that although 'few, if any [of the variants in Bridgewater] have authority for Milton's text', the cuts 'were probably excluded by Milton'. Neither cuts nor variants should, I think, be assumed to carry the weight of Milton's decision.

One cannot mention the idea of censorship or the fact that some of the cuts in the Bridgewater text concerned the Lady's speaking explicitly about her sexual fears, without recalling the impact of the Castlehaven scandal of 1631. On the whole, I want to play down the specific influence of the scandal on the *Comus* text. Yet the matter is complicated and largely in the realms of speculation,

Appendix

and since there is no doubt that Milton would have known of the affair or that the President and his family wanted to forget it, it might be worth thinking the issue through at this point.

Articles that have connected the Castlehaven trial directly with *Comus* have assumed that it had a formative influence on the choice of theme for the masque, whoever exactly had the responsibility for that choice. I think that it is rather unlikely to have been a chief determining factor in the choice of device for Ludlow. If one is concerned, as an inventor of a masque, to be decorous, and one knows, because decorousness would require one to find out, that the earl had kept a rather discreet distance from the public manifestations of the affair, then one does not frame an action in a gratulatory masque so as to remind him of all he was trying to forget. What is more, the terms of the moral debate in the masque are not simply about chastity and sexual perversion, but rather are more generally about the whole process of the degradation to bestial riot, seen in the context of aristocratic festivity, and also about providential aids, some of which adhere to the Welsh occasion. Didacticism, or exemplary demonstration, in masques and other occasional writings, normally takes the form of generalities. Once the general yet occasional reference to the *kōmos* was decided on, the paths to unchastity were bound to be shown, if the analysis was to have its proper moral realism.

That moral realism is the heart of the matter and the most important focus of critical speculation. Thinking of the realism of *Comus* in relation to the other writings of Milton, one would say that there is nothing uncharacteristic about it: moral realism was the pillar of all his major work. The question is whether the poet's acute moral realism in general was not too strong for a 'censor', whose function was to screen for tact and decorum. We shall never know how much the Castlehaven affair featured in Milton's mind with other instances from literature and life that went towards a recognition of the pernicious power of the *kōmos* amongst sons of Belial. Young and idealistic though he was, he would not have been fool enough to want to be thought to be writing *about* the scandal, for this family, at this time, but it may be that the inclusive realism of the dangers of *kōmos* struck the censor as inadvertently foolish, for this occasion.

In this matter, there are two sets of evidence to discuss: the

Authenticity of the Bridgewater manuscript

deletions in the Bridgewater text (connection with Castlehaven by Breasted), and the additions for *1637* (brought into discussion by Rosemary Mundhenk). With regard to the additions for *1637*, I have already tried to argue that they should be seen as a whole, as symptoms of a decision to exploit the new function of the text as 'poem' from author to reader. A greater urgency was possible in that situation, now free from some of the constraints of original occasion, but the 'new' dimension is not likely to be determined by specific persons and places any more. The tendency is precisely opposite, towards greater generality in the definition. Whether memories of the Castlehaven trials contributed to Milton's mental picture of aristocratic effeminacy, of slackening of the people, and (since Castlehaven was accused as papist) of the ravages of the 'privy wolf', is a matter nice to speculate about but impossible to determine.

With regard to the cuts in the Bridgewater text, it must be admitted that the omission of the Lady's fears in her soliloquy looks like tact in a sexual context. Similarly with the 'likerish baits' passage, or Comus' invitation to 'daintie lims' or his passage against virginity. But, as we have seen, the 'censor' was concerned with a variety of things, including his sense of proper dignity for the boys and for Wales, and perhaps the church. There may have been as much 'offence' in the suggestion of the extreme vulnerability of the Lady as in the sexual nature of the challenge. Some pretty explicit sexual stuff was left elsewhere in the masque, though perhaps not so much coming from her mouth. The virginity speech of Comus may have been too strong partly because of its blatant association of sexual depravity with masques, an association that was liable to recall the party of Prynne. Also, Milton's text was written in a language more determined by moral and religious seriousness than any normal masque or entertainment, so that many aspects of his expression were liable to find themselves modified, in various areas of reference, according to the sense of customary propriety in these things. In other words, a censor's sensitivity to passages of sexual explicitness, especially perhaps those put into the mouth of the Lady, may have been sharpened by a memory of the Castlehaven affair, but this kind of censorship was likely to arise in any case out of Milton's habitual moral realism and is only a part of a more

Appendix

various review of the text in Bridgewater, a review which tried generally to protect the dignity of the aristocratic parties. All in all, we need to sense a complex set of relevances and constraints, in connection with occasion, and to see the *whole* relationship between Milton's apparent intentions and what was actually played at Ludlow, without attributing overmuch to the influence of Castlehaven alone.

Throughout my account, I have deliberately kept to the non-committal formula of the 'censor' rather than try to name the party or parties. Of course Henry Lawes is likely to have been heavily involved. Some of the changes in Bridgewater are production changes and to do with the music. Yet it does not seem to me safe to take it for granted that the censor was simply Henry Lawes. There is not enough evidence to know. Lawes worked out of a brief as royal musician who was also 'Thyrsis', servant to the family. It may well be, even if he had something like overall control of preparations for 29 September, that he consulted members of the family or household, at all stages, in more delicate matters. If he had sole responsibility for the masque, he must have occupied a place of considerable trust in the earl's house.

A NOTE ON THE GOLDEN GROVE PORTRAIT

The charming three-quarter-length portrait of a girl standing against a pastoral background, with a church and other buildings seen at a distance (reproduced in Plate 14), brings with it a series of legends connecting it with Milton's masque. Sadly, they must be dispelled. The painting was in the collection of the Vaughan family of Golden Grove, Carmarthenshire. Traditionally the subject was identified as Lady Alice Egerton, the Lady of the masque, who many years later married Richard Vaughan, second Earl of Carbery, who himself became President of Wales at the Restoration. The assumption was that Alice had taken the portrait of herself as a girl with her to her married home, where it had remained until the house was given up as a private residence earlier this century. It has been inherited with the Vaughan estate by the Earl of Cawdor and is now at Cawdor Castle, Nairn.

Nineteenth-century legend embroidered the literary possiblilities. It claimed that the Lady in the portrait was dressed for Milton's masque, and that the background was a romanticised Staywood Forest, with Ludlow Castle and Church in the distance. This idea may itself have been encouraged by an earlier legend about Milton's masque, initiated by the antiquary William Oldys in the eighteenth century, that the Egerton children had actually been lost in a wood on their way to Ludlow in 1634. As late as 1948, when the portrait was exhibited with other portraits in an exhibition made up from collections in Welsh houses, the legendary identification with Lady Alice was repeated. Tradition also attributed the painting to Gerard Soest.

Despite the tempting-seeming appropriateness of the portrait to the masque, it cannot be a picture of Lady Alice in 1634. To begin with, the girl in the painting is rather too young for the fifteen-year-old Alice. Then also, the style of the painting and the

Note on the Golden Grove portrait

dress of the subject suggest a date later, not earlier, than 1634. I quote Sir Oliver Millar, in a private letter: 'On stylistic grounds I doubt if it could be dated earlier than c.1650. The costume may lead to the same conclusion.' What is more, Sir Oliver is sure that the painter is Lely: 'The drawing of the draperies and the placing of the figure seem inescapably Lely's.'

The fact is that we have no idea of the identity of the girl, whose facial type however makes identification with the Egertons understandable enough, as comparison with some of the other portraits shows.

NOTES

Introduction

1 George Wither, *The Hymnes and Songs of the Church ... Translated and Composed by G. W.* (London, 1623), p. 182.
2 'My strength is made perfect in weakness.' Both entries, Columbia XVIII 271.
3 *The Poems and Masques of Aurelian Townshend*, ed. Cedric C. Brown (Reading: The Whiteknights Press, 1983), p. 100.
4 The Castlehaven scandal is referred to below, pp. 20–3, 74, 175–8; the issue of the Evans case is raised by Leah S. Marcus, 'The Milieu of Milton's *Comus*: Judicial Reform at Ludlow and the Problem of Sexual Assault', *Criticism*, XXV (1983), 293–327.
5 Richard Helgerson, *Self-Crowned Laureates: Spenser, Jonson, Milton and the Literary System* (Berkeley, Los Angeles and London: University of California Press, 1982), p. 272. Although my approach is largely through Milton's sense of vocation and the address to occasion in individual texts, rather than by the 'laureate' role, I find myself in a good deal of agreement with Helgerson about Milton's self-presentation.
6 The kind of issue reviewed by Philip Edwards in his essay on Ben Jonson in *Threshold of a Nation* (Cambridge University Press, 1979), pp. 131–173, where some earlier speculation is summarised and assessed. The pursuit is somewhat similar to that of Leah S. Marcus in a series of articles: 'Present Occasions and the Staging of Jonson's Masques', *ELH*, XLV (1978), 201–205; 'The Occasion of Ben Jonson's *Pleasure Reconciled to Virtue*', *SEL*, XIX (1979), 271–293; 'Masquing Occasions and Masque Structure', *Research Opportunities in Renaissance Drama* (*RORD*), XXIV (1981), 7–16.
7 Kenelm Digby, *Observations of the 22. Stanza in the 9th Canto of the 2d Book of Spencer's Faery Queene* (1643).

1 · Contexts and occasions

1 The clients of Milton senior would of course provide another possible source of introduction. The most obvious contact would seem to be Sir

Notes to page 13

Francis Leigh, Lord Dunsmore, later Earl of Chichester, nephew to the Earl of Bridgewater and godson of the Dowager Countess of Derby. Dunsmore had been a client of Milton senior, borrowing money, since 1624 (W. R. Parker, *Milton: A Biography*, Clarendon Press, 1968, I, 688, 697, 735, 759) and was a visitor to Harefield, as at the farewell visit of Bridgewater at the end of June 1634 (Harefield accounts, in Huntington Library, Hastings papers, w/e 3 July 1634).

2 Apart from Lawes' dedication of the *1637* text of the Ludlow masque, in which he acknowledges 'many favours', see especially his dedication of the first book of his *Ayres and Dialogues* (1653) to Lady Alice, now Countess of Carbery, and Lady Mary, now Lady Herbert of Cherbury: 'most of them being Composed when I was employed by Your ever Honour'd Parents to attend Your Ladishipp's Education in Musick ... my Gratitude ... to both Your Ladiships; and to manifest that Honour I bear to the Memory of Your deceased Parents, whose Favors it is impossible should ever be forgotten ...' The fullest speculations on Lawes' life are to be found in Willa McClung Evans, *Henry Lawes: Musician and Friend of Poets* (New York and London, 1941).

3 Murray Lefkowitz, *William Lawes* (London, 1960), pp. 187–204; John P. Cutts, 'British Museum Additional MS. 31432: William Lawes' Writing for the Theatre and the Court', *Library*, VII (1952), 225–232; Margaret C. Crum, 'Notes on the Texts of William Lawes' Songs in B.M. MS. ADD. 31432', *Library*, X (1955), 122–127.

4 Mr David Lloyd, of the Ludlow Historical Research Group, passes on to me the intriguing information that in the Ship Money assessments for 1635, in the Shropshire Record Office, for Castle ward, Ludlow, there is reference to 'William Law and Thomas Ludnam, musicians'. If 'Law' is 'Lawes', this would be the first connection of any kind to appear to link him with Ludlow, most of his known activities rather suggesting London. Even if 'Law' is not 'Lawes', the entry serves as an indication that there would have been some resources in music available in Ludlow itself for the masque night.

5 See below, pp. 22, 25.

6 Harefield accounts, w/e 11 Dec. 1634, stables account: 'Bate by Mr Lawes horse'; w/e 25 Dec. 1634, extraordinary expenses: 'To Hussie for fetching Mr Lawes horse & his brothers from Lond.'. There was resident music at Harefield as well. See accounts, w/e 26 March 1635: 'To Mr Alhoun & Mr Cotton to find there violls wth till Michaelmas next'. (Also w/e 20 Nov. 1634) W/e 11 Dec. 1634: 'To Mr Walran for tewning a harpsicall & my la: virginalls'. W/e 26 Mar. 1635: 'To Mr Vaux for a kaye for the harpsicall'. W/e 7 Aug. 1634: 'To Mr Vaux for harpsicall strings'.

7 D. Masson (*The Life of John Milton*, Cambridge and London, 1859) put the necessary note of caution, whilst speculating delightfully (and on the whole with very full information) on the possibilities: 'We are apt to forget that every life has many minute ramifications in addition to the few which biography can trace' (I, 563).

Notes to pages 13–16

8 Lawes' dedication to the *1637* masque text; Milton's sonnet to Henry for the Lawes brothers' *Choice Psalms* (1648); Lawes' letter to Milton in 1638, helping him to get permission to go abroad (Columbia XII 325–326).
9 See below, p. 45.
10 British Library Add. Ms. 53723.
11 Assuming that the contact was made with Harefield first. In past and present a good many members of the family had taken their religion seriously and had played their part in pious patronage. Something of Bridgewater's attitude to religion is revealed in his letter to his son-in-law William Courteen (quoted, p. 33), where he makes his dutiful observance plain but does not wish to seem overpious. John Collinges' *Par Nobile: Two Treatises* (1669), gives puritan approval to two of the Egerton daughters, Frances (wife of Sir John Hobart) and Katherine (wife of William Courteen), claiming that one of the Egerton daughters had had qualms about masquing on Sundays. Various branches of the family had supported good reformist causes, but the likelihood is that Collinges' retrospective account is biassed and that most of the family would have hesitated to cast themselves as puritans. It should be noticed that whoever was responsible for cuts in the Bridgewater manuscript text (see Appendix, above) took the edge off the ardent religiousness of some passages in Milton's text. The religious predispositions of the family are reviewed briefly by John Creaser, 'The present aid of this occasion': the Setting of *Comus*', in *The Court Masque*, ed. David Lindley (Manchester University Press, 1984), pp. 111–134.
12 Questions of vocation are taken up in the last chapter, and questions of dating in my forthcoming article, 'The Date of *Arcades*'.
13 Steven May, 'Spenser's "Amyntas": three poems by Ferdinando Stanley, Lord Strange, fifth Earl of Derby', *MP* LXX, 1 (1972), 49–52.
14 See *Stanley Papers*, Chetham Society, vols. XXIX and XXXI (1853). Material on the earlier life of the countess is most conveniently summarised in French Fogle's Clark lecture, '"Such a Rural Queene": The Countess Dowager of Derby as Patron'. I wish to express my gratitude to Professor Fogle, who has made a study of the countess for many years, with whom I compared notes and who allowed me to read his Clark lecture whilst still in typescript.
15 The British Library copy of Daniel's masque (161. a. 41) has manuscript notes in a contemporary hand identifying Proserpina as the Countess Dowager; her part in Jonson's masque is known through an Italian description: see John Orrell, 'Antimo Galli's Description of *The Masque of Beauty*', *HLQ*, XLIII, 1 (1979), 13–23.
16 In the Elizabethan period other writers dedicating works to the family include Robert Greene and Thomas Nash; in the Jacobean Sir John Davies (an Egerton protégé), John Davies of Hereford and Thomas Gainsford. See Fogle, 'Such a Rural Queene'.
17 See *The Poems of Sir John Davies*, ed. R. Krueger (Oxford, 1975), pp. 409, 431–435.

Notes to pages 16–22

18 *The Poems of John Marston*, ed. A. Davenport (Liverpool, 1961), pp. 40–45, 189–207, 376–379.
19 I have used the survey made in 1636 now in the possession of the Fitzroy-Newdigate family at Arbury Hall, Warwickshire. There is a similar document in Middlesex Record Office, Newdegate Papers, General Management, E.M.2.
20 Huntington Library MS. EL 6481.
21 Parish Registers at Harefield: 22 July 1624.
22 Huntington Library MSS. EL 6841, 6846, 6848.
23 Charles Hamilton, 'The Bridgewater Debts', *HLQ*, XLII, 3 (1979), 217–229; E. Hopkins, 'The Re-leasing of the Ellesmere Estates, 1637–1642', *Agricultural History Review*, x (1962), 15.
24 I have not been able to be sure about the name or date of birth of the second daughter, but Huntington Library MS. EL 6524 is a copy of an agreement about the portion of Frances, daughter of Anne, Countess of Castlehaven, in a marriage with Mr Edmund Fortescue, dated 14 May 1635.
25 Leicester Record Ofice, DE 500, bundle 25.
26 Huntington Library MS. HA 5514 (slightly repunctuated), letter to Lord Marlborough of 22 Jan. 1626–7. Masson (1 559–560) and Davenport, ed., *Poems of John Marston* (pp. 40–45) comment on the apparent lavishness of the 1607 entertainment at Ashby, but a more modest impression of the household is given in Claire Cross, *The Puritan Earl* (London and New York, 1966). Cross (pp. 61–111) gives an account of the financial struggles of the fourth and fifth earls.
27 Huntington Library MS. HA 4845.
28 I have supplied previously uncertain dates of birth from the parish register of Ashby de la Zouch, now in Leicester Record Office.
29 Printed source: *The Arraignment and Conviction of Mervin Lord Audley, Earl of Castlehaven* ... (1642). Fullest MS source: SP Dom. 207.
30 Barbara Breasted, '*Comus* and the Castlehaven Scandal', *Milton Studies*, III (1971), 201–224; Dean A. Reilein, 'Milton's *Comus* and Sabrina's Compliment', *Milton Quarterly*, 5 (1971), 42–43; Rosemary Mundhenk, 'Dark Scandal and the Sun-Clad Power of Chastity', *SEL*, XV, 1 (1975), 151–152; A. N. Wilson, *The Life of John Milton* (Oxford University Press, 1983), pp. 39–50; W. B. Hunter, Jr, *Milton's 'Comus': Family Piece* (New York, Whitston Publishing Co., 1983), pp. 23–35. Scholarship using the Castlehaven scandal is reviewed in John Creaser's article, 'Milton's *Comus*: the Irrelevance of the Castlehaven Scandal', *N&Q*, XXXI (1984), 307–317. I am grateful to him for showing me the typescript.
31 SP Dom. 192.11; cf. her letter to the king, 192.11.1.
32 SP Dom. 198.18; the decision given in 195.30.
33 SP Dom. 203.25 & 100; for Elizabeth 14 November, for Lady Castlehaven 30 November.
34 Harefield accounts, w/e 10 July 1634.
35 Middlesex Record Office, Newdegate Papers, court books. The Earl of

Notes to pages 22–8

Manchester (Lord Privy Seal) and Lord Coleraine were appointed to look after the estate during Chandos' minority.

36 HMRO Hastings I 341.
37 Arbury Hall MS., see above, note 19.
38 Huntington Library MS. HA 4839.
39 Huntington Library MS. HA 4388. Cf. also HA 481 (1627?): 'your Dawters are very well I thank God and well growne'.
40 The wedding took place several weeks before the beginning of the account book, but on w/e 11 Sept. 1634 there is noted a sum to the confectioner 'for banquetting sweetmeates served in my La: Eliz. wedding & other times not entered before'.
41 The death of the Countess of Huntingdon earlier in the year may have eased the finding of a dowry for the daughter, but the dowager may also have helped.
42 Huntington Library MS. HA 5533.
43 Harefield accounts, w/e 20 Nov. 1634.
44 The Countess of Huntingdon's letter to her husband (HA 4839) shows her nervous to disagree wth her mother's plans for Alice's marriage.
45 Huntington Library MS. EL 6522; I. F., *A Sermon preached at Ashby-de-la-Zouch . . . At the Funerall of . . . Lady Elizabeth Stanley . . . late Wife to Henrie Earle of Huntingdon* (London, 1636).
46 Huntington Library MS. HA 2516.
47 Harefield accounts, w/e 11 Dec. 1634.
48 Huntington Library MS. HA 2515.
49 Breasted, '*Comus* and the Castlehaven Scandal', 216.
50 Huntington Library MS. EL 6522.
51 Huntington Library MS. EL 6481.
52 Harefield accounts, w/e 3 July 1634.
53 Harefield accounts, w/e 22 Jan., 29 Jan., 5 Feb. 1634/5.
54 Information on the Council drawn chiefly from Caroline A. J. Skeel, *The Council in the Marches of Wales* (London, 1904); Penry Williams, *The Council in the Marches of Wales under Elizabeth I* (Cardiff, 1958); 'Government and Politics in Ludlow, 1590–1642', *Transactions of the Shropshire Archaeological Society*, 56 (1957–1960), 282–294; 'The Activity of the Council in the Marches under the Early Stuarts', *Welsh Historical Review*, 1 (1961), 133–160; 'The Attack of the Council in the Marches, 1602–42', *Transactions of the Honourable Society of Cymmrodion* (1961), part 1, 1–22.
55 Marcus, 'Milieu', above.
56 Of the many extant copies I have used Huntington Library MS. EL 7397.
57 Skeel, *Council in the Marches*, p. 129.
58 The Instructions laid down the rules for keeping up a sufficient staff, usually consisting of three judges resident in term time, and provided for a vice-president or for the Chief Justice of Chester to act in the president's absence.
59 Williams, *The Council*, p. 17.
60 Huntington Library MSS. EL 7066–7070; 7072–7078.

61 See the introduction to Lady Alix Egerton (ed.), *Milton's Comus, being the Bridgewater Manuscript, with Notes and a short Family Memoir* (London, 1910).
62 Huntington Library MSS. EL 6669.
63 For information of Bridgewater's attendances at Privy Council and Star Chamber see *Acts of the Privy Council*.
64 Huntington Library MSS. HA 4851.
65 Bridgewater suffered severely from the gout, which crippled his hands; he also had 'weak eyes' and since quite an early age had been lame. Back in the winter of 1626/7 he had been very seriously, even critically, ill, of fever – see Huntington Library MS. HA 4839, letter of Lady Huntingdon to her husband of 18 Jan. 1626/7 (misdated 1632/3 in HMRO Hastings report; also HA 4838). He was ill again in February 1632/3 (see HA 4851) and absent from Privy Council, 16 Jan. to 3 May.
66 This is a nice feminine explanation of 'extraordinary occasions' provided by Lady Alix Egerton in her edition. Lady Penelope Egerton was married to Sir Robert Napier of Luton Hoo at some time after 22 February 1631, when, still unmarried, she played in the masque *Chloridia*; Lady Katherine married William Courteen some time after 14 February 1632, when she was a masquer in *Tempe Restored*; and at some time in 1633 Lady Magdalene married Sir Gervase Cutler of Stainburgh, Yorks.
67 Details of Bridgewater's itinerary to Wales drawn mainly from Huntington Library MSS. EL 6674–6676.
68 Shropshire RO, 212/B, draft of letter from Bridgewater to William Courteen, 14 July 1634, quoted below, p. 33.
69 Shropshire RO, 212/B, draft of letter to Sir William Courteen, 14 July 1634.
70 Noted above, p. 25 and note 52. Young William Courteen was present, and his father declares in a letter (Shropshire RO, 212/B, 19 July) that he had intended to be there 'but some unexpected occasion befell me'.
71 Shropshire RO, 212/B, draft of letter from Bridgewater to William Courteen, 14 July 1634: '... I hope y^u will remember the last words I spoke to y^u in my Coache at Harfielde when we parted: I assur y^u I will not forgett them as time & my pressing occasions will p^{rmitt} at this distance & for that purpose I have already sent for some of my servantes to come to speake wth me.'
72 Shropshire RO, 212/B, draft of letters of Bridgewater to both Courteens, 14 July 1634.
73 Bridgewater was at Towcester on the road home on 19 October (Huntington Library MSS. EL 6519), so he probably arrived at Ashridge on 20 or 21 October. He visited Harefield for a day during the week ending 30 October and attended his first Privy Council on 5 November.
74 Fragmentary accounts between Ludlow and Lyme, Huntington Library MSS. EL 6678–6683.
75 There is one page recording gratuities to footmen, for their 'running' from place to place, apparently for longer days of travel. Information about

Notes to pages 31–8

Ruthin and the muster from *Y Cwtta Cyfarwydd: The Chronicle, Written by The Famous Clarke, Peter Roberts, Notary Public. For the Years 1607–1646*, ed. David R. Thomas (London, 1883), p. 155. I am grateful to Dr Peter W. Thomas for this reference.

76 Family history: Evelyn Legh (Lady Newton), *The House of Lyme from its Foundation to the End of the Eighteenth Century* (London, 1917).
77 John Rylands Library, Legh of Lyme papers, correspondence (unnumbered). This archive is on deposit from Lord Newton.
78 Dates of terms taken from books of hearings, Huntington Library MSS. EL 7574–7578.
79 Shropshire RO, 212/B, draft of letters from Bridgewater to William Courteen, 26 July 1634, and to Sir William, 14 July 1634.
80 Shropshire RO, 212/B, draft of letter from Bridgewater to William Courteen, 19 July 1634.
81 Huntington Library MSS. EL 6863: 'Rules how to compose'.
82 Huntington Library MSS. EL 6495. Herbert's book is incorrectly called 'The Church Porch'.
83 Edited and described by the author in 'The Chirk Castle Entertainment of 1634', *MQ*, XI, no. 3 (October, 1977), 76–86. The present account gives a more precise dating than the article.
84 See below, Appendix.
85 See note 4 above. There may have been other music, not composed by Lawes, and a whole group of musicians would have been required.
86 Phornutus (L. A. Cornutus), *Speculatio de Deorum Natura*, index *s.v.* 'Comus', in the collection beginning with Hyginus, *Fabularum* . . . *liber* (Leyden, 1608).
87 Most notably, among those who have studied the subject closely, by J. G. Demaray, *Milton and the Masque Tradition* (Cambridge, Mass., 1968), pp. 77, 100–101. See Parker, *Milton*, I, 791.
88 *The Autobiography of Richard Baxter*, ed. J. M. Lloyd Thomas (London, 1925), pp. 7–8.
89 Shropshire RO, Ludlow papers, 1634.
90 Hunter, *Family Piece*, p. 48.
91 Demaray, *Milton and the Masque Tradition*, p. 99.
92 *1637* and *1645* both say that the Spirit 'descends or enters', which had also been the reading of the Bridgewater manuscript.
93 Glynne Wickham, *Early English Stages, 1300–1660*, vol. II, part 2 (London and New York, 1972), p. 121.
94 Performances of plays in the provinces, of course, frequently took place in great halls smaller than Ludlow's. See for example David George, 'Jacobean Actors and the Great Hall of Gawthorpe, Lancashire', *Theatre Notebook*, XXVII, no. 3 (1983), 109–121, where some comparisons are also made with other stages.
95 James G. Taafe, 'Michaelmas, the "lawless hour", and the occasion of Milton's *Comus*', *ELN*, VI (1969), 257–262; William B. Hunter, Jr, 'The

Liturgical Context of *Comus*', *ELN*, IX (1972), 11–15; M. S. Berkowitz, 'An Earl's Michaelmas in Wales', *MQ*, XIII (1979), 122–123; Hunter, *Family Piece*, pp. 23–36.
96 The election of a new mayor was a Michaelmas event, even though the festivity came a month later.
97 Published in London in 1605; no pagination.
98 'Everlasting God, which hast ordained, and constituted the services of all Angels and men in a wonderfull order; mercifully grant that they which alwayes doe thee service in heaven, may by thy appointment succor and defend us in earth, through Jesus Christ our Lord', BCP quoted in edition of Barker (London, 1633).
99 Wither, *Hymnes and Songs*, p. 182.

2 · The Arcadians

1 I am referring to the interpretation of J. M. Wallace, which has been influential and which is discussed below, note 4 and p. 50 and note 25.
2 For the sake of consistency with the quotations from *Comus* in the rest of this book I quote *Arcades* in the text of the Trinity manuscript. However, the manuscript is quite badly torn at this point, and where I need a passage from a damaged area I have used *1645*, acknowledging when I have done so.
3 In the manuscript Milton first wrote Juno, then substituted Ceres, then finally restored Juno by underlining.
4 I would want to point out the range of significances in these various divinities, including the cancelled Ceres. Taken *together* they add up to an appreciation of the dowager. The allegorical reading of J. M. Wallace selects as primary the significance of wisdom, building on 'wise Latona' and seeing an adaptation of the description of the visit of the Queen of Sheba to Solomon in 1 Kings 10.6–7: 'And she said to the king, It was a true report that I heard in mine own land of thy acts and of thy wisdom. Howbeit I believed not the words, until I came, and mine eyes had seen it; and, behold, the half was not told me: thy wisdom and prosperity exceedeth the fame which I heard.' It would be foolish to deny the possibility of an allusion to this biblical formula, fitting a kind of quest and the idea of wisdom. Nevertheless I would want to point to the dangers of subordinating the whole appreciation of the dowager to one idea: the ideas of motherhood and regality (that is, nobility) are equally important to the expression of the familial tribute.
5 Milton's verses have not always been seen as the opening business of the night. John T. Shawcross, for example, in 'The Manuscript of "Arcades",' *N & Q*, CCIV (1959), 3, sees it as the close.
6 'Milton's "Arcades" in the Trinity Manuscript', forthcoming in *RES*.
7 Harefield accounts, w/e 20 Nov., 1634.

Notes to pages 45-50

8   See above, pp. 15-26.
9   These two lines were marginal insertions in both of the concluding songs before the refrain 'such a rurall Queene . . .' Milton then seems to have struck through the insertion in the first song, and in *1645* the additional lines appear only in the last song.
10 *Ben Jonson*, ed. C. H. Herford and P. and E. Simpson (Oxford, 1925-52), VII 121 (hereafter cited as H & S).
11 My forthcoming article, 'The Date of *Arcades*'.
12 When I first wrote on these issues in *Renaissance Drama*, the article of Mary Ann McGuire, 'Milton's *Arcades* and the Entertainment Tradition,' *SP*, LXXV (1978), 451-471, had not appeared. I share many points of reference with this article, in connection with country-house entertainments, though I do not agree on the matter of outdoor staging.
13 *Variorum Commentary*, II, ii, 526.
14 But see Parker, *Milton*, I, 83.
15 See *Variorum Commentary*, II, ii, 542.
16 Some notable seventeenth-century examples available to Milton in print: Ben Jonson's entertainment at Althorp (1603), Highgate (1604) and Theobalds (1607), all in the 1616 Folio (H & S, VII), and Campion's Caversham entertainment of 1613 (*Works*, ed. Walter R. Davis (London, 1969), pp. 231-248). Examples not available to him in print: Sir John Davies' entertainment at Harefield of 1602 and John Marston's entertainment for the countess herself at Ashby of 1607 (*The Poems*, ed. J. Davenport, Liverpool, 1961), pp. 189-207 (see above, p. 16 and notes 17 and 18 of Chapter 1). Contemporaneous examples: Jonson's entertainments at Welbeck (1633) and Bolsover (1634) (see H & S, VII, 787-814) and the anonymous Chirk Castle entertainment (see my article, *Milton Quarterly*, XI (1977), 76-86, and above, pp. 30 and 34). Of course there were many others, and many Elizabethan examples, on which see Bruce R. Smith, 'Landscape with Figures: The Three Realms of Queen Elizabeth's Country-House Revels', *Renaissance Drama*, VIII (1977), 57-115, and Jean Wilson, *Entertainments for Elizabeth I* (Brewer: Woodbridge, 1980). It should be noted also that Sidney's Wanstead entertainment (*The Lady of May*) was frequently reprinted with the *Arcadia* in the 1620s and 1630s, so was a familiar model.
17 McGuire, 'Milton's *Arcades*', 454-458.
18 *The Poetical Works of John Milton*, ed. H. J. Todd, 2nd edn (London, 1809), VI, 151-156.
19 Masson, *Life of Milton*, I, 563-564.
20 Parker, *Milton*, I, 81; Demaray, *Milton and the Masque Tradition*, p. 49 (see also his '*Arcades* as a Literary Entertainment,' *PLL*, VII (1972), 15-25); *Variorum Commentary*, p. 531; McGuire, 'Milton's *Arcades*', 459-461; Hunter, *Family Piece*, p. 15; Wilson, *Life*, p. 41.
21 Parker has 'the grand old lady peering into the darkness beyond from a shining and canopied throne'; Woodhouse, in the *Variorum*, merely makes the state 'visible from without' also without mentioning hearing;

Demaray indicates a 'suitable distance' between the position of the first song and the countess' chair.
22 S. Orgel and R. Strong, *Inigo Jones: The Theatre of the Stuart Court* (London, Berkeley & Los Angeles, 1973), I, 128–129.
23 An idea of C. Brooks and J. E. Hardy in *Poems of John Milton: the 1645 Edition* (New York, 1951), pp. 163–168; adapted by S. Blau in 'Milton's Salvational Aesthetic', *Journal of Religion*, XLVI (1966), 282–295.
24 D. Daiches, *Milton* (London, 1957), p. 62.
25 Apart from Brooks and Hardy, the most elaborate allegorisation is by J. M. Wallace, 'Milton's *Arcades*', *JEGP*, LVIII (1959), 627–636, mentioned above, notes 1 and 4. Many editors cite this article, and Hunter (*Family Piece*, p. 15–20) builds on the allegorical reading to connect it with readings for 2 May, in an attempt to date the entertainment. On the improbability of his dating, see my forthcoming article, 'The Date of *Arcades*'.
26 Blau, see note 23 above.

3 · 'Kōmos' – the adversary for the occasion

1 See my article, "Milton's 'Arcades' in the Trinity Manuscript", forthcoming in *RES*.
2 Phrase from Tertullian, *De Spectaculis*, quoted in Commonplace Book (Yale I 362). Although the entry has been dated in the latter 1630s, it is of interest for the aristocratic entertainments, since Tertullian was censuring drama and spectacle.
3 Encomia rehearsed in the opening pages of Camden's *Britannia* (1610 edition, p. 2) and in Hieronymus Commelin, *Rerum Britannicum* (Heidelberg, 1587), p. 1.
4 Virgil, *Aen.* 1.21.
5 An obvious literary reference is in Herbert's 'The Church Militant'. Some analogies are given in the unpublished PhD dissertation of Graeme Watson, 'The Eschatological Thought of Henry Vaughan' (Reading, 1983), pp. 163–166.
6 *PL* 9.79–80: '... thus the Orb he roam'd / With narrow search'; *PR* 1.33–35: '... That heard the Adversary, who roving still / About the world, at that assembly fam'd / Would not be last'; *PR* 2.178–180: '... Before the Flood thou with thy Lusty Crew, / False titl'd Sons of God, roaming the Earth / Cast wanton eyes on the daughters of men.'
7 The lines beginning 'amidst th'Hesperian gardens...' On the dating of this passage, see Sprott. Moralised uses of the Hesperides are noticed below, Chap. 6.
8 Phrases from Romans 13.12–13; see below, p. 65.
9 The phrase is H. Estienne's translation of *Kōmos heortēs*, from Nonnus' *Dionysiaca*, in the entry on *kōmos* in *Thesaurus Linguae Graecae* (1572), II, 531.

Notes to pages 63–6

The Stephanus entry gives all the common senses of the word recognised at that time and includes several allusions. The definition of Philostratus' god is given only at the end of the meanings of the common noun, assuming a personification of those activities. A similar set of references can be found in the lexicon of Guillaume Budé (Buddaeus), *Lexicon graeco-latinum* (Geneva, 1584).

10 Metres do not translate, but there are signs that the heptasyllabic line was adopted as equivalent to the Anacreontic. See for example the translations of Stanley: *Poems and Translations of Thomas Stanley*, ed. G. M. Crump (Oxford, 1972), pp. 74–100.

11 Thomas Randolph, 'Upon Love fondly refused for Conscience' sake', line 4. An example of the expression of a familiar sentiment.

12 Randolph, 'An Eclogue to Master Johnson', line 98. However, that 'purer fire' is a familiar phrase is suggested by its occurrence in Carew's *Coelum Britannicum*, describing dancers as stars (*The Poems of Thomas Carew*, ed. Rhodes Dunlap (Oxford, 1949), p. 179).

13 Because of confusion in the transmission of manuscript texts, Philostratus 1.2 and 1.3 appeared as the last two items in editions of Phornutus, *Speculatio de Deorum Natura*. Phornutus was available in many editions, usually printed with other mythographical material: with Aesop and Palaephatus, from Venice 1505 onwards; and then also with Hyginus, from Basle 1549 onwards. Cornutus, a first-century AD stoic, lived before Philostratus, of course.

14 For the several appearances of Comus as god of cheer in Jonson, and in Dekker and other writers, see the summary in *Variorum Commentary*, pp. 768ff. The Philostratus/Phornutus material is examined fully by John Arthos, *On a Mask Presented at Ludlow Castle* (Michigan and Oxford, 1954).

15 Erycius Putaeanus (van der Putten), *Comus, sive Phagesiposia Cimmeria: Somnium* (Louvain, 1608; Oxford, 1634). Possible influence is fully discussed by R. H. Singleton, 'Milton's *Comus* and the *Comus* of Erycius Putaeanus', *PMLA*, 58 (1943), 949–957. The reprinting of this text in Oxford in the same year as Milton's masque makes an additional reason for taking the possibility of influence seriously, but it may simply be that those responsible for the new edition were commenting on current aristocratic luxury, that is, were responding to the present historical context in a way similar to Milton's.

16 My approach is philological rather than simply iconographical. For iconographical comment on Comus the reader is once again referred to the references given in the *Variorum Commentary*. I should also like to mention the article of John Steadman, 'Iconography and Renaissance Drama: Ethical and Mythological Themes', *RORD*, XIII–XIV (1970–71), 72–123, which gives a very full account of Comus in tradition. My research into the *kōmos* was done many years ago, before I had seen Steadman's essay or talked with him on the subject. I owe to him the reference to Caseneuve. My account places more emphasis on biblical influence, on glosses in Greek texts, and interprets the use of Circe rather

differently. About the discussion of *kōmos* in Georgia B. Christopher's *Milton and the Science of the Saints* (Princeton University Press, 1982) I should like to observe that the documentation of the Christianised use of the word in literary texts is much too short, being limited to Erasmus.

17 TMS f. 34, the page beginning 'The Deluge. Sodom'.

18 I have quoted from the second edition. The first reads '... Dores / Yielded thir Matrons to prevent worse rape'. More damning, this was biblically inaccurate.

19 The earliest use listed in dictionaries is Homeric *Hymn to Hermes* (481), in which the joy of festivity is said to belong to day and night.

20 For example: Plato, as well as those places noted below, *Theat.* 173D; Xenophon, as well as the Babylonian victory mentioned below, *Symp.*, 2.1, *Cyr.* 7.5.25; Heliodorus, rape of Chariclea, IV.12 (17); many references in Euripides, as *Alc.* 343, 804, 918; *Bacc.* 836, 1167; *Cyc.* 451, 492, 508; *Hipp.* 55; *Ion* 1197; *Phoen.* 791; *Supp.* 390; *Helen* 1469.

21 Robert Gell, *Remaines* (London, 1676), II, 515. On Gell see note 33 below. Many dictionaries pointed to symposia and after-dinner parties.

22 The subject is treated at length in Francis Cairns, *Generic Composition in Greek and Roman Poetry* (Edinburgh, 1972).

23 e.g. Vincenzo Cartari, *Le Imagini* (Venice, 1571), p. 416; (Lyons, 1581), p. 278.

24 Plato, *Laws* 637B: 'I saw the whole city drunk at the Dionysian festival.'

25 *Testamenti Veteris Biblia Sacra ... ex Hebraeo facti ... brevibusque illustrata ab Immanuelle Tremellio et Fransisco Junio ... novi Testamenti libros ... a Theodoro Bezo ... conversi* (London, 1581), under Romans 13.12.

26 John (Giovanni) Diodati, *Pious and Learned Annotations upon the Holy Bible* (2nd edn, London, 1648) under Amos 6.2. With regard to *kōmos* in the Bible, seventeenth-century scholars often noticed also two passages in the Apocrypha: II Macc. 6.4 and Wisd. 4.23. See for example Hugo Grotius, *Annotata* (Paris, 1644) on Rom. 13.13, where he refers to Theocritus Idyll 3 and these two passages. II Macc. has a feast and procession of Bacchus.

27 *Hieroglyphicorum et Medicorum Emblematum DŌDEKAKROUNOS* (Lyons, 1626), pp. 31–39. After Philostratus the most significant description of the god is in Cartari's *Imagines*. There is a brief mention in L. G. Gyraldus' *De Diis Gentium* (Basle, 1560, p. 46), and related figures in the various editions of Ripa's *Iconologia* are Convito (Banquet), Allegrezza (Mirth) and Ubriachezza (Drunkenness).

28 Blaise de Vigenère (tr.), *Les Images ou Tableaux ... des deux Philostrates* (1614, 1615 and 1629), article on Comus. First editions of the Anacreon translations: *Anacreontis Teii odae ... Ab Henrico Stephano ... Latinate nunc primum donatae* (Paris, 1554); *Anacreontis et aliquorum lyricorum odae ... ab Helia Andrea factae* (Paris, 1556).

29 *Aeschyli tragoediae septem ... versione et commentario Thomae Stanleii* (London, 1663), p. 377.

30 Ann Lefèvre, *Les Poésies d'Anacréon et de Sapho, traduites ... avec des Remarques* (1681, 1698, 1699, 1716); *Works of Anacreon*, tr. Joseph Addison (London,

1735), pp. 7–8; *Odes of Anacreon*, tr. Thomas Moore (London, 1800), p. 160.
31 Johann Wilhelm Stuck (Stuckius), *Antiquitatem Convivialem* (Frankfurt, 1613), I.x (my translation). A connection between CAMAS, 'to hide or conceal', and Milton's 'conceal'd solemnity' is of course tempting.
32 Joannes Drusius, *Annotationes in Pentateuchum*, on Numbers 21.29; reprinted in J. Pearson (ed.), *Critici Sacri* (London, 1660).
33 Robert Gell, *Remaines: or Several Select Scriptures of the New Testament Opened and Explained* (London, 1676), I, 622: 'Men receive and believe in their Mammon, trust in their Riches, receive and believe in *Chemosh*, the God of riot and drunkenness...' Gell had been fellow of Christ's College, Cambridge, in the 1630s, and some of these addresses were given in college. He also refers to *kōmos*/Chemosh (with Bacchus) at I, 585 and again at II, 515.
34 Edward Leigh, *Critica Sacra* (2nd edn, 1650), Part II, p. 154; Part I, p. 112.
35 Clement, *Paedagogus*, 114. Typically, the sixteenth-century Latin translation of Gentian Hervert (1590) assumes the word *kōmos* to be personified: ... *a Christiano convivio vult abesse Comum*.
36 Compare also the mention of 'The Book of Sports' in *The Reason of Church-Government* (Yale I 819).
37 Gyraldus makes a satirical aside, much in the same spirit, about Comus: 'He [Philostratus] portrays him crowned, because he subjects a great many agreeable places to his decrees.'
38 The word is that of Ben Jonson adopted by Rosemund Tuve, *Images and Themes in Five Poems by Milton* (Cambridge, Mass.: Harvard University Press, 1957), p. 115.
39 The linking of blindness with unbelief would seem to recall II Cor. 4.3–4. Though he used the biblical sense of blindness (associated with hardness of heart) twice elsewhere in his poetry, Milton never again used the pious 'unbeliefe' in his verse.

4 · The young heroes – realism and idealism

1 See for example Malcolm M. Ross, deploring a puritan spirit: 'Faith, Hope, and *Chastity*. And the greatest of these is chastity! ... the substitution is too startling, too exposed, to have been accidental' (*Poetry and Dogma: The Transformations of Eucharistic Symbols in Seventeenth-Century English Poetry* (Rutgers University Press, 1954), p. 196).
2 William Ames, *The Marrow of Sacred Divinity* (London, 1643), p. 324, a translation of the *Medulla Theologiae* (1623, 1627), a popular book which Milton's Commonplace Book shows he had read at some time. See also Ames on charity, p. 232.
3 Ovid, *Met.* 3.359–401.
4 *Variorum Commentary*, pp. 891–892. A recent discussion of the problem is in

Thomas N. Corns, 'A Mask Presented at Ludlow-Castle, 1.231'. *N & Q*, CCXXVII, ns XXIX (1982), 22–24.

5 Ovid, *Met.* 9.451: *totiens reduentis eodem*. See also *Met.* 8.162–167, a long simile about Meander suggesting uncertainty and irresolution.

6 *Od.* 6.149; *Aen.* 1.327–28; *Met.* 4.320; *Faithful Shepherdess*, II i 58–65; *Temp.* I II 421–427. See also, for example, William Browne, *Britannia's Pastorals*, 1.4.272–276 (probably imitating *Faithful Shepherdess*) and Fletcher, *The Sea Voyage*, II i, the entry of Albert and following exchange (imitating *Tempest*).

7 The phrase 'seat of the scorners' from Ps. 1.1, a famous verse of some suggestiveness for the masque: 'Blessed is the man that walketh not in the counsel of the ungodly, Nor standeth in the way of sinners, Nor sitteth in the seat of the scornful.' It was picked up (as 'seat of pestilences') by Tertullian (*De Spectaculis*, XXVII) to describe the moral effects of attendance at theatres. The treatise was referred to by puritan writers against 'pagan' shows. We cannot be sure that Milton read *De Spectaculis* until about 1637 (see Yale I 362), but when he did he used a passage adjacent to this as first entry in the Commonplace Book.

8 The perversion begins in the first speech, signalled by 'from these gates / sorrow flies farre'. 'Gates', besides the Circean palace, seems to recall Is. 3.26: 'And her gates shall lament and mourn . . .' The judgement is against idolatrous, luxurious cities. Comus' statement that sorrow will fly recalls another formula in Isaiah: 'And the ransomed of the Lord shall return . . . they shall obtain joy and gladness, and sorrow and sighing shall flee away' (35.10, cf. 51.11). Such joy is meant for the good. Again, the biblical passages act as judgement upon the speaker.

9 *Milton's Arcades and Comus*, ed. A. W. Verity (Cambridge, 1891), p. 163.

10 As usual the details are exact. Helen's drug banished pain, anger and sorrow and was associated, like julep, with the luxurious east. Milton took the trouble to write *nepenthes* in the margin of the Trinity manuscript, because the word means 'removing sorrow'.

11 C. L. Barber, 'A Mask Presented at Ludlow Castle: The Masque as Masque', in *A Maske at Ludlow: Essays on Milton's Comus*, ed. John S. Diekhoff (Cleveland, 1968), p. 199. This essay was reprinted from *The Lyric and Dramatic Milton*, ed. Joseph H. Summers (New York, 1965), 35–63.

12 Reviewed in *Variorum Commentary*, pp. 773–775.

13 There is the celebration of moon and stars as aid to travellers, the old association of Chaos and Night (cf. *PL* 1.543; 2.894), the 'double' night of Ovid (*Met.* 11.550), and the educated distinction between the steering-star of Greeks and Phoenicians, 'Starre of Arcadie' or 'Tyrian Cynosure'. See *Variorum Commentary*, p. 903.

5 · Spiritual instructions

1. The following section about Haemony and the shepherd lad is a shortened and somewhat modified version of my article, 'The Shepherd, the Musician, and the Word in Milton's Masque'. For the long bibliography on the Haemony debate the reader is referred once again to the *Variorum Commentary*, 929–939. Since then, Charlotte F. Otten, 'Milton's Haemony', *ELR*, 5 (1975), 81–95; John C. Ulreich, Jr, '*A Bright Golden Flow'r*: Haemony as Symbol of Transformation', *SEL*, 17 (1977), 119–128.
2. My arguments about Haemony were of course formulated before the appearance of Georgia B. Christopher's book (see also above, Chap. 3, note 16). My definition of the word is far simpler than hers. Encouraging though it is to find another scholar expressing the centrality of the word to Milton's poetry, I am puzzled that she does not see it actually represented in the masque in the Haemony allegory.
3. *Animadversions*, sect. 13; Yale I 716.
4. This was first noted in print by J. M. Steadman, 'Milton's Haemony: Etymology and Allegory', *PMLA*, 77 (1962), 206. The biblical text is Hebrews 11.15–16: '... the better country, that is, an heavenly'.
5. *PL* 3.352–357; 11.78 ('amarantine'). Amaranthus as religious flower derives from words meaning unfading, as in I Pet. 1.4 and I Pet. 5.4. It seems to have been Clement of Alexandria (*Paedagogus*, II, 8) who was responsible for putting a symbolic flower into Peter, recalling a long-lasting bloom called *amarantos* used in funerals and festivals (cf. *Lyc.* 149). In Milton's time Peter's words were still often construed to refer to a real flower, as Diodati reports: 'Others translate it, as Amaranthus, which is a flower that fadeth not away' (under I Pet. 5.4, p. 417). Note the resemblance to the plant Fame in *Lycidas* (78–82), which like amaranthus thrives in heaven not on earth. Marvell worked similarly with the plant Conscience in *Upon Appleton House*, st. 45. For amaranthus as emblem, see for example Alciati, *Emblemata: cum commentariis* (Paris, 1583), no. 135: 'Strenuorum immortale nomen'.
6. Cf. also Heb. 10.29: 'Of how much sorer punishment ... shall he be thought worthy, who hath trodden under foot the Son of God.'
7. *Annotations*, Ps. 18.12.
8. Yale I 826.
9. Cf. II Cor. 6.9: 'as unknown, and yet well known'.
10. Henry More, *Philosophicall Poems* (Cambridge, 1647), pp. 50, 483. Compare *PR* 2.458–460: 'yet not for that a crown, / Golden in show, is but a wreath of thorns, / Brings dangers, troubles, cares ...'
11. So also in *PL* 3.170; 7.175, 208. Compare Rom. 9.6: 'the word of God hath taken none effect'; and I Thess. 2.13: 'the word of God, which effectually worketh'.
12. In II Cor. 6.7, 'power of God' and 'word of truth' were understood in these ways: 'Either by this power which manifested itself in my effectual and

powerful ministry, or the power of God, whereby I wrought many miracles among you' (*Annotations*). The healing was a fulfilment of Hebrew prophecy: 'He sent the word, and healed them, and delivered them from destruction' (Ps. 107.20).

13 *Reason of Church-Government*, II, iii (Yale I 837). Milton often applies the word efficacy to the true ministry, as in 'spirituall efficacy' (Yale I 833).
14 First discussed in print in *The Poems of John Milton*, ed. Thos Keightley (London, 1859), I, 108. Cf. Thomas Cooper, *Thesaurus Linguae Romanae et Britannicum* (London, 1565), proper name list, 'Thessalia': 'the women there, beinge wonderfull witches, transfourmed men into the figure of beastes'.
15 In association with Medea and Circe, *Ars Amatoria*, II 99; *Remedium Amoris* 249. Waters with magical effects are called Haemonian, *Fasti*, II, 40; *Amores*, II, i, 9. In the stilted wit of the second *Elegy*, the younger Milton had already used the adjective in the same way: 'Yet you deserved to be made young again with Haemonian medicine (*Haemonio . . . succo*); you deserved to go on living, like Aeson', said the student poet to the aged beadle claimed by death. For the associations of Aeson and his son Jason with Haemonian arts, see *Met.*, VII, 264, and VII, 314.
16 Compare Milton, *An Apology*: 'in all plenteous dispensation of the word' (Yale I 932).
17 'The Shepherd, the Musician, and the Word', pp. 526–527.
18 *Reason of Church-Government*, II, i (Yale I 825). On the paradox of humility and exaltation in an inglorious messiah, see Phil. 2.7–9, and various OT passages, e.g. Ps. 78.70–72. Calvin prefaced his commentary on the Psalms with the thought that he had shared David's providential progress from 'base' beginnings, so as to be able to act for the good of the people: 'But like as he was advaunced from the sheepfolds to the high estate of a kingdome: even so God drawing mee from base and slender beginnings, hath vowtsaved me this honorable office, to make me a preacher and a minister of his Gospel' (*Psalmes*, trans. Golding, 'To the Reader').
19 *Reason of Church-Government*, I, iii (Yale I 766).
20 Diodati, under Psalms, 'Argument'.
21 *Variorum Commentary*, p. 929: Hanford, Wright, Prince and Frye see a reference to Milton himself.
22 When he dedicated the *Choice Psalms* to King Charles, Lawes himself predictably thought of David: Henry and William Lawes, *Choice Psalms put into Musick* (London, 1648), dedication.
23 On this role see Franklin R. Baruch, 'Milton's *Comus*: Skill, Virtue, and Henry Lawes', *Milton Studies*, v (1973), 289–308.
24 The question of Sabrina, skirted by so many, was attempted by John D. Cox, 'Poetry and History in Milton's Country Masque', *ELH*, 44 (1977), 622–640. My conclusions, reached independently, have some similarities to Cox's, but they rest on different sets of evidence and differ in argument in the following important ways: (a) I wish to push the vision associated with the river towards a model for the nation, which Cox does not (hence

his suppression of the Trojan/British references); (b) I see the potentialities of courtly 'visitors' and pastoral location *coming together* in celebration, rather than 'country' simply overcoming 'court', with the political attitude that idea implies; (c) I wish to pick up the idea of providential 'pity', which Cox ignores, and also not to deny elements of 'grace'; (d) I do not wish to take the Castlehaven affair so seriously as primary context as Cox appears to do; and (e) I try to base my analysis more closely than Cox does on the masque text in its various states.

25 Ovid, *Met.* 4.237–238: *ille ferox immansuetusque precantem / tendentemque manus ad lumine Solis.* Milton transfers the epithet 'lovely' to the hands. For allusions in the imagery of this whole passage, see the summary in *Variorum Commentary*, pp. 964–965.

26 In an early version of Trinity, Milton wrote that the emeralds were set into the wheels of her sliding chariot: 'that my rich wheels inlayes'.

27 After touching the chair Sabrina has to move back to her chariot and to descend. Her remaining lines are not long enough to accompany the descent. Was she to speak them as she crossed the stage back to the chariot?

28 One is intrigued as to why music has not survived for Sabrina's song. Could it be because other people were involved, including other musicians, and only the Lawes/Egerton memorials have survived? Similarly perhaps with the music for the dance of Comus' rout, though this need not have been newly composed.

29 *Met.* 2.364–366; *Aen.* 8.74.

30 Milton, *Poems* (1645), pp. 71–72.

31 *Od.* 10.388–399; *Met.* 14.299–301; George Sandys, *Ovid's Metamorphoses English'd, Mythologiz'd* (Oxford, 1632), p. 481. Considering the 'magic' invocations of song in this episode, one might note a possible reversal of Virgil, *Ecl.* 8.70: *carminibus Circe socios mutavit Ulixi* (Circe changed the companions of Ulysses with the power of song).

32 'Precious cure' sounds redemptive (see, e.g., the coupling of redemption with 'precious blood' in I Pet. 1.18–19) but it is also in the pietistic manner of Fletcherian pastoral: the rhyme pure/cure was in fact a favourite in *The Faithful Shepherdess*, as Warton noted (pp. 244–245).

33 Prov. 4.23.

34 e.g. the 'sealing' of baptismal cleansing, or even the blessing of temporal governors, as in the coronation ceremony.

35 A. S. P. Woodhouse, 'The Argument of Milton's *Comus*', *UTQ*, 11 (1941–42), 46–71, reprinted in *A Maske at Ludlow: Essays on Milton's Comus*, ed. John S. Diekhoff (Cleveland: Case Western, 1968), pp. 17–42; '*Comus* Once More', *UTQ*, 19 (1949–50), 218–223. Early reactions can be seen for example in C. Clarke, 'A Neglected Episode in *Comus*', *The Wind and the Rain*, 6 (1949), 103–107; J. Arthos, *On a Mask Presented at Ludlow Castle*, p. 71; A. E. Dyson, 'The Interpretation of *Comus*', *Essays and Studies* (1955), 89–114; W. G. Madsen, 'The Idea of Nature in Milton's Poetry', in *Three Studies in the Renaissance*, R. B. Young et al. (New Haven, 1958),

pp. 211–217. That the effects of Woodhouse's theological scheme are still being felt even now, especially in relation to Sabrina, is attested by the reference to him by Cox (see above, note 24), pp. 636–637, where 'nature' in Sabrina is held up to deny Woodhouse's 'grace', confusingly and largely because of adopting Woodhouse's division.

36 Cox seems to be striving against such a hierarchy in his qualifications (p. 636) of the word 'goddesse'.

37 There is a slight but significant difference between this account and that of Cox in connection with court and country. Cox sees the masque as a uniquely 'country' masque, asserting the values of 'country' over 'court'. That seems to me to express a lot, yet finally to simplify: the court comes into the principality, and the potentialities of both are exploited in the celebration of the masque. (*Comus*, incidentally, is not unique as a country masque, though it is the best known.)

38 The possible influence of Drayton has been examined most fully, and perhaps with some overstatement, by Jack B. Oruch, 'Imitation and Invention in the Sabrina Myths of Drayton and Milton', *Anglia*, 90 (1972), 60–70, where earlier discussions are also reported. Drayton associated Sabrina with the unity of Wales and England and he notes, with the patriotic wish for British unity in mind, that Gwendolen's wars were the Britons' 'first intestine strife, / Since they were put a-land upon this promis'd shore' (VI 131).

39 Cox, 'Poetry and History, p. 625.

40 I do not think that *Polyolbion* says what Marcus (p. 320) implies, that Sabrina's unifying, judgemental powers were those incorporated in the Welsh presidency, the jurisdiction of which was under discussion in James' reign. In Drayton Sabrina's prophetic role concerns not the presidency but the royal house in the nation.

41 Songs, trinal sprinklings, images of purity, actions of purgation and the display of chaste womanhood are all common features of pastoral fictions. In *Comus*, as in *The Faithful Shepherdess*, a virgin comes to the aid of one like herself – 'will be swift / to aide a virgin such as was her selfe'. The language is also peculiarly mannered in this section. The words 'shrewd', 'medling', 'elfe', 'urchin' and 'ill-luck' are used here only in his poetry, and 'pinches' come elsewhere only in the comic pastoral of *L'Allegro* (line 103). Some of these features suggest Shakespeare in the mood of *A Midsummer Night's Dream*. The movement of the heptasyllabic lines is, once again, most like that of Fletcher in ritualistic situations.

42 The two lines about healing the cattle were censored from the Bridgewater text. Perhaps the trouble was the suggestion that there might be something wrong with the Ludlow livestock. The second of the two lines was kept in *1637*, thereby maintaining 'precious viold liquor' to reinforce 'drops of precious cure'. Milton wanted to emphasise purity and healing. Mention of crops and disease had belonged to pastoral poetry back as far as Virgil's first eclogue (49–50), but the young Milton seems to have found figures of pestilence and demonic evil particularly congenial,

perhaps because they had literary sanction yet were also religiously expressive.
43 See Warton, p. 249–251: *Faithful Shepherdess*, III i 461–472; *Britannia's Pastorals*, Book I, Song 2, 272–292.
44 See for example II Chron. 9.11; 14.7; 26.10; 27.4; Ps. 48.12; Song 8.12; Is. 30.25; 33.18; Ezek. 26.4; compare also *PR* 4.54.
45 Virgil *Ecl.* 2.33. The tradition is very clearly expressed in Jonson's *Pan's Anniversarie* in the second choric hymn.
46 See esp. v.v.194–197; 207–210; 218–237.
47 *PL* 11.429–447; 12.6–24; 12.350–352.
48 Yale 1 382, on poetry, entry conjecturally dated about 1639–41; 1 489–491, on spectacles, entry conjecturally dated about 1637–38. With regard to public shows Milton allows Tertullian's arguments against them in *De Spectaculis* to be valid only for pagan games, presumably of the kind crushed by God in *Samson Agonistes*. He will not accept the arguments of Tertullian, the pseudo-Cyprian, and Lactantius against drama, at least drama of the right kind. He thinks that Tertullian demonstrates the refutation of his own case in the closing parts of the treatise, where the father uses raised style to 'stir up the mind of the Christian to better plays, that is to say, divine and heavenly plays, which, in great number and of great value, the Christian can anticipate concerning the coming of Christ and the Last Judgement'.

6 · 1634 and 1637 – texts, epilogues, audiences

1 On the history of '1637' changes regarded purely textually I am in general agreement with Sprott, whose symbols I re-use. Amongst recent more critically interpretative discussion of these changes mention must be made of George William Smith, Jr, 'Milton's Revisions and the Design of *Comus*', *ELH*, 46 (1979), 56–80. Smith links textual revisions to a possible symmetry in design between the two 'debates', that of the brothers balanced by revisions in the 'temptation' scene. As a means of accounting for the reasons for textual change his case is I think overstated.
2 These are the omission of the four lines of the Lady beginning 'hast thou betrayd my credulous innocence' and the whole of Comus' diatribe against virginity ('list ladie be not coy . . .'). Despite Sprott's technical arguments that these may have been omitted by Milton himself in a refining of the text, I find it difficult to believe that he would have wished to suppress such morally and religiously acute lines as those of the Lady. With both omissions it seems to me likely that as elsewhere the poet's determined moral realism has been tempered by, or come under pressure from, other parties more concerned with decorum for the occasion.
3 Todd first made the reference, p. 361; more recently, see Carey, p. 215, and *Variorum Commentary*, p. 952.

Notes to pages 139-45

4 Diodati on Rev. 12.1: '... many circumstances induce us to understand this of the Jewish nation, and of that which hath befallen it since the birth of Christ'. Assembly Annotations, on the same verse: 'Representing the Christian Church, compared to a virgin espoused to Christ, 2. Cor. 11.2. to a bride, chap. 19.7 & 21.9 & 22.17. to a wife, Eph. 5.15, 26, 27, 32'.

5 For example, Assembly Annotations cross-refers Rev. 12.1 with Rev. 19.8, and Matt. 13.43 with Dan. 12.3 and Jud. 5.31 and 17.2, as all expressing righteousness in terms of glorious clothing.

6 Warton, p. 228; *Variorum Commentary*, p. 954, where Bush notes: 'In Milton's mind the recollection may have been more than verbal: Hughes (1937) notes that Horace is describing "the earth as shaken by a thunderbolt so marvellous that it shook his scepticism about the gods".'

7 In *The Poems of Horace... rendered in English verse by Several Persons* (London, 1666, 1680); Fanshawe's version was first published in 1652 (*Selected Parts of Horace*, tr. R. F.).

8 *quo bruta tellus et vaga flumina / quo Styx et invisi horrida Taeneri / sedes Atlanteusque finis / concutitur* ...

9 That is to say, the open dwelling *by the Lady herself* on chastity and virginity might have been resisted by the 'censor', as it was in her soliloquy.

10 I am referring to the cancelled passage in the prologue in the Trinity manuscript elaborating the 'Hesperian' abode of the Spirit as a place of eternal happiness guarded by watchful dragons or dragon. The rich, even paradoxical eclecticism of this passage is of some interest, not only for itself, as an ambitious if somewhat dubiously controlled version of the *topos*, but also because its indecisions in some ways prefigured the '1637' changes in the equivalent passage in the epilogue. In the early version of the prologue Milton allowed the far west by Ocean to be associated with a heavenly abode, then seemed even to blur the distinction (articulated elsewhere) between the heavens and heaven itself. The *topos* was allegorised. The happy abode was described as the reward for the trial of virtue, using a common Christianised reading of the myth of Hercules and the golden apples of the Hesperides (cf. Alexander Ross, *Mystagogus Poeticus* (3rd edn, London, 1653), p. 175; Sandys, p. 334). The dragon to be overcome was satanic; 'Uninchanted' had biblical authority (Jer. 8.17; Ps. 58.5; cf. Eccl. 10.11); and the 'faire tree' was that of immortal life. The hellish alternative was also given, in the (Virgilian) hellish 'Stygian pool' (*Aen.* 6.323; cf. *PL* 3.14). It would seem that Milton had always been tempted to allegorise 'Hesperian' material, as he would in the expanded epilogue.

11 As before, quotations follow H & S.

12 Townshend, ed. Brown, p. 89.

13 The *topos* examined in A. Bartlett Giamatti, *The Earthly Paradise and the Renaissance Epic* (Princeton, 1966).

14 There may be other ways in which the epilogue looks back to masquing. The happy repose may make an ironic contrast with the delusive ease and refreshment of Comus' feast: this is the repose of the pure in spirit. The

1634 Trinity epilogue also shows a simple organisation which may comment on occasion: there are joyful sounds (cosmic harmonies of Hesperus and daughters), sweet smells (borne by Zephyr, etc.), then through Iris the impression of colourful sights. Is this a feast of senses to reflect back upon the masque-feast?

15 *De Raptu Proserpinae* 2.71ff. The passage in Ovid is remembered in the fifth elegy, 69–70. On the conventionality of this complex, see *Variorum Commentary*, pp. 281–283.

16 Giamatti (p. 70) noted that Christian paradises often stressed the sense of smell; Milton's western gardens take on the aromas of the east.

17 Cf. Ps. 45.8: 'All thy garments smell of myrrh, and aloes, and cassia, out of the ivory palaces, whereby they have made thee glad.'

18 Manna for example may be interpreted as 'the everlasting benefits of my heavenly kingdom' (Diodati on Rev. 2.17).

19 See the discussion in *Variorum Commentary*, p. 980.

20 On Matt. 11.15 Diodati comments: 'A frequent admonition in the Gospels, & Rev. 2 & 3, to stir up beleevers who have received the gift of faith which is the eare of the soul, to exercise it in apprehending, and executing those things, the revelation of which was properly directed only to them.'

21 This is another set of conventional, probably largely Ovidian, associations. In Milton's own verse, hyacinths and roses are associated with sweet scent (*PL* 5.349; 8.517; 9.426; *Elegy* 3.48), with richness of colour (*PL* 3.43; 4.698, 701; *Elegy* 1.6; *In Ob. Procanc.* 44), with spring or summer freshness (*PL* 3.43; 9.1041; *L'Allegro* 22), and with love (*PL* 4.773; 9.218; *Horace* 2; *Elegy* 1.84; 3.20; 5.60; 6.21). Roses are associated with death at *PL* 9.833 (Adam's faded love-garland), and hyacinths and roses grow as compensating beauty out of the grave in the elegy on the Vicechancellor (43–44), where Milton also described a kind of Elysian repose. In the third elegy Venus' rose withers in death, and in the consolation Adonis is seen in some ideal landscape in the heavens, where there are flowers, including dewy, scented roses. These appearances of hyacinth and rose in a sensuous landscape associated with death may owe something to Ovid's description of the gardens of Henna (*Fasti* 4.429ff), whilst the story of Hyacinthus was of course best known in the *Metamorphoses* (10.162–220).

22 Sandys' commentary on Ovid, giving the usual details, mentioning Solomon's worship of Astarte, reports a statue of her on Mount Libanus, which is in a 'mournful posture', having 'her head covered with a vaile; leaning on her cheek and on her left hand, and sustaining her mantle with the other, into which her teares appeared to descend. Now Adonis was no other then the Sun, adored under that name by the Phœnicians, as Venus by the name of Astarte' (pp. 366–367). A measure of the commonplace nature of these ideas may be taken from the following passage from Thomas Godwyn's *Moses and Aaron*, an elementary handbook about the Hebrews which many schoolboys and students of Milton's time would have known:

> The Sun was also worshipped by the house of Judah, under the name of Tamuz; for Tamuz, saith Hierom, was Adonis, and Adonis is generally interpreted the Sun from the Hebrew Adon, signifying Dominus . . . namely, the Lord or Prince of the Planets. The month which we call June, was by the Hebrews called Tamuz; and the entrance of the Sun into the sign Cancer was, in the Jews Astronomy, termed Tekupha Tamuz, the revolution of Tamuz. Concerning Adonis whom sometimes ancient Authors call Osiris, there are two things remarkable, *aphanismos*, the death or loss of Adonis and *heuresis*, the finding of him again. As there was great lamentation at his loss, especially amongst the Women; so there was great joy at his finding. By the death or loss of Adonis, we are to understand the departure of the Sun; by his finding again, we are to understand his return. Now he seemeth to depart twice in the year: . . . And of this the Prophet Ezekiel is thought to have spoken, Ezek. 8. 14. There sate women weeping for Tamuz.
>
> (10th edn, London, 1671, pp. 151–152)

23 I have in mind chiefly the progressive Platonic scheme in Wright and Arthos (reported in *Variorum Commentary*, p. 986) and Carey (p. 227), working from Plutarch's account of the 'second death' (*Moralia* 942F). In confirmation of the religious allegory one might consider the use of the word 'advance' (lift up, rise up) applied to Cupid here and played with elsewhere by Milton (*PL* 4.90; 5.185–191; 9.148–151) in connection with man or Christ-as-man, expressing the paradoxes of humiliation and exaltation, death and resurrection: 'Yet so much bounty is in God, such grace / That who advance his glory, not thir own, / Them he himself to glory will advance' (*PR* 3.142–144).

24 Columbia XVIII 206–207; Yale I 489–490.

7 · The sense of vocation in the 1630s

1 Lawrence Stone, *The Crisis of the Aristocracy, 1558–1641*, abr. edn (Oxford, 1967), p. 6.
2 *Par Nobile*, pp. 3 and 36. However, with relation to Milton's later views of these families, one might consider Creaser's remark ('Present aid', p. 117) that 'It may well be significant that Milton removed all explicit reference to the Egerton family from the 1673 edition of his shorter poems . . . whereas the headnote relating *Arcades* to the Countess Dowager of Derby was retained without change.'
3 Yale I 820.
4 Yale I 639.
5 Yale I 590.
6 With regard to the occasion of the death of the righteous man Milton's *Lycidas* has some common ground with Henry Vaughan's *Daphnis*, the elegy for his twin brother Thomas. I have sketched some parallels, and given some further documentation of Isaiah's ominous device in an essay, 'The Death of Righteous Men: Prophetic Gesture in Vaughan's *Daphnis*

and Milton's *Lycidas*', to appear in a special number of the *George Herbert Journal* to be devoted to Henry Vaughan.
7 The fullest recent treatment of Milton and prophecy is Joseph A. Wittreich's, *Visionary Poetics: Milton's Tradition and his Legacy* (San Marino: Huntington Library, 1979), in which much earlier scholarship is also recorded. Wittreich's book is however mainly centred on Revelation, and he does not mention the device from Isaiah on which the transmutation of elegy rests.
8 Nicholas Bernard, *The Life and Death of the Archbishop of Armagh* (London, 1656), p. 90.
9 Quoted from *The Remains of that Sweet Singer of The Temple, George Herbert* (London, Pickering, 1848), p. 88.
10 The parallel polemical use of this passage in Isaiah in *An Apology* comes at Yale I 932.
11 Critical interpretations of the passage are summarised in *Variorum Commentary*, 672–706. I should stress that I wish only to sketch an approach to *Lycidas* as prophetic document in this chapter, not to engage the notorious interpretative debate. Many have of course identified the 'engine' as the sword of the word, the symbol of reformation.
12 The base text is of course Matthew 16.19: 'And I will give unto thee the keys of the kingdom of heaven: and whatsoever thou shalt bind on earth shall be bound in heaven: and whatsoever thou shalt loose in earth shall be loosed in heaven.'
13 Columbia XVI 327.
14 Yale I 816.
15 Yale I 827. The two-edged sword of Hebrews was of course linked with the 'sharp two-edged sword' of Revelation 1.16 and with 'the sharp sword with two edges' of Revelation 2.12.
16 It seems that there may be two interpretations of the power of the word of God against hypocrites, not mutually exclusive: either a manifestation to the subjects themselves, inwardly, pierced by the sword in their consciences; or an imminent public manifestation, including judgement and execution. The point of the wit is in the *means* to justice in the exposure to the truth, in the word, the 'tenting and searching to the core'.
17 John Spencer Hill, *John Milton: poet, priest and prophet* (London: Macmillan, 1979).
18 Yale I 816.
19 In the development of Milton's sense of this role Hill points to two periods: first to 1641, citing Milton's dismay at the Bishops' War and his decision to join the controversy against the bishops; secondly to the time about the Restoration in 1660, when, he says, Milton's identification with the prophetic role became complete. Whereas in 1642, in *The Reason of Church-Government*, the role is seen 'as a distant analogue to his own experience', by 1660 Milton 'speaks as a prophet rather than of the prophets'. The argument is illustrated by a reference to Jeremiah in particular.

20 There is every sign that Henry Lawes had much to do with the publication of the masque, but Milton cannot have been a wholly passive partner: he took his opportunity to speak out. One should not confuse the poet's many protestations of unreadiness, of practising flight, at this period, including the modest disclaimer on the title page – 'alas, what am I doing, letting the west wind blow among my flowers' – with uncertainty as to vocational aims or reformist purposes.

21 On the title page of the Bridgewater copy of the *Defensio* (1651) now in the Huntington Library. That was last mentioned by William Ingoldsby in 'Intramuralia', *HLQ*, XXXVII (1973), 89–90.

Appendix. The authenticity of the Bridgewater manuscript and the idea of the censor

1 Sprott, esp. pp. 17–23; J. S. Diekhoff, 'The Text of *Comus*, 1634 to 1645', *PMLA*, LII (1937), 705–727, reprinted in Diekhoff (ed.), *A Maske at Ludlow: Essays on Milton's Comus* (Cleveland, 1968), pp. 251–275. See also his introductory essay in that volume, pp. 1–16.
2 This passage may however have been written after the copying of the manuscript on which Bridgewater was based.
3 Diekhoff, ed., *Maske*, p. 7.

INDEX

Addison, Joseph, 71, 192–3
Adonis/Adonia, 148–51, 201–2
Aeschylus, 71, 192
Alciati, *Emblemata*, 195
Allen [Alhoun], Mr, servant, 46, 182
Amaranthus, 105–6, 195
Ames, William, 82, 193
Anacreontea, 62–71, 192–3
André, Elie, 71, 192
Arcadia/Arcadianism, 41, 43, 46–7, 53–4, 57–8, 126
Aristotle, 94–5
Ashby de la Zouch, 16, 49, 184
Ashridge, 24, 29–30
Assembly Annotations, 107, 195–6, 200
Astraea, 125, 143
Audley, James Touchet, Lord (later third Earl of Castlehaven), 20, 25
Audley, Elizabeth (see Brydges)

Bacchus, 58–60, 64–71, 76, 192–3
Barber, C. L., 93, 194
Barnard, Nicholas, *Life of Armagh*, 161, 203
Baxter, Richard, 36, 187
Belial/sons of Belial, 67–9, 73, 176
Betts, Capt., of Ludlow Castle, 28
Bible, 109
  Septuagint, 71
  Genesis, 90
  Numbers, 193
  Judges, 66–7, 200
  I Kings, 188
  II Chronicles, 199
  Job, 61, 82
  Psalms, 85, 88, 98, 107, 111–12, 122, 145, 194–6, 199–201
  Proverbs, 82, 89, 121, 197
  Ecclesiastes, 200
  Song, 71, 199
  Isaiah, 71, 90, 159, 194, 199

  Jeremiah, 168, 200, 203
  Ezekiel, 82, 110, 127, 149, 159, 199
  Daniel, 90, 200
  Amos, 71, 192
  Matthew, 40, 82, 106–7, 139, 148, 200–1
  Luke, 106, 108
  Romans, 62, 65, 69, 72, 82, 107, 190, 192, 195
  II Corinthians, 3, 77, 107, 110, 181, 195
  Galatians, 71, 82
  Ephesians, 82, 200
  I Thessalonians, 107, 195
  Philemon, 196
  Hebrews, 77, 90, 106, 108, 163, 195
  I Peter, 61, 71, 106, 110, 195, 197
  II Peter, 82
  Revelation, 91, 127, 138, 148, 150, 200–1, 203
  Apocrypha, 192
Brackley, John Egerton, Lord (*plates 9 and 12*), 6, 9, 18, 34–5, 47, 78, 170
  as 'Elder Brother', 40–1, 92–102, 104–5, 115–16, 141, 174
Breasted, Barbara, 177, 184–5
Bridgewater, Frances, Countess of (*plate 8*), 6–7, 16–18, 24–5, 33, 75
Bridgewater, John Egerton, first Earl of (*plate 7*), 6–7, 12, 16, 18, 24–35, 41–2, 59, 114, 130, 182–3, 186–7
  presidential journeys in 1634, 7, 27–35, 186–7
Britain, 59, 61, 113–14, 124–5, 157–64, 173
Brooks, C., and Hardy, J. E., 93, 190
Browne, William, *Britannia's Pastorals*, 127, 194, 199
Brydges, Elizabeth, 19, 21, 44, 47, 184
Brydges, Frances (?), 19, 22, 184
Brydges, William, 18, 22–5, 44, 47

205

Index

Budé, Guillaume, *Lexicon*, 191
Bush, Douglas, 140

Calverly, Hugh, 23
Calvin, Jean, psalm commentary, 196
Cambridge, 10, 12–13, 158, 164–5
Camden, William, *Britannia*, 59, 190
Carey, John, 199, 202
Carbery, Richard Vaughan, second Earl of, 25, 143, 191
Carew, Thomas, *Coelum Britannicum*, 25, 143, 191
Cartari, Vicenzo, *Le Imagini*, 65, 192
Campion, Thomas, Caversham entertainment, 189
Caseneuve [Casanova], Louise de, *Hieroglyphics*, 70, 191–2
Castlehaven, Mervyn Touchet, second Earl of, 4, 14, 17, 18, 20, 28, 74, 175–8, 184
Cerdogni, Count Camillo, autograph book, 3
Chair of state, 41, 43, 50–1
Chandos, George Brydges, sixth Baron (*plate 6*), 13, 18, 22, 25, 44, 47
Chandos, Grey, fifth Baron, 18
Charles I, King, 46, 142–3, 196
Chemosh/Baal-Peor, 71–2, 74
Chirk Castle, 7, 30–1, 34–5, 42
  the entertainment, 34–5, 42, 189
Cholmondley Hall, 31
Christopher, Georgia B., 11, 192, 195
Circe, 58–61, 75–7, 79, 104, 112, 116, 120, 191, 194, 197
Claudian, *De Raptu Proserpinae*, 145
Clement of Alexandria, *Paedagogus*, 72, 193, 195
Cockpit-at-Court, theatre, 37
Codrington, Ralph, 22
Collier, John Payne, rogue scholar, 34
Collinges, John, *Par Nobile*, 154, 183
Commelin, Hieronymus, *Rerum Britannicum*, 59, 190
Comus (personification): see *Kōmos*
Comus (masque): see Milton, John
Cooper, Thomas, *Thesaurus*, 196
Coprario, Giovanni (John Cooper), 33
Corns, Thomas N., 194
Cotton, Mr, servant, 46, 182
Courteen, Sir William (father), 18, 29–30, 186
Courteen, William (son), 18, 29–30, 33, 183, 186
Cox, John D., 183–4

Cross, Claire, 184
Cupid, 90, 150–1
Cyprian, the pseudo-, 199

Dacier, Mme (Ann Lefèvre), *Les Poésies d'Anacréon*, 71, 192
Daiches, David, 52, 190
Dance
  in the Harefield entertainment, 48–9
  in the Ludlow masque, 37–8, 48, 63–5, 79
Daniel, Samuel, *Vision of Twelve Goddesses*, 15
David, 111–12, 196
Davies, Sir John, 20–1, 183
  Harefield entertainment, 16, 50, 189
Davies, John, of Hereford, 183
Demaray, John G., 36, 187, 189–90
Derby, Alice, Countess Dowager of (*plates 2 and 3*) 13–26, 41–56, 154, 182–3
  as patron, 13, 15–16, 183
  celebrated in *Arcades*, 41–56
Derby, Ferdinando Stanley, fifth Earl of, 15, 183
Derby, William Stanley, sixth Earl of, 16
Diekhoff, J. S., 171, 175, 204
Digby, Sir Kenelm, 11, 181
Diodati, John (Giovanni), biblical commentator, 70, 113, 160, 163, 192, 195–6, 201
Donne, John, 55
Dorchester, Secretary, 21
Douglas, Lady Eleanor, 20
Drayton, Michael, *Polyolbion*, 11, 123–4, 127, 198
Drusius, Joannes, biblical commentator, 72, 193
Dunham Massey Hall, 31

Echo/echo song, 83–5
Edwards, Philip, 181
Egerton, Lady Alice (*plates 11 and 14*), 9, 12, 18, 34–5, 45, 47, 179–80, 182
  as 'The Lady', 41–2, 78–92, 102–3, 104, 120–2, 133–41, 169, 173–4
Egerton, Lady Alix, editor, 186
Egerton, Lady Frances, 183
Egerton, Lady Katherine, 47, 183, 186
Egerton, Lady Magdalene, 186
Egerton, Lady Mary, 12, 45, 182
Egerton, Lady Penelope, 186
Egerton, Sir Thomas, Lord Chancellor, 15–18, 26, 31

Index

Egerton, Thomas (*plates 10 and 13*), 9, 18, 25, 34–5, 47
  as 'Younger Brother', 41–2, 78, 82–102, 104–5, 115–16, 118
Elizabeth I, Queen, 15, 50, 155
Epicureanism, 140
Etienne, Henri (Stephanus)
  Anacreontis Teii odae, 71, 192
  Thesaurus, 190–1
Erasmus, 164, 192
Euripides, 68–9, 192
Evans, Margery, 4, 26, 86, 90, 97
Eve, 86, 90, 97
Eyton Hall, 30

Fanshawe, Richard, *Poems of Horace*, 140, 200
Ferrar, Nicholas, 161
Fletcher, John
  The Faithful Shepherdess, 54, 83, 86, 99, 115, 127–8, 194, 197–9
  The Sea Voyage, 194
Fogle, French, 16, 183
Fortescue, Mr Edmund, 184

Gainsford, Thomas, 183
Gell, Robert, *Remaines*, 68, 72, 192–3
Genius of the Wood, 41, 43–6, 50–1, 53–6, 125
Gil, Alexander, 166
Godwyn, Thomas, *Moses and Aaron*, 201–2
Greene, Robert, 183
Grotius, Hugo, *Annotata*, 192
Guarini, *Il Pastor Fido*, 43, 83
Gyraldus, L. G., *De Diis Gentium*, 192–3

Haemony, 11, 104–10, 113, 115, 123, 139, 163, 167, 169, 173
Hammersmith, 12
Harefield, house and estate, 1, 6, 12–26, 29, 41, 182, 186
  in *Arcades*, 41–52
  church, monument (*plate 4*), 17–18
Hastings, Ladies Alice and Elizabeth, 19, 22–3, 44–5, 47, 185
Hastings, Ferdinand, Lord, 19
Hastings, Henry, 19
Hastings, Lucy (née Davies), 19, 23
Helgerson, Richard, 8, 181
Heliodorus, 192
Herbert, George, 161
  The Temple, 33
  'Dooms-day', 108

'Church-Militant', 190
Henrietta Maria, Queen, 46, 162
Hermes/Mercury, 79, 104–5, 112
Hercules, 147, 200
Hesperus, Hesperides, 62, 142, 144–7, 200
Hill, John Spencer, 11, 164–8
Holyday, Sir Leonard, mayor, 39
Homer, *Odyssey*, 41, 61, 77, 79, 86, 89, 92, 104, 106, 116, 120, 145, 197
Homeric *Hymn to Hermes*, 192
Horace, 3, 69, 140, 200
Hughes, M., 140, 200
Hunter, W. B., Jr, 184, 187–8, 189
Huntingdon, Elizabeth Hastings, Countess of (*plate 5*), 19, 22–3, 28, 33, 185–6
Huntingdon, George Hastings, fourth Earl of, 19
Huntingdon, Henry Hastings, third Earl of, 19
Huntingdon, Henry Hastings, fifth Earl of, 16, 19, 22–3

Jackson, Dr Thomas, 161
Jones, Inigo, 3
Jones, Mr, servant, 23, 46
Jonson, Ben, 2, 151, 181, 199
  Althorp entertainment, 46, 189
  Chloridia, 142
  Forest, 155
  Golden Age Restor'd, 143
  Haddington Masque, 142
  Highgate entertainment, 189
  Love's Triumph, 142
  Masque of Beautie, 15
  Masque of Oberon, 142
  Neptune's Triumph, 143
  New Inn, 33
  Pan's Anniversarie, 43, 143, 199
  Pleasure Reconcil'd, 65, 181
  Theobalds entertainment, 189
  Vision of Delight, 142, 146
Jove, 43, 45, 53, 57, 84, 140, 174
Juno, 43, 84, 89

Keightley, Thomas, 196
King, Edward, 2, 133, 158–64
Kōmos/Comus, 4, 33, 35–6, 40, 169
  history and significance to occasion, 58–77, 94, 152, 176–7
  Comus' opening speech, 62–5
  Comus and youth, 35–6, 40, 60, 62–5, 69, 72, 79, 169

207

Index

Kōmus/Comus (*cont.*)
  Kōmos and chastity, 81–3, 97–9, 137–41, 174, 177
  Comus and The Lady, 79–80, 85–92, 96, 98, 133–41, 173–4
  education to counter *kōmos*, 104–5, 108 (see also Haemony)
  Comus and Sabrina, opposing spirits, 120–2, 126, 129
Knowsley, 15

Lactantius, in Milton's commonplace book, 199
Laud, Archbishop, 166
Lawes Henry (*plate 1*), 7, 12–13, 30–1, 34–8, 45, 54, 111–12, 146, 172, 178, 182–3, 196–7
  as Attendant Spirit, 6, 45, 54, 79, 86, 102, 110–12, 114–15, 123, 162, 174, 196
  Spirit and Genius compared, 53–6, 104–12
  with the boys, 59–62, 79, 93
  in the Sabrina scene, 115–20, 129–30
  and the epilogue, 150–1
  as index of vocation, 167, 169
Lawes manuscript (Add. Ms. 53723), 13, 183
Lawes, William, 12–13, 182–3, 196
Lee, Bishop, president, 27
Legh, Evelyn (Lady Newton), 187
Legh, Sir Peter, 31
Leigh, Edward, *Critica Sacra*, 72, 193
Lely, Peter, 180
Lloyd, David, 182
Ludlow, 12, 26–38, 41–2, 124–5, 128
  great hall, 36–7, 96
  in 'scene', 121, 128
Lyme Park, 30–2, 34–5

McGuire, Maryann Gale, 10–11, 189
Marcus, Leah S., 4, 11, 26, 126, 181, 185, 198
Marston, John, Ashby entertainment, 16, 184
Marvell, Andrew, 155, 195
Masson, David, 22, 50, 182, 189
Meander, 84–5
Meliboeus, 109, 130–1, 167
Michaelmas, 2, 7, 34, 38–40, 123
Middleton, Sir Thomas, of Chirk, 30
Millar, Sir Oliver, 180
Milton, John, Snr, 12, 166, 181–2

Milton, John
  autographs, 3, 181
  commonplace book, 59, 66–8, 130, 193–4, 199
  Letter to a Friend, 13, 165
  sense of vocation, 153–70
  POEMS:
  Ad Patrem, 166
  'Arcades': contexts for, 6, 12–26; dance in, 48–9; form, 48–52; changes in, for *1645* text, 7–8, 57–8
  'At a Solemn Music', 12, 122
  'At a Vacation Exercise', 165
  Elegies, 196, 201
  Horace, 201
  'How soone hath Time', 165
  'Il Penseroso', 76, 168
  In Ob. Procanc., 201
  'L'Allegro', 201
  'Lycidas', 2, 5, 39–40, 110, 114, 132–3, 157–64, 166–70, 195; Peter's speech in, 104, 108, 139, 159–64; prophecy in, 8–10, 133, 139, 141, 159–64; vocation in, 8, 153, 164, 166–70
  'Masque at Ludlow Castle': occasion, 6–7, 26–40; staging, 36–8; device of journey in, 41–2; exemplifying conduct in the feast, 4, 58–77; chastity in, 4, 20, 81–3, 97–9, 121–2, 129, 135–9, 174; roles of children in, 78–103; pastoral and romance in, 10, 63, 75–7, 80–5, 93–6, 99, 104–31; spiritual instructions in, 4–5, 104–31; true poet in, 5, 130–1, 151, 167; theme of youth in, 60–5, 68, 72, 75, 77, 78–122, 148–52; suasive design of, 5, 121–2, 128–31, 145, 167; sense of vocation in, 8, 153–8, 164–70; epilogue, 2–3, 141–52; in version of Bridgewater MS, 2, 7–9, 11, 20, 35, 81, 83, 85, 90, 92, 95, 97, 99–100, 102, 113, 116–19, 134–5, 146, 171–8, 183, 187, 198; changes in Trinity MS text, 2, 7–9, 12, 13, 26, 34–5, 43, 45–9, 57–8, 62, 66, 81, 91–2, 94–5, 97, 99–101, 105, 109, 116–18, 133–52, 162, 166, 171–2, 188–9, 192, 194, 200; text developed for publication, 7–9, 58, 90–2, 99–100, 132–52
  Paradise Lost, 60–1, 63–4, 67, 73, 86–7, 101, 106, 129, 144, 147, 170, 190, 194–5, 199, 200–2
  Paradise Regained, 61, 67–8, 75, 87, 111,

208

Index

190, 195, 199, 202
Psalm paraphrases, 85
Samson Agonistes, 73, 199
'To Lawes', 183
PROSE:
Animadversions, 105, 125, 195
An Apology, 77, 93, 98, 159, 196, 203
Christian Doctrine, 163
Defensio, 170, 204
Of Reformation, 74–5, 129, 158–9
Reason of Church-Government, 107, 110, 163, 165, 193, 196, 203
Moly, 104–7
Moor Hall, manor, 17, 22
Moore, Tom, *Odes of Anacreon*, 71, 193
More, Henry, 107, 195
Mostyn, 31
Munday, Anthony, 39
Mundhenk, Rosemary, 177, 184

Nash, Thomas, 183
Nepenthes, 92, 134–5, 194
Neptune, 59, 118

Odysseus, 79, 112, 116, 197
Oldys, William, antiquarian, 179
Oley, Barnaby, *Life of Herbert*, 161
Orgel, S. and Strong, R., 190
Orpheus, 129
Ovid, 86
   Amores, 69, 109, 196
   Ars Amatoria, 109, 196
   Fasti, 109, 196
   Metamorphoses, 59, 83–4, 86, 104, 109, 117, 119–20, 124, 145, 193–4, 196–7
   Remedium Amoris, 109, 196

Pan, 43, 46–7, 128
Parker, W. R., 165–6, 182, 187, 189
Petrarch, 138
Philostratus, *Imagines*, 65, 70–1, 191–2
Phornutus (L. Annaeus Cornutus), 65, 187, 191
Plato, 68–9, 98–101, 192
Plutarch, 69, 202
Prophecy, 9–10, 91–2, 95, 98, 126–7, 141, 150, 158, 160–4, 167–70
Propertius, 69
Providence, 57, 81, 84, 86, 94, 98, 116–17, 122–31, 170
Prynne, William, *Histriomastix*, 73–4, 177
Psyche, 150–1
Puteanus, Erycius (van der Putten), *Comus*, 65, 191

Quarles, Francis, *Emblems*, 23

Randolph, Thomas, 'An Eclogue to Master Johnson', 63–4, 191
   The Muses Looking-Glass, 94–5
Redcross, 96
Righteous man, death of, 10, 160–4
Ripa, Cesare, *Iconologia*, 192
Roberts, Peter, notary, 31, 187
Ross, Alexander, *Mystagogus Poeticus*, 193
Ruthin, 31

Sabrina, 5, 35–7, 42, 57, 79, 115–31, 145, 167, 174, 197
Salusbury, Sir Thomas, 34
Sandys, George, Ovid translation, 120, 197, 200–1
Satan, 59–61, 86–7, 97, 200
Saturn/saturnalia, 60, 71–2, 138, 140
Shakespeare, 173
   A Midsummer Night's Dream, 54, 115, 145, 198
   The Tempest, 81, 86, 115, 138, 145, 194
'shepheard lad', 11, 110–2, 115, 167
Shirley, James, *Triumph of Peace*, 142
Sidney, Sir Philip, *Arcadia*, 53
   Defence, 5, 30
   Lady of May, 55, 155, 189
Smith, George W., 199
Spenser, Edmund, 5, 13, 61, 154, 165
   Colin Clout's Come Home Again, 15
   Faerie Queene, 11, 76–7, 96, 98, 102, 109, 149
   Shepheardes Calendar, 110, 159
Sports, Book of, 11, 74
Sprott, S. E., xiii, 8, 11, 132, 171
Stanley, Thomas, Aeschylus translation, 71, 192
   Anacreon translation, 191
Steadman, John, 76, 191, 195
Stone, Lawrence, 154, 156
Stuck, Johann Wilhelm, *Antiquitatem Convivialem*, 71, 193
Syrinx, 43, 46–7, 55

Tammuz, 149, 202
Tertullian, *De Spectaculis*, 59, 190, 194, 199
Theocritus, 69, 112, 192
Thessaly, 109, 196
Tibullus, 69
Todd, H. J., 49, 189, 199

Index

Townshend, Aurelian
   Albions Triumph, 142, 146
   Tempe Restored, 3, 181
Tremellius, Emanuele, and Junius,
   Francisco, Bible translators, 70, 192
True pastor, the, 5, 111–12, 157–70
Tuve, Rosemund, 76, 193

Una, 96, 98
Ussher, Archbishop, 161

Vaughan, Henry, 'Daphnis', 202
Vaux, Mr, servant, 182
Venus/Astarte, 64, 149–52
Vigenère, Blaise de, Philostratus
   translator, 71, 192
Virgil, *Eclogues*, 53–4, 112, 128, 197–9
   Aeneid, 59, 86, 119, 124, 190, 197, 200

Wales, 5–7, 15, 24, 27, 29–35, 57–9, 61,
   117, 123–30, 173
   Council of, 26–8, 32–3, 36, 42
Wallace, J. M., 188, 190
Walran, Mr, instrument tuner, 182
Warton, Thomas, 140, 197, 199, 200
Wentworth, Sir Thomas, 27
Williams, Penry, 185
Wilson, A. N., 50, 184
Wither, George, 160
   Hymns of the Church, 2–3, 40, 181, 188
Woodhouse, A. S. P., 11, 122–3, 197–8
Word of God, 105–11, 113, 138–41, 158,
   162–4, 173
Wotton, Sir Henry, 119

Xenophon, 69, 192

Zouch, Lord, president, 27